The English *Aeneid*

Edinburgh Critical Studies in Literary Translation
Series Editors: Stuart Gillespie and Emily Wilson

The series reflects the current vitality of the subject and will be a magnet for future work. Its remit is not only the phenomenon of translation in itself, but the impact of translation too. It also draws on the increasingly lively fields of reception studies and cultural history. Volumes will focus on Anglophone literary traditions in their foreign relations.

Published Titles

The English Aeneid*: Translations of Virgil, 1555–1646*
Sheldon Brammall

Forthcoming Titles

The Many Voices of Lydia Davis: Translation, Rewriting, Intertextuality
Jonathan Evans

The English *Aeneid*

Translations of Virgil, 1555–1646

Sheldon Brammall

EDINBURGH
University Press

Edinburgh University Press Ltd
The Tun – Holyrood Road
12(2f) Jackson's Entry
Edinburgh EH8 8PJ

www.euppublishing.com

Typeset in 10.5/13 Sabon by
Servis Filmsetting Ltd, Stockport, Cheshire,
and printed and bound in Great Britain by
CPI Group (UK) Ltd, Croydon CR0 4YY

A CIP record for this book is available from the
British Library

ISBN 978 0 7486 9908 7 (hardback)
ISBN 978 0 7486 9909 4 (webready PDF)
ISBN 978 1 4744 0452 5 (epub)

Contents

Series Editors' Preface viii
Acknowledgements ix
Notes on the Text xi

Introduction 1
Current Critical Approaches and the Aims of This Study 4
Lawrence Humphrey and the Duties of a Translator 8

1. **The Search for a Lofty British Virgil: The Early Elizabethan *Aeneids* of Thomas Phaer, Thomas Twyne and Richard Stanyhurst** 19
The English Renaissance *Aeneid* 19
Thomas Phaer and the 'Privilege Vertue Gives' 23
Thomas Twyne and the 'Unperfect' *Aeneid*: Reverence, Continuity and Change 31
Aeneas the Martyr: Richard Stanyhurst and the Lofty Irish Virgil 37
The Highpoint of Humanist *Aeneids* 49

2. **'Sound this Angry Message in Thine Eares': Sympathy and the Translations of the *Aeneid* in Marlowe's *Dido Queene of Carthage*** 55
Marlowe's *Dido* and the Renaissance *Aeneid* 57
Translations of the *Aeneid* in *Dido* 63
Dramatic and Epic Voices in *Dido* 70

3. **Courteous Virgil: The Manuscript Translations of an Anonymous Poet, Sir John Harington and Sir William Mure of Rowallan** 78

An Anonymous Manuscript Translation and Dido's Passionate Complaint 79
Virgil Corrected: Sir John Harington and Book 6 of the *Aeneid* 88
Virgil Interrupted: Sir William Mure's 'Dido and Æneas' 100

4. Virginian Virgil: The Single-Book Translations of Sir Thomas Wroth, Sir Dudley Digges and George Sandys 116
The Spectre of Creusa: Prophetic Closure in Sir Thomas Wroth's *Destruction of Troy* 118
Eyes of Judgment: The Two Dedications in *The Destruction of Troy* 118
'Translated Hence Out of This Mortall Life': Rewriting the Role of Creusa 121
The 'Schoole of Virtue': Sir Dudley Digges's *Didos Death* 125
Antique Discipline: The Martial Virgil of the *Foure Paradoxes* 126
From November to December 1621: The Genesis of Digges's Translation 130
'What Hercules Would Be': George Sandys's Essay upon the *Aeneid* 133
The Leaves of the Sibyl: Virgilian Credibility in *A Relation of a Journey* 135
'The Two Maine Columnes of a Common-wealth': Virgilian Politics in the 1632 *Ovids Metamorphosis* 139

5. Rome at War: The Military Virgils of John Vicars, Robert Stapylton and Robert Heath 149
A Horrible Travesty in Earnest? Providence and Parliament in John Vicars' *The XII Aeneids* (1632) 150
'Virgiliae Vindiciae' in Bodleian MS. Ashmole 38 152
Englands Hallelu-jah: The Context of Vicars' *XII Aeneids*, 1617–31 153
Providence and Parliament in *The XII Aeneids of Virgil* 157
Arms and the Man, or Merchandise and the Woman? Robert Stapylton's *Dido and Aeneas* 165
'Drad Wars, and that Brave Hero's Fame': Robert Heath's Manuscript 'Æneis' (1645–6) 171
'Girt a la mode with Skins': The Attribution to Robert Heath 172
A Song Sung in a Siege: Robert Heath's 'Æneis' 174

Conclusion 187

Bibliography 194
Index 208

Series Editors' Preface

Translators, Pushkin's 'post-horses of enlightenment', play a central role in every society's reception of other cultures. The study of translation – in theory, in practice and in relation to broader narratives in literary and cultural history – is now a vibrant scholarly field. It is key to current debates on literary canons in an increasingly global world, and on the possibility of World Literature. Edinburgh Critical Studies in Literary Translation addresses translation as a literary and historical phenomenon and is the first monograph series to do so.

Some of these studies engage with the approaches individual authors have taken to translation. Some deal with the impact of particular source texts or of particular translations on the societies in which they were produced. A central concern of the series is with interactions between translation and other forms of creative work and with the part translation can play in forging the identity of individual authors. We are no less interested in the way translation can set directions for literary cultures at large.

There are no constraints on historical period. The emphasis of the series is in the first instance on translations involving the English language, whether in the context of ancient or modern literature. Our scholarly territory straddles the disciplines of English Literature, Classical Studies, Comparative Literature and Modern Languages. Contributors necessarily work at their frontiers, using innovative tools on interdisciplinary topics.

Stuart Gillespie and Emily Wilson

Acknowledgements

Shorter versions of three sections in this book have previously appeared in *Translation and Literature* (Edinburgh University Press) and the *Review of English Studies* (Oxford University Press), as follows. An earlier version of Chapter 2 appeared as '"Sound this Angrie Message in Thine Eares": Sympathy and the Translations of the *Aeneid* in Marlowe's *Dido Queene of Carthage*', *RES* 65 (2014), 383–402; a version of Section 1 of Chapter 3 appeared as '*Aeneid* 4 in BL Add. MS 60283: A New Assessment and Text', *T&L* 23 (2014), 68–109; and a much shorter version of Section 2 of Chapter 4 appeared as 'The Politics of the Partial Translations of the *Aeneid* by Dudley Digges and Marie de Gournay', *T&L* 22 (2013), 182–94.

I have accrued many debts to people who have helped me with my work towards this book. It is a pleasure to be able to thank some of these people now.

At the University of British Columbia, where I studied as an undergraduate and where I still feel very much at home, I must thank three individuals who have taken a long-term interest in my work: Lee Johnson, Dennis Danielson and Eva-Marie Kröller. Their friendship and untiring support over the years have been invaluable.

The present book had its genesis during time I spent in the Master of Studies programme at Magdalen College, Oxford. The idea of writing on the English Renaissance translations of Virgil came about through conversations I had with John Pitcher, David Norbrook and Stephen Harrison. I am grateful for their guidance in finding and focusing the topic.

To be able to carry out my research on this subject, I have received financial support from Trinity College, Cambridge, an Overseas Research Scholarship and the Cambridge Commonwealth Trust. Since then, I have held a Research Fellowship at the Ludwig Boltzmann Institute for Neo-Latin Studies in Innsbruck and have begun a Leverhulme Trust

Early Career Fellowship at the University of Oxford. These have made the current project possible.

Many scholars have generously helped me out at various stages, either by reading drafts of chapters or by giving me pointers in my research. These include: Colin Burrow, Gerard Kilroy, Adrian Poole, Jason Scott-Warren, Edward Wilson-Lee, Mark Vessey and Arnoud Visser. I owe special debts to Helen Cooper and Philip Hardie who have given me much helpful advice. I would like to thank Emily Wilson for the great care with which she has read and commented on my typescript.

There are two people, however, I would like to single out. The first is my PhD supervisor Raphael Lyne. He has not only been guiding my thoughts through their many metamorphoses, but also guided me through the doctoral studies with his particular intelligence, warmth and wit. The other is Stuart Gillespie, whose unfailing energy and support have been extraordinary. This project would have been inconceivable without his help.

Lastly, it is the greatest pleasure to be able to thank my family. It is to them that I have dedicated this book. They have supported me, in every way.

Oxford
October, 2014

Notes on the Text

Throughout this book I quote from the Loeb edition of Virgil's *Aeneid*. I have used this edition for ease of reference. However, for historical accuracy I have checked all quotations from the *Aeneid* against the popular *Universum poema* edition (Venice, 1558), or the equally popular, later edition by Pontanus, the *Symbolarum libri XVII* (Augsburg, 1599). Whenever there is a discrepancy of note, I have mentioned this in a footnote. Similarly, other references to classical texts in this book are usually made to the Loeb series.

I quote early modern works in their original spelling. The only changes I make are to normalise i/j and v/u when I quote directly from an early modern edition. Unless otherwise noted, italics are in the original text. The only exception is in Latin quotations, where I have used italics to represent my expansions.

For my family:
Mom, Rose, Brendan, Justin and Anna

Introduction

On 13 April 1594, King James VI of Scotland wrote a letter to Queen Elizabeth I in which he complains about her generous treatment of the Scottish rebel, the earl of Bothwell. James expresses his horror at 'how my avowed traitor hath not only been openly reset in your realm, but plainly made his residence in your proper houses'.[1] Recalling to the Queen her promise that Bothwell 'should have no harbor' within her country, James hopes that she will not let her subjects overrule her – for surely that is the only reason she would allow this traitor to reside in her land. Permitting James's avowed enemy to live in England would be 'so far against all princely honor as I protest I abhor the least thought thereof'.[2] To plead with her, James sent this letter with two ambassadors to the Queen in London. He concludes the letter with an allusion to Virgil's *Aeneid*:

> I trust ye will not put me in balance with such a traitorous counterpoise, nor wilfully reject me, constraining me to say with Virgil, *Flectere si nequeo superos, Acheronta movebo* ['if Heaven I cannot bend, then Hell I will arouse']. And to give you a proof of the continuance of my honest affection, I have directed these two gentlemen unto you, whom I will heartily pray you to credit as myself in all that they have in charge to deliver unto you; and because the principal of them goes to France, to return the other back with a good answer with all convenient speed. And thus assuring you that friendship shall never fail upon my part, I commit you, madame and dearest sister, to the holy protection of the Almighty. From Edinburgh the 13 of April, 1594.[3]

Quoting from the seventh book of the *Aeneid*, James warns Elizabeth that if she refuses to aid him, he will be forced to seek other methods. If need be, like Juno, he will not hesitate from stirring up hell.

Elizabeth was furious with James's letter. In her reply she writes, 'I am that prince that never can endure a menace at my enemy's hand, much less of one so dearly treated.'[4] She had interpreted James's allusion to Virgil as a threat. She read it as a proclamation that James would not hesitate either to invade England with the help of other countries or to attack her own person.[5] In his answer to Elizabeth's angry letter, James devotes a large section to explain what precisely he meant by the quotation and how she has supposedly interpreted it incorrectly:

> now the other point of mistaking is of yon Latin verse in the hinder end of my letter, which I perceive ye interpret to be a threatening of you. But I doubt not ye will conceive far otherways of my meaning thereby, if ye will [be] pleased to weigh first the meaning of the author that first wrote it, and since consider what precedes and follows in my letter that alleges it. For Virgil feigneth that Juno – being in a rage that the rest of the gods through Venus' persuasion nold [i.e. would not] consent to the wreck of Aeneas, whom against she bare inveterate hatred as against all Troy – she not only pronounceth these words of my letter but immediately goes to Alecto, one of the hellish Furies, and persuades her to stir up Turnus in Italy to war against Aeneas, thereby to hinder his conquest there. Now, to make the allusion then: suppose (*Omnis comparatio claudicat uno pede* ['every comparison limps on one foot']) I am Juno, ye are the rest of the gods, Bothwell is Aeneas, and other foreign princes are Acheron. Juno's seeking aid of Acheron, then, was only for the wrack of Aeneas, and no ways either for the invading or threatening of the rest of the gods. On the other part, where this verse is set down in my letter, I say not that I am of mind so to do, but by the contrary I say I trust you will not constrain me so to do. And the very next words I subjoin are 'and to give you a proof of my honest affection.' And thus, madame, my intention was to complain unto you, not to threaten you, thereby seeking your aid and neither seeking nor leaning to the aid of others. So in a word my prayer was to you as we all pray to God, 'Lead us not into temptation.'[6]

Elizabeth had read herself as Aeneas, whom James was threatening to overthrow with the forces of hell (presumably Spain). Such a reading would constitute a serious threat against her state. But the Scottish king's reply realigns the characters, so that the brunt of his threat is directed towards Bothwell himself, not Elizabeth. It is hard to imagine that James had not seen how the quotation would be 'misread'. Rather, he used this line from the *Aeneid* to provoke Elizabeth – conveying his full resentment at her treatment of Bothwell – while at the same time allowing him to plead innocence by claiming that his allusion has been misinterpreted.

James's crafty use of Virgil in these letters is a fitting place to begin this book, which tells the history of English translations of the *Aeneid* from 1555 to 1646. In these two letters, a line of Virgil's epic was nearly enough to launch England and Scotland into a war. The letters thus dramatically illustrate just how much could be invested in a political application of the *Aeneid* during this period. At a time when Virgil was regarded as the 'prince of poets' and his work was cited by monarchs with easy familiarity, it would be hard to overstate how important the

Aeneid was as a cultural reference point. The translators in this study range from courtiers at the palaces of Elizabeth and James to obscure figures from the far corners of their kingdoms. But they shared with their monarchs the practice of turning to the *Aeneid* to comment upon contemporary circumstances.

The specificity with which James and Elizabeth apply the *Aeneid* to their own concerns shows that it is worth examining a single linguistic and national tradition of reading Virgil's epic. It has been said that the English *Aeneid* was the same as the French or Italian, since the scholarly commentaries on Virgil were shared all over Europe.[7] But even if it is true that the Latin texts available were international, vernacular translations helped to develop nationally specific traditions of *Aeneid* reception. This book will explore how the *Aeneid* came to have certain associations in English culture and how particular readings developed and preoccupied different English communities of translators. The focus will be exclusively on translations of the *Aeneid* rather than of the *Eclogues* or *Georgics*. No English translator of the *Aeneid* before John Ogilby translated Virgil's other works as well. Therefore, in the period I am discussing, translations of the *Eclogues* and *Georgics* should be treated as a separate tradition. They represent different genres and pose different challenges. Translators of the epic are rarely interested in them, and complete Virgils are a phenomenon of a later era of English translation. They come into their own in the second half of the seventeenth century. Concentrating on the *Aeneid* will allow me to focus specifically on how political, literary and pedagogical readings of this epic developed over the course of the century.

The letters are also a fitting place to begin because they illustrate one of many ways that the *Aeneid* could be used for a cause other than conservative panegyric. James quotes Virgil in order to make a threat, and the topical allegory that he pursues is anything but obvious. Many studies still tend to present the *Aeneid* in this period as a stable tool for royalist platitudes. But its reception is full of surprises. There was a wide range of traditions of reading the *Aeneid* available in Renaissance poetry and scholarship. As I will show, the English translators creatively engaged with the full epic and its long interpretive history. The result was a series of competing translations that aimed to do such disparate things as educate the nation, question structures of power, lament lost virtues, incite people to love or war, or, indeed, issue threats. Only rarely did anyone translate Virgil's epic simply to praise.

In the course of this study, I will explore thirteen translations of significant portions of the *Aeneid*. Usually this means that the translator has completed at least one full book of the poem. However, I have made an exception in the case of Marlowe, because *Dido Queene of Carthage* includes a wide range of translations that are among the most distinguished in the period. Aside from Marlowe, the main figures in this study are: Thomas Phaer, Thomas Twyne, Richard Staynhurst, an anonymous courtier, Sir John Harington, Sir William Mure, Sir Thomas Wroth, Sir Dudley Digges, George Sandys, John Vicars, Robert Stapylton and Robert Heath. I argue that these translators deserve to take their due places in the study of Virgil's reception in this period. Several display considerable poetic merit in their creative engagements with Virgil and, collectively, their texts offer the material to develop a new picture of the *Aeneid*'s reception in early modern England.

Current Critical Approaches and the Aims of This Study

In the scholarship on English Renaissance translations of the classics, politics has been one of the most enduring concerns. Two seminal studies that were undertaken in the first half of the twentieth century – C. H. Conley's *The First English Translators of the Classics* (1927) and F. O. Matthiessen's *Translation: An Elizabethan Art* (1931) – established the initial parameters of the discussion. In these two books, the political implications of Renaissance translations were painted with very broad brushstrokes. Conley focused on the group of translators who appeared in print between 1560 and 1572.[8] He argued that these translators were an organised movement centred upon the Inns of Court.[9] Stirred by their youthful spirits, the early Elizabethan translators were non-scholarly, Protestant and nationalistic. Their purpose was to disseminate Renaissance ideals while challenging the traditionalists (represented by university scholars), Catholic sympathisers and supporters of the Spanish alliance.[10] Moreover, these youths were a liberalising movement, and the revolutionary act of translation conveyed their new rationalism.[11] Conley's arguments were eventually to reach a wide audience through the work of Christopher Hill, who accepted Conley's thesis that 'the first English translators of the classics were a homogeneous group of non-university Protestants and Puritans, mostly young and inspired by an ardent patriotism'.[12] But already four years after Conley, Matthiessen had published a rather different account of the Elizabethan translators, in which their politics of translation was less polemically divisive. In his book, Elizabethan translation was an act of patriotic conquest.[13] Just as the voyager or merchant could do some good for his country, so could the translator. He or she could bring literature into England, 'not for the learned alone, but for the whole country'.[14]

Matthiessen stressed how these early translators strove for linguistic purity and a colloquial quality in their English. These translations would affect the daily lives of all Englishmen by bringing 'new blood and vigor to the stock of England'.[15]

Since the appearance of Conley's and Matthiessen's books, the political nature of early English translations has remained at the forefront of discussion. However, their accounts have gradually been challenged and refined. This has been especially apparent in the past twenty years, when the study of historical translations has become more intensive. Conley's account has thus been the subject of some strong censure. Margaret Tudeau-Clayton, for example, has undermined Conley's connection of translation and 'liberalism' by showing how early modern translations could be used to stabilise a sense of hierarchy within the vernacular.[16] Tudeau-Clayton called for more attention to be paid to the particular text being translated: one cannot generalise.[17] Likewise, Matthiessen's claim for the unproblematic patriotic spirit of the English translators has been challenged by recent work. In *Ovid's Changing Worlds*, for example, Raphael Lyne has demonstrated how early modern Ovid translators were working from a 'position of inferiority' in relation to texts they translated.[18] Consciousness of their inferiority mitigated any sense of a grand triumph. Sometimes translations display an anxiety that underpins their patriotic ventures, and in some of them, instead of displacing authority from the source text to the English, the place of prestige is preserved for the Latin. What recent scholarship has accomplished is a more variegated account of the possibilities in such acts of translation. The present book will continue this process of variegation.

So far there have been only three brief surveys of the English Renaissance translations of the *Aeneid*. In 1982, William Frost published an essay in which he overviewed the translators of Virgil from Gavin Douglas to John Dryden. Frost focused on the biographies of the translators. He noted that these biographies contain a curiously high degree of political involvement. 'It is thus probably no accident that Virgil drew to himself, as political life revived in Europe after sixteen centuries, so many writers who were themselves personally committed to public involvements of a political, religious, or generally ideological kind.'[19] Beyond that, however, Frost made no specific claims. In an essay in the *Cambridge Companion to Virgil*, Colin Burrow argued that, far from being at the centre of power, the translators of Virgil have generally been proponents of losing causes who sought 'the consolation of [Virgil's] authority'.[20] The two causes the Renaissance translators of Virgil identified with were, in Burrow's account, Catholicism (Phaer, Stanyhurst) and royalism (Sandys). More recently, in the *Oxford*

History of Literary Translation in English, Gordon Braden has offered a survey of the translations of the *Aeneid*.[21] Braden takes into account the work of Burrow and Tudeau-Clayton, noting that the translators 'are frequently involved in public life, but with diverse allegiances'.[22] Being a survey, however, Braden's account is unable to explore in any detail the fascinating question it raises: namely, how the many translators of Virgil's *Aeneid* were able to utilise the epic for these diverse causes.

Aside from these brief pieces, however, there has been no study of the Elizabethan and Jacobean translations of the *Aeneid*. The only book-length treatment of early modern English *Aeneid*s was Leslie Proudfoot's monograph from 1960, in which he discussed some of the seventeenth-century texts and viewed them as literary stepping stones towards Dryden.[23] The lack of a study of the earlier translations is all the more striking given the amount of attention that the reception of Virgil in the Renaissance has received. In the past twenty-five years, there have been English books specifically on Virgil's Renaissance reception by Craig Kallendorf, Donna B. Hamilton, John Watkins, Heather James, Margaret Tudeau-Clayton, Andrew Wallace and David Scott Wilson-Okamura.[24] That is only to list some of the English works in which Virgil's reception is the primary concern. Countless others touch on the subject incidentally. But the translations of Virgil's epic between 1555 and 1646 still do not play the prominent role they deserve in our understanding of the epic's English reception. In 2011, Stuart Gillespie argued that 'translation should move towards the forefront of the study of reception'.[25] This book is an attempt to effect such a change.

The sequence of translations of the *Aeneid* in early modern England provides a solid material foundation for a fresh consideration of Virgil's role in this period. While translations do not, of course, represent an exhaustive overview of contemporary readings of the poem, they can present a useful, well-founded guide. I will chart how the *Aeneid* was first translated according to continental, humanist readings of epic poetry (Chapter 1). These epideictic translations appeared from the 1550s until the 1580s. In the following decades, translators produced more provocative and playful works: these include Marlowe's dramatic adaptation (Chapter 2) as well as courtly and amatory versions that circulated in manuscript (Chapter 3). These later translators isolated smaller portions of the epic to create shorter texts that challenged the 'grave' and 'lofty' humanist translations. In the early Stuart era, explicitly political versions then came to the forefront. In 1620–32 there was a series of translations by prominent members of the Virginia Company (Chapter 4). Militaristic renditions of the epic appeared on the eve of the

Civil War (Chapter 5). These texts helped shape trends in the epic's early modern English reception.

The English *Aeneids* also have great explanatory value as tests of some of the current trends in Virgilian scholarship. Arguably the most controversial development in the study of the Virgilian tradition has been the extension of the debate over 'optimistic' and 'pessimistic' readings of the *Aeneid* into reception studies. Two books in particular have been at the centre of this controversy: Richard F. Thomas's *Virgil and the Augustan Reception* (2001) and Craig Kallendorf's *The Other Virgil: 'Pessimistic' Readings of the 'Aeneid' in Early Modern Culture* (2007).[26] In the middle of the twentieth century, essays by classical scholars such as R. A. Brooks, Wendell Clausen and Adam Parry attempted to shift the focus from the public, imperial 'voices' in Virgil's epic to the private voices of suffering.[27] Making a striking claim, Parry argued that 'the satisfaction of "having arrived" in Italy means less to [Aeneas] than his own sense of personal loss'.[28] Virgil's poem was said to undermine its own portrayal of the glories of the Roman Empire. A heated debate among classical scholars was carried out over the course of several decades.[29] One of the main arguments against Virgilian pessimism was the apparent lack of pessimistic readings before the 1960s. Reacting to this point, Richard F. Thomas has shifted the focus to reception studies and has gone in search of historical pessimistic readings. Despite hostile critiques of Thomas's book, other scholars have joined him in this pursuit.[30] Most notable among these is Craig Kallendorf, who has alerted us to the possibility of alternative Virgils in early modern Europe.[31] As a consequence, in reception studies the debate over Virgilian 'pessimism' is far from over. The present study of translations can supply new evidence for this debate. I will suggest that there is one exceptional case of a pessimistic translation of the *Aeneid* in the English Renaissance. However, this does not mean that all of the other translations simply praise those in power. Several of the texts I discuss reveal, if not 'pessimistic', then definitely oppositional perspectives. Militaristic translations of the *Aeneid* in Jacobean and Caroline England, for example, challenge the perceived effeminacy of the Stuart court. This book seeks to redefine, more historically, what an alternative reading of Virgil's epic could be in the English Renaissance.

By focusing on the period from 1555 to 1646, I hope that this book avoids a teleological reading of early modern translations of the *Aeneid*. Most of the scholarship on translations in the English language has focused upon the literature of the 'Augustan Age'. Paul Davis has described this period as 'the golden age of poetic translation in England' and has charted the relative stress given to this period by scholars.[32] While this bias is certainly defensible, given the large number of translations and imitations produced during this later period,[33] it has often led to the earlier works being treated as nothing more than a lead-up to the great flowering in the age of Dryden. Leslie Proudfoot's monograph treats seventeenth-century *Aeneid* translations as important only in so far as they pave the way for Dryden. This teleology is likewise apparent in more recent studies such as Robin Sowerby's *The Augustan Art of Translation* and Gordon Braden's survey of translations of the *Aeneid* from 1550 to 1660. For example, Braden remarks that the search for a metre to recreate Virgil's hexameters 'can seem to find a fulfilment in Dryden's translation'.[34] Such a focus on Dryden and the Augustan translators has distorted our understanding of an earlier era of translation. This is due in part to a lack of attention being paid to the earlier texts. But it is also apparent that the labels suited to many of the later, Augustan translations – *royalist*, *stately*, *panegyric* – are often projected backwards. Close attention to the prior period makes evident how it differs from the age that follows. And although I will not discuss the early Augustan tradition, my readings of these other translations may open new ways to think about Augustan Virgil. The first years of this prominent tradition can only be properly understood with a thorough grounding in the context of the previous translations.

Lawrence Humphrey and the Duties of a Translator

The approach in this book will be chronological and I will offer individual readings of the translations. These readings are grouped into chapters according to the primary 'community' to which the translators most closely belonged. This format will allow a history of the early English *Aeneid*s to develop over the five chapters. However, two concerns will underlie all readings. I draw these from a text on translation by Lawrence Humphrey, a renowned English scholar of the late sixteenth century. Humphrey's *Interpretatio linguarum* is a little-known treatise, but the 622-page work is arguably the magnum opus of Renaissance translation theory. In sheer size, it dwarfs any other work on the theory and practice of translation produced in the European Renaissance. Humphrey had a well-earned reputation as a man of great erudition, and nowhere is his learning on such clear display as in this book. I hope to accomplish two things by using the *Interpretatio* to frame my argument. The first is to bring Humphrey's text into a more central position in translation studies and to show that its ideas can lead to compelling readings. The second is to avoid some of the anachronisms that come from taking modern theories as points of departure. Humphrey's treatise can help us explore both how early modern practitioners fit into contemporary theories of translation and how such theorising might help us understand their practice.

The genesis of the *Interpretatio* took place while Humphrey was in exile during the reign of Queen Mary. It was during the six years he spent in Switzerland from 1554 to 1560 that Humphrey became involved in the continental debates about translation. Before this period, Humphrey was a lecturer in moral philosophy at Magdalen College, Oxford. In 1553, when the Catholic Queen Mary came to the throne of England, she sent Stephen Gardiner to remove the more troublesome Protestants from the universities. Some thirty fellows from Magdalen were expelled in the course of two years.[35] Humphrey was not one of these thirty fellows, as he seems to have fled to Basel before they could expel him. Since he was not forcibly removed, he kept being funded by Magdalen until 1556, when he was finally stripped of his fellowship. After his stipend from Magdalen College was cut off, Humphrey worked at the printing house of Froben in Basel and was employed in particular on projects in translation.[36] The *Interpretatio* displays a keen awareness of controversies surrounding the Latin translations of Aristotle (Périon), Homer (Wolf) and the Bible (Erasmus, Castalio), which were being printed in Basel at the time. However, the *Interpretatio* was not only written for a continental audience. Published one year after Elizabeth acceded to the throne of England, it is one of several works Humphrey had printed in order to advertise his new learning before he returned home. In the preface 'De laude interpretationis', he writes, 'O happy exile, which sends men back more learned; o happy court, which receives noble and learned exiles!'[37] The *Interpretatio* is thus a text that bridges two cultures. It engages with debates that were especially relevant in Basel in the 1550s, but it also aims to show off Humphrey's learning and erudition to an English audience.

Humphrey's desire to display the range of his learning perhaps explains the extraordinary breadth of the *Interpretatio*. George Steiner has rightfully described it as 'one of the summarizing statements in the history of translation'.[38] However, its significance for specifically English translation history has not yet been brought to light.[39] In the *Oxford History of Literary Translation in English*, Gordon Braden has argued that since Humphrey's work 'was written in Latin, published in Basle, and never reprinted', its position is marginal: 'there is no reason to think the work circulated at all widely'.[40] It is true there is no clear evidence of the work being quoted. But there are several copies of Humphrey's treatise in the libraries of Oxford and Cambridge, suggesting that there was at least some audience in England. There is also evidence that Humphrey was still studied by continental scholars over a century after his work was printed. In the *De interpretatione* of 1680, Pierre-Daniel Huet cites Humphrey as one of the few English contributors to the theory of translation.[41] But what is more important for this particular book, Humphrey was a celebrated pedagogue who taught several generations of students at Oxford and was known to many of the translators of Virgil.[42] He wrote commendatory verse for Richard Stanyhurst (Chapter 1) and dedicated his treatise on translation to the grandfather of Thomas Wroth (Chapter 4), with whom (the grandfather) he attended lectures while in exile. In the *Metamorphosis of Ajax*, Sir John Harington (Chapter 3) summarises Humphrey's reputation, declaring that Humphrey was 'a sound authoritie indeed, and in so serious a matter as under heaven is no weightier, to such a person, as in the world is no worthier, from such a scholer, as in Oxford was no learneder'.[43] Just as Harington's description suggests, Humphrey had immense sway at Oxford: at the height of his career, from 1571 to 1576, he was Vice-President of the University, Regius Professor of Divinity and President of Magdalen College. Even if Braden's analysis is correct and the *Interpretatio* had a limited readership, Humphrey's reputation and rapport, especially with the translators of the *Aeneid*, is far too great to ignore. And the treatise represents some of the most sophisticated reflections on the art of translation during the Renaissance.

The *Interpretatio*, which I can only briefly overview here, is divided into three sections. These treat the art of translation, its relationship to imitation and practical exercises. In the first book, Humphrey offers a picture of the ideal translator. Such a translator must serve the source text by opening its virtues to a new audience. According to Humphrey, good translators operate on the *via media* between excessive literalism and excessive freedom. To do so, they must cultivate four virtues: *plenitudo*, *proprietas*, *puritas* and *aptitudo*. Humphrey discourses at length on each of these and then explains how translators must be nurtured. In particular, they should possess four qualities: *natura*, *doctrina*, *fides/religio* and *diligentia*. The second book of the *Interpretatio* then looks at imitation. The discussion broadens out from translation to how translation and imitation are connected. During the Renaissance, translation was often regarded as akin to imitation. Thus Jacques Peletier writes, 'La plus vr*a*ee espece d'imitacion, c'est de traduire.'[44] However, Humphrey was especially concerned to establish the boundaries between the two disciplines in Book 2. The final part of the *Interpretatio* constitutes a sort of study book. It contains advice on everything from working with manuscripts to detailed analysis of how to translate all of the various tropes and figures in a language.

There are two concepts I want to draw from the *Interpretatio*. The first of these is prominent in the first book of Humphrey's treatise and offers a way of approaching the cultural politics of the early English translations of the *Aeneid*: this concept is the *utilitas* of translation. Humphrey emphasises the social and political usefulness of translation more than any earlier Renaissance writer on the subject. There is no equivalent discussion in the Latin treatises by Bruni, Manetti, Vives or Périon. The only real precedent for Humphrey's treatment of this theme is in Longiano's Italian treatise on the Ciceronian rules for translation.[45] But unlike Longiano, Humphrey makes *utilitas* an organising principle of his work. From the beginning of the preface, he writes about the 'fellowship and very manifest utility' of translating.[46] He stresses that 'indeed no part or performance of life can be without this skill of translating.'[47] The utility of translation is ostensibly quite simple for Humphrey. First, since one cannot know all of the languages in which knowledge is mediated, one must rely upon translators. Second, following a common humanistic assumption, Humphrey imagines the great philosophy and poetry of the ancients as having an active power to lead us towards virtue. This power is useless if a text cannot be understood. Here Humphrey invokes the humanists' rhetorical theory of translation, in which the affective energy of the original must be recreated.[48] The key virtue to make a translation useful is *perspicuitas*. This quintessential virtue involves more than just clarity. Humphrey presents perspicuity as 'the attendant of all other virtues'. It must be 'diffused through all parts of a discourse, just like blood', since it is the virtue that is 'necessary for the utilisation' of a text.[49] Translators who work with perspicuity can contribute invaluably to a commonwealth. They can spread knowledge and actively promote virtue and religion. Humphrey thus exclaims, 'blessed is that republic which has translators!'[50]

This conviction of the public utility of translation also comes through in the metaphors he uses. A recent trend in relating the theories and practice of translation has been to explore the dominant metaphors for the art in a given culture or author. Matthew Reynolds has argued that the metaphor *translation* (that is 'carrying-across') rarely reveals much about a text, since it is common to almost all practitioners of the art. However, the other metaphors that translators select to describe their practice often shape their entire poem-translations. Concepts such as 'opening', 'friendship', 'desire', 'taking a view', 'zooming', 'resurrection' and 'metamorphosis' provide readers with a better way of grasping the unique aims of these texts.[51] Although Reynolds's study does not try to map the popularity of metaphors across time, he does acknowledge that certain metaphors will flourish in certain periods. A similar approach has been taken by Paul Davis in his more historical study, which focuses on how Augustan translators drew on predominantly negative metaphors (exile, secrecy, slavery) that were current in their culture.[52] In the preface to the *Interpretatio*, Humphrey offers the reader two metaphors for what he glosses in the margin as 'utilitas linguae et interpretationis' ('the usefulness of language and translation'):

> That the use of language is multifold, everyone who speaks can witness. If you use a language well, it will be an ornament and assistance for a republic. If you should never bring it forth, but only know it, it will be as if you have a treasure locked up uselessly at home; it will be as if you have a sword, but that sword is hidden in its scabbard. The usefulness of a sword is its use: and likewise the edge of language shines with use, but grows dull by concealment.[53]

In both of these metaphors, the translator is someone who activates the latent powers of a foreign language. Humphrey's translator is far removed from the negative images that dominate Davis's study. Instead, Humphrey provides us with two metaphors that show how a translator could be seen as an active contributor to early modern society. This translator is an *adiumentum* that can provide wealth, ornaments and incitement.

However, Humphrey's discussion of the ideal translator in the first book of the *Interpretatio* is always tempered by an awareness that translation is never perfect. It is this awareness that gives an edge to all of his discussions.[54] There are two sides to this problem as Humphrey conceives it. One part is linguistic. He insists that translation is ultimately not a substitute for language learning, because no translation can be a replacement for the original. Each language has its own innate genius that is made up of the *proprietas* of its individual words and the *puritas* of its eloquence. These unique qualities cannot be directly recreated. It is impossible to reproduce the collocation of the original words without ruining the purity of your own language. The second side of the problem is personal. It is impossible to find a translator whose character corresponds precisely to that of the original author. Humphrey's fourth virtue, *aptitudo*, includes this quality of correspondence between the translator and the writer. Each author has a certain power or inspiration that Humphrey believes is a gift of God; to be a good translator one must be given a correlating gift (pp. 116–17). But even when blessed with this rare capacity, a translator never has precisely the same character as the original author, and each translator brings a distinctive set of tools to the task. The problem Humphrey sees is not only a question of the capacity each translator has as a writer, but also their modes of reading.

Humphrey acknowledges that different translators will see different qualities in a source. At the outset of Book 1, he writes, 'it is commonly but truly said that there are as many understandings as there are heads; or there are as many opinions as there are people. Each has their own eyes with which they may see what escapes others. And all do not have a similar nose for smelling or a similar judgement.'[55] Humphrey compares translation to painting another person's mind, but each person will see something slightly different. To make a perfect translation, we would have to be greater than the angels (p. 232). While Humphrey thus seeks to adumbrate the ideal translator, he constantly qualifies his own text with an awareness of the problems with which translation is fraught.

Throughout this book, I will explore how different translators of Virgil's *Aeneid* conceived their acts of translation. The standard approach to the *Aeneid* in the Renaissance was to read it as a model of epideictic poetry: it promoted virtue in its readers by providing, in Aeneas, a perfect example to follow.[56] Accordingly, the poem was regarded as an extremely useful text to disseminate in English. Most of the translators felt they were doing a great service to their nation by recreating the *Aeneid* in the vernacular. Their *utilitas* was a central motivation for them. A few, however, did not translate with the public good in mind. The stern Humphrey would certainly have condemned these men as writers of low character, because they preferred their own amusement to the commonwealth's good. As I will show in Chapter 3, these translators circulated their work in manuscript and delighted in mischievous readings of the *Aeneid*. For those who published translations of Virgil's epic in print, however, the *utilitas* of translating the *Aeneid* is a constant concern. And in the case of the printed early modern English *Aeneid*s, the key question to be asked is, what sort of virtues did the translators believe the poem promoted? As Humphrey notes, translators do not all have the same characters or read with the same eyes. For example, in the eyes of one translator, the *Aeneid* could provide a model of aristocratic, pacific policy for the king; in another's eyes, it might be meant to promote militant godliness in the common reader. By focusing on how different translators conceived the *Aeneid*'s *utilitas* I hope to break down some of the royalist/republican and optimistic/pessimistic dichotomies that are prevalent in contemporary criticism.

The second concern that this study will borrow from Humphrey is the role of emulation in translation. As G. W. Pigman III has shown in a classic essay, emulation was just beginning to be theorised in the early sixteenth century.[57] One of Humphrey's unique contributions to Renaissance theory is his extensive treatment of emulation in Book 2 of the *Interpretatio*. In this part of his treatise, Humphrey considers how translation relates to literary imitation. While acknowledging that there is a close relationship between the two, he laments that they were often being confused. His analysis of this confusion centres on the question of emulation. According to Humphrey, the main difference between an imitator and a translator is that the imitator is free to emulate the original text, whereas the translator is not. In this way, he offers a fascinating theory on the distinction between translation and imitation in the Renaissance.[58]

Arguing in particular against Joachim Périon, an infamous French translator of Aristotle, Humphrey posits that a translator's duty means that emulating the source text is out of the question. As soon as one presumes to emulate, then one is no longer an *interpres* but an *imitator*. To make his point, Humphrey offers a long and involved discussion of Cicero's and Périon's comments on 'free' translation (and the dangers of misinterpreting them).[59] The outcome of this discussion is Humphrey's declaration that 'it is the duty of the translator, in my opinion and understanding, to equal the author, not to surpass; to pursue, not to run ahead; and to aim to be alike, not greater than'.[60] The translator's duty to the reader is to provide something that either imparts knowledge or promotes virtue; the corresponding duty towards the source is to render the text as accurately as possible. Consequently, Humphrey makes one of the most radical claims for fidelity in sixteenth-century writing on translation. Even when the author is pagan and teaches something contrary to Christianity, the original meaning must be preserved: 'This fidelity is to be performed for all authors, even if they are very far removed from Christ.'[61] By enforcing this duty upon the translator, Humphrey makes a case for an ethics of translation that is impressively uncompromising.

This emphasis on a translator's duty, however, does not mean that emulation has no place in Humphrey's theory. On the contrary, he defends it in strong terms. He simply stresses that the target of one's emulation is not the source author, but rather the previous translators. For example, towards the end of the *Interpretatio*, in a section on the benefits of collating texts, Humphrey writes:

> Emulation is a great spur and incitement so that we translate correctly, and we contest with others who translated before us, so that we may struggle for the victory with them. Indeed this kind of emulation has not ignoble exemplars.[62]

Humphrey suggests that the most dynamic literary predecessor for a translation is often not the source, but the previous translators of that source text. Correspondingly, one of the great virtues of his treatise is how carefully he weighs different translations against each other. We have seen how for Humphrey all translations are inevitably imperfect and how translators will bring different perspectives to an author. This means that there will never be an end to translations of a specific text. Indeed, it is a great virtue to have multiple translations of a single work, because the translators can then emulate each other and produce something better. Several scholars have observed that early modern translators worked with other versions in front of them. In the tradition of English *Aeneid*s, the most notable examples of this have been John Dryden and William Wordsworth.[63] But already in the middle of the sixteenth century, Humphrey shows a theoretical awareness of this practice and encourages it.[64] Perhaps Humphrey's promotion of emulation among translators also provides some theoretical reasoning as to why, as Stuart Gillespie recently observed, 'classic' translations did not deter further translators but rather acted as a spur to them.[65]

In the course of this book, I will pay special attention to the question of how later translators seek to vie with their predecessors. I argue that this is not only a question of surpassing artistically, but also of supplanting old readings with new ones and contesting the cultural applications of Virgil's epic. Later translators could seek to offer a text with improved perspicuity, aptitude, elegance or cultural utility. The *Aeneid* is a unique opportunity to study this process of rivalry because of the number of translations that appeared in a short period of time. In the first chapter, I begin with a translation that became the first classic of early modern English *Aeneid*s: the version of *Aeneid* 1–9 by Thomas Phaer. Phaer's translation becomes a dominant influence on later translators of the epic, and it is even used in the versions that John Vicars and Robert Heath composed almost a century later. In the first chapter, I will begin by studying Phaer's translation itself, and then show how it affected the work of his two most immediate followers, Thomas Twyne and Richard Stanyhurst. I will show that translations from the English Renaissance need to be read together as a self-conscious tradition. The whole book will trace one such tradition and delineate its twists and turns.

Notes

1. James's full letter can be found in Elizabeth I, *Collected*, p. 375.
2. Ibid., p. 376.
3. Ibid., pp. 376–7.
4. Ibid., pp. 378–80.
5. A parallel can be drawn with George Peele's Neo-Latin poem *Pareus* (1585). In this poem, Juno summoning Allecto in Book 7 of the *Aeneid* is

the model for Pluto summoning Fraud in order to inspire William Parry to assassinate Elizabeth. Compare ll. 53–5 with *Aen.* 7.568–71. Peele's poem influenced later Anglo-Latin poetry (Sutton, *Oxford Poetry*, pp. 153–75), and it is not unlikely that Elizabeth was familiar with this application of Book 7 of the *Aeneid.*

6. The full letter can be found in Elizabeth I, *Collected*, pp. 380–2. Here, I quote p. 381.
7. Wilson-Okamura, *Virgil*, p. 9.
8. Conley, *First English Translators*, p. 2.
9. Ibid., pp. 23–5.
10. Ibid., pp. 32–3.
11. Ibid., pp. 57–63.
12. Hill, *Intellectual Origins*, p. 27.
13. Matthiessen, *Translation: An Elizabethan Art*, p. 3.
14. Ibid., p. 3.
15. Ibid., p. 26.
16. Tudeau-Clayton, *Jonson, Shakespeare and Early Modern Virgil*, p. 37.
17. Tudeau-Clayton, 'The Politics of Translating Virgil', pp. 507–9.
18. Lyne, *Ovid's Changing Worlds*, pp. 12–19.
19. Frost, 'Translating Virgil, Douglas to Dryden', p. 273.
20. Burrow, 'Virgil in English Translation', p. 21.
21. Braden, 'Epic Kinds', pp. 167–74.
22. Ibid., p. 167.
23. Proudfoot, *Dryden's 'Aeneid'*.
24. Kallendorf, *In Praise of Aeneas*; Kallendorf, *Virgil and the Myth of Venice*; Hamilton, *Virgil and 'The Tempest'*; Watkins, *The Specter of Dido*; James, *Shakespeare's Troy*; Tudeau-Clayton, *Jonson, Shakespeare and Early Modern Virgil*; Wallace, *Virgil's Schoolboys*; Wilson-Okamura, *Virgil in the Renaissance*.
25. Gillespie, *English Translation*, p. 1.
26. Thomas, *Virgil and the Augustan Reception*; Kallendorf, *The Other Virgil*.
27. Brooks, '*Discolor Aura*'; Clausen, 'An Interpretation of the *Aeneid*'; Parry, 'Two Voices of Virgil's *Aeneid*'.
28. Parry, 'Two Voices of Virgil's *Aeneid*', p. 80.
29. For some 'pessimistic' readings, see Putnam, *The Poetry of the 'Aeneid'* and Lyne, *Further Voices*. For distinguished 'optimistic' accounts in English, see: Otis, *Virgil: A Study in Civilized Poetry*; Hardie, *Virgil's 'Aeneid': Cosmos and Imperium*; and Cairns, *Virgil's Augustan Epic*.
30. Galinsky, 'Clothes for the Emperor'.
31. Kallendorf, *The Other Virgil*, p. 14.
32. Davis, *Translation and the Poet's Life*, p. 2; see also Braden, Review.
33. Gillespie, 'Translations from Greek and Latin Classics, Part 2'.
34. Braden, 'Epic Kinds', p. 167.
35. Kemp, 'Laurence Humphrey', pp. 8–9.
36. For details on his exile, see Kemp, 'Laurence Humphrey', pp. 6–15. Here, pp. 11–12.
37. Humphrey, *Interepretatio*, a8^{r}: 'O felix exilium quod homines remittit doctiores, o felicem aulam quae nobiles et doctos exules recipiet.'
38. Steiner, *After Babel*, p. 277.

39. In 2013, for the first time an excerpt of the *Interpretatio* has appeared in English translation in Neil Rhodes's collection. Rhodes, *English Renaissance*, pp. 263–94.
40. Braden, 'Translating Procedures in Theory and Practice', p. 89. This point is repeated in Gillespie, *English Translation*, p. 36.
41. See Steiner's discussion of Huet's relation to Humphrey: Steiner, *After Babel*, pp. 276–80.
42. Kemp, 'Laurence Humphrey', p. 134.
43. Harington, *New Discourse*, p. 104.
44. Peletier, *L'Art poetique*, p. 30.
45. Longiano, *Dialogo*, fols. 7v–8v.
46. Humphrey, *Interpretatio*, sig. a2v: 'communitatem utilitatemq*ue* late patentem'.
47. Ibid., sig. a5v: 'deniq*ue* nulla vitae pars aut functio hac interpretandi arte vacare potest: sive populu*m* doceas ut concionator, siue Scripturas interpreteris ut Theologus, siue tradas artes, ut Professor: siue iuventutem informes, ut Ludimagister: imo si teipsum erudias, haec semper utilis est, nunquam otiosa.'
48. On this theory of translation, see part 3, 'The Vocabulary of Expression', in Norton, *Ideology*, pp. 185–322.
49. Ibid., p. 114: 'Pedissequa*m* harum uirtutum omniu*m* nunc addo perspicuitate*m*, cognitione facillima*m*, usu necessaria*m*: ut quae per omnes partes orationis tanq*uam* sanguis quidam, sit diffusa.'
50. Ibid., sig. a5v. 'Foelix illa demum Respublica quae habet Interpretes.'
51. Reynolds, *The Poetry of Translation*, pp. 6–7.
52. Davis, *Translation and the Poet's Life*, pp. 6–7.
53. Humphrey, *Interpretatio*, p. 1: 'Usumfructum Linguae multiplicem esse, omnes qui loqui norunt, testari possunt: qua si utaris, magno erit ornamento et adiumento Reipubl*icae*. sin proferas nunquam, scias tantum: thesaurum quidem habes, sed domi clausum et inutilem: et gladium tenes, at in vagina reconditum. Gladii utilitas est usus: sic acies Linguae splendescet promendo, hebescet condendo.'
54. Norton's claim (*Ideology*, pp. 11–13) that Humphrey believed all translation could be perfectly and reductively schematised into a set of calculations ignores Humphrey's frequent assertions that there can be no universal, reductive doctrine of translation. See, for example, Humphrey, *Interpretatio*, p. 31.
55. Humphrey, *Interpretatio*, p. 10: 'Vulgo sed vere iactatum est, Quot capita, tot sensus, quot homines, tot sententiae. Sunt et cuiq*ue* sui oculi, quibus uideat, quae alios praeterea*nt*: nec similem in rebus olfaciendis nasum habent omnes et iudicium.'
56. See Kallendorf, *In Praise of Aeneas*. I will discuss this model of reading the *Aeneid* at greater length in Chapter 1.
57. Pigman, 'Versions of Imitation', pp. 22–5.
58. I am preparing an article on this topic, titled 'Joachim Périon, Lawrence Humphrey, and the Place of Imitation in Sixteenth-Century Translation Theory'.
59. Humphrey, *Interpretatio*, pp. 24–57.
60. Humphrey, *Interpretatio*, p. 251: 'Est autem interpretis officium, mea

quidem sententia et ratione, autorem aequare, non superare, assequi non praecurrere, et ut similis esse studeat non superior.'

61. Humphrey, *Interpretatio*, p. 176: 'Haec in omnibus autoribus praesta*n*da fides est, licet sint a Christo alienissimi.'
62. Humphrey, *Interpretatio*, p. 536: 'Aemulatio magnum calcar est et incitamentum ut recte vertamus, contendamusq*ue* cum aliis qui ante nos quippiam verterunt, ut cum illis de palma certemus. Hoc enim genus aemulationis non ignobiles autores habet.'
63. Proudfoot has described Dryden's translation as 'a tissue of adaptations' (*Dryden's 'Aeneid'*, p. 73). Wordsworth himself comments on his debts to previous translators in letters to Lord Lonsdale: see Wordsworth, *Translations*, pp. 562–7. For analysis of Wordsworth's relationship to Dryden and Pitt, see Graver, 'Wordsworth', and Gillespie, *English Translation*, pp. 150–5.
64. The practice of emulating previous translators has a long history among the humanists, but Humphrey is the first of the major theorists to focus on the term *aemulatio*. On the history of competitive translation, see Botley, *Latin Translation*, pp. 170–2.
65. Gillespie, *English Translation*, pp. 116–22.

Chapter 1

The Search for a Lofty British Virgil: The Early Elizabethan *Aeneids* of Thomas Phaer, Thomas Twyne and Richard Stanyhurst

The English Renaissance *Aeneid*

The complete translation of the *Aeneid* by Thomas Phaer and Thomas Twyne has every reason to be considered the central English Renaissance *Aeneid*.[1] The publication history tells the story succinctly. Whereas no other translation of Virgil was printed in England more than twice until the 1650s (and only the Earl of Surrey's translation of Book 4 was printed more than once in England during this time), the translation by Phaer and Twyne went through eight editions, running from 1558 through to 1620. It influenced the translations by Richard Stanyhurst (1582), Sir John Harington (1604) and Sir Thomas Wroth (1620), and it was still one of the most important subtexts for John Vicars' *The XII Aeneids of Virgil* (1632). Much as the translation by Annibale Caro came to dominate the market for Virgil in Italian, the Phaer-Twyne *Aeneid* became the English standard. It was not until the eighteenth century that any English translation of Virgil's epic went through more editions.[2]

That this translation would become so successful would have been difficult to predict from its inauspicious beginnings. The initial translator, Thomas Phaer, was a physician and solicitor in the Marches of Wales. He published nothing else in verse and would have made an unlikely candidate for a great interpreter of Virgil. Nevertheless, in 1555 he began work, hoping to be the first to 'sette open' the gate so that future translators could follow. Although Phaer seems to have been aware of both the Middle Scots translation by Gavin Douglas and the two books by the Earl of Surrey, he presented his version of the *Aeneid* as the start of a new line of translations.[3] By December 1557, Phaer had completed a version of Books 1–7. He had these printed in 1558. By April 1560, he had completed up to the end of Book 9. But late in that spring, he suffered a riding accident that ruined his hand and would soon cost him his life. Before his death on 12 August, he sent all that he had finished of his translation – which was then up to line 286 of Book 10 – to William Wightman, a friend of his in Pembrokeshire. This friend fervently believed in Phaer's literary gifts and, after Phaer had passed away, he searched the deceased's house for any trace of remaining verses. But there was none to be found. In 1562, Wightman resigned himself to publishing what he had of Phaer's Virgil, hoping that another author might complete the project. Just over a decade later, the work was taken up by Thomas Twyne, who was a physician in London. He completed the fragment of the *Aeneid* left by Phaer and had it printed in 1573. Another eleven years later, Twyne produced an edition with a translation of Maffeo Vegio's Book 13 added as a supplement. Composed by a distinguished fifteenth-century Neo-Latin poet, Book 13 was a popular continuation of the *Aeneid* that appeared in many Renaissance editions. The thirteen-book Phaer-Twyne *Aeneid* thus took just under thirty years to reach its completion: the publication in 1584 of a handsome quarto titled *The .xiii. Bookes of Æneidos* marked the end of the project that Phaer had originally embarked upon in May 1555.

The response to the translation was extremely positive. In his preface to Greene's *Menaphon*, Thomas Nashe noted that Phaer's 'famous *Virgill*' contained 'heauenly verse'.[4] Barnabe Googe wrote admiringly about the translations of the Earl of Surrey, Nicholas Grimald and Gavin Douglas, but he judged Phaer the greatest translator by far: 'But all these same dyd *Phayre* excel, I dare presume to wryte, | As muche as doth *Apolloes* Beames, the dymmest Starre in lyght.'[5] In Chapter 31 of *The Arte of English Poesie*, titled 'Who in any age have been the most commended writers in our English poesy', George Puttenham declared that 'in Queen Mary's time flourished above any other Doctor Phaer'.[6] Likewise, in *A Discourse of English Poetrie*, William Webbe stated that among translators, 'I ever esteemed, and while I lyve, in my concept I shall account Master D. Phaer: without doubt the best.'[7] Another admirer of Phaer's work was Arthur Hall, who was the first English translator of Homer. He tells us that reading Phaer's Virgil made him dumbfounded and ashamed by his own attempts at the *Iliad*: 'I was so abashed looking upon M. Phaers Heroicall Virgill, and my Satiricall Homer, as I cried out, envying Virgils prosperitie.'[8] Such comments clearly show the immense enthusiasm with which this Virgil was greeted. No other early modern English translation of a classical poet received such universal high praise.

The contemporary responses are also instructive because they sketch the initial impression that the translation made. They provide us with a hint about what made Phaer's work seem so exceptional. Common to all contemporary responses was a sense of what Richard Stanyhurst describes as the work's 'loftiness'. Stanyhurst states, 'the gentleman [Phaer] hath translated *Virgil* into Englishe rythme with such surpassing excellencie, as a very few (in my conceit) for pickte and loftie words can bourd him, none, I am wel assured, overgoe him'.[9] *Loftiness* was the choice word for Stanyhurst and, although other writers couched their praise in different terms, the message was the same. In the eyes of William Webbe, Phaer's *Aeneid* was a sign that English poetry can 'be brought to the very majesty of a ryght Heroicall verse', since it embodies a 'gallant grace'.[10] And in a particularly curious comment Thomas Nashe even went so far as to state that Phaer's verse was 'blemished by his hautie thoughts'.[11] In early modern English, 'haughty' could be a synonym for lofty and, through its derivation from 'haut', it also carried a sense of height.[12] Thus Googe begins his 'Epytaphe of Maister Thomas Phayre' by writing about the 'hawtye verse y^{t} *Maro* wrote', which Googe will eventually praise Phaer for recreating.[13] Phaer's poetry was perceived as lofty, gallant, majestic: it pursued no middle flight. No modern critic, however, has attempted to explain why this translation garnered this early reception.

Instead, recent critical responses have focused on the 'popularising' aspect of Phaer's *oeuvre*. Scholars such as Rick Bowers and Steven Lally have insisted on understanding the translation in the larger context of Phaer's lifelong project. He was a great populist polymath. Phaer spent one part of his life as a physician and public servant, and the other part following a personal mandate to promote the spread of knowledge by writing and translating into English scientific (*Natura Brevium*, *c.*1530), legal (*Newe Boke of Presidentes*, 1543), medical (*The Boke of Chyldren*, 1544) and classical texts (*The Nyne Fyrst Bookes of the Eneidos*, 1562). Many of these works contain notes about his aims in their introductions. For example, in Phaer's *Boke of Chyldren*, his intention is 'to distrybute in Englysshe to them that are unlerned part of the treasure that is in other languages, to provoke them that are of better lerning, to utter theyr knowledge in suche lyke attemptes'.[14] In an impassioned introduction to his translation of Jean Goeurot's *The Regiment of Life*, Phaer cites Galen, Pliny, Avicenna and Ficino as examples to show that the wisest of men write in their own language so that their ideas can reach wide audiences: 'the entent of all that ever set forth any noble studye have ben to be redde, of as many as wolde.'[15] Christ says that 'no man lyghteth a candle to cover it with a bushel', and those who would conceal knowledge in a foreign language are doing something 'eccedynge dampnable and devylyshe'.[16] For Bowers and Lally, Phaer's translation of the *Aeneid* was a continuation of his lifelong ambition to spread knowledge in the vernacular. His *Aeneid* was a national, democratic and educational project.[17]

The counter-argument, however, has been made in an article by Margaret Tudeau-Clayton. She argues that in the case of these early translations that claim to be promoting 'English', one first needs to ask *whose* English is being promoted.[18] The translators do not necessarily promote a universally available model of 'English' and critics need to pay greater attention to the specific 'linguistic ideology' of each individual translation. When this subtle form of ideology is studied, then one realises that translations of Virgil 'could rather serve attempts at stabilising the vernacular and, with it, the social hierarchy, the "Language" of the "gentleman" being distinguished as his "proper" property'.[19] In spite of Phaer's pronouncements that he is translating to spread knowledge, Tudeau-Clayton reads Phaer's work as promoting an 'exclusive', 'polished' and 'ornate' gentleman's language. Her awareness of the potential for translations to be elitist is an important correction to Bower and Lally. And her claim that Phaer's *Aeneid* is more exclusive than democratic is also intriguing, especially when considering the contemporary responses to the translation. However, Tudeau-Clayton does not offer any evidence to show what this noble, gentleman's language actually entails. She does not explain what makes Phaer's translation in any way exclusive, aside from noting that he addresses 'the nobilitie' in his closing remarks to the readers.

In this chapter, my aim will be to uncover what the 'loftiness' that contemporaries found in Phaer's *Aeneid* involves. As this translation came together in many different stages, any thorough study must consider it one stage at a time. In the first section, I focus exclusively on Thomas Phaer's rendition of Books 1–9. I begin by exploring how from his marginal position he was able to create an *Aeneid* that became so central in English Renaissance culture. In contemporary commentaries, Virgil's *Aeneid* was always associated with the 'grand' style: Badius states that Virgil wrote the *Eclogues* in the 'humile genus', the *Georgics* in the 'mediocre' and the *Aeneid* in the 'sublime'.[20] I will show that Phaer's translation fulfilled the demands of the high style in three ways. First, he conveyed a loftiness of language and versification; second, he stressed the importance of historical Roman nobility in the poem, bringing out the epic's treatment of noble heroes; and, most importantly, he read the *Aeneid* as a humanistic expression of the lofty potential of man. In the second section, I explore how Phaer's *Aeneid* was later continued by Thomas Twyne. I show that Twyne's extension of Phaer's work was undertaken with reverence for Phaer's achievement; even if Twyne shows some hesitations about Phaer's Catholicisim, he faithfully imitates his predecessor's reading of the epic. Their combined efforts thus produced a coherent, standard translation that appealed greatly to English readers and had an immense influence. To conclude the chapter, I will consider the first example of this translation's sway over later poets. Richard Stanyhurst's distinctive style of translating Virgil into dactylic hexameters sprang out of his attempt to emulate the loftiness of the Phaer-Twyne *Aeneid*. History has not dealt kindly with Stanyhurst's efforts, but one can appreciate his translation better by understanding how it emerged out of his reaction to his chief predecessors. His translation develops the English *Aeneid* in directions that were not to be taken up by any of his followers. As such it offers a fascinating glimpse into a potential world of English *Aeneid*s that (thankfully) never were.

Thomas Phaer and the 'Privilege Vertue Gives'

At the beginning of the twelfth chapter of *The Light in Troy*, Thomas Greene traces the development of early English humanism by charting the growth of a historical consciousness in English literature. Greene places the development of an early English historicism at the end of the fifteenth century and the beginning of the sixteenth. He sketches its progress in four stages that he illustrates with translations of the *Aeneid*.[21] The first stage, anachronism, is reflected in William Caxton's *Eneydos* of 1490, which reveals a complete lack of perception of historical change. The second phase, early humanism, is then exemplified by Gavin Douglas's *Aeneid* (1513), which is still full of anachronisms (knights and ladies people the landscape), but is nonetheless aware of the gulf between classical Rome and early modern Scotland. For the third stage, mature humanism, Greene turns away from Virgil translators and uses Sir Thomas More's epigrams. The final stage, full heuristic imitation, is illustrated by the complex imitations of Wyatt and Surrey. It would have been interesting to know where Greene would have placed Phaer's translation in this outline. Borrowing his model, I would suggest that Phaer's *Aeneid* fits somewhere in between the early humanism of Gavin Douglas and the full historical consciousness of Sir Thomas More. His treatment of history jumps back and forth between their models. In this quality, Phaer's *Aeneid* is perhaps most typical of sixteenth-century English humanism, which Greene characterises as being less polemically divided from its medieval past than the French or Italian versions.[22]

One place in which one can see this 'in between' position is the metre Phaer uses for his translation. The iambic heptameter can be read as a version of the standard, medieval ballad metre. One could rewrite the opening of Phaer's translation as a ballad, and it would flow very convincingly:

I that my slender Oten Pype
    in verse was wont to sounde
Of woodes, and nexte to that I taught
    for husbandmen the grounde
How frute unto their gredie luste
    thei might contrayne to bryng,
A worcke of thankes: Lo now of Mars
    and dreadfull warres I syng.[23]

The exact fit of the caesuras to the divisions of the ballad metre is common in the early parts of Phaer's translation. In the address to his readers, Phaer asks them 'to pardon my first booke, wherin I found this new kinde of fingering somewhat straunge unto me'.[24] The word 'fingering' evokes the image of Phaer tapping out the rhythms on his desk as he worked out his versification. It seems that as he started working with fourteeners, Phaer relied especially on the underlying ballad rhythm to make his verse flow. In the later books, however, it is not so easy to find verse that reveals its affinity to the ballad. While Phaer begins by adapting a medieval English verse form, he ends with something he believed to be much more fitting for classical, Roman epic.

In the *Aeneid* translations before Phaer, one can trace a progression towards imitating dactylic hexameter in English. In 1490, William Caxton displayed no interest in the Latin hexameter at all, translating from a French text into English prose. In Douglas's 1513 *Eneados*, Virgil's poetic line becomes the typical unit of translation, although Douglas tends to render every one of Virgil's lines into at least two lines of Scots.[25] In the 1540s, the Earl of Surrey, who has been described as 'the first English classical poet', moves much closer to the Latin line. In W. A. Sessions's account, Surrey's blank verse originated from the dialectic between his meditations upon the Latin hexameter and his experiments in reproducing the human voice.[26] Surrey's blank verse could thus be said to represent the first full heuristic imitation of Virgil's dactylic hexameter in English. But Phaer found a distinctly different possibility in the fourteeners. The essential formal structure, the unit by which he translated, is Virgil's poetic line. He takes the liberty of changing the phrasing freely, but he tries to keep the same content in the same position in the poetic line as it is in Virgil's Latin. This practice is not found in any other major translator of mid-sixteenth-century England, but it was a controversial concept on the continent. Several French theorists, such as Dolet and Sebillet, attacked those who felt that a translation should follow the lines of the original.[27] Phaer would have disagreed with these theorists, since Virgil's line is integral to his method of composition. A comparison of how many lines the translators needed to render Book 2 of the *Aeneid* into English can demonstrate just how different Phaer's translation was from his predecessors. Book 2 has 804 lines in the original, 1,442 lines in Douglas's translation and 1,070 lines in Surrey's translation. Phaer uses 812.[28] And perhaps the clearest signal of this new imitation of Virgil's Latin hexameters is that Phaer is the first English translator to reproduce all of Virgil's conspicuous half-lines.

To see how this method of translation works in action, we can look at a passage from Book 8, where Phaer follows Virgil to the exact position in the line. Here, Venulus is told what to report to Diomedes:

> Dilating more, howe many nations be yt joyne their dedes
> With Troy: & how the Trojan name in Latium shrewdly spredes
> What these beginnings meane, & if his chaunce shuld give successe
> What sequel worke he would: more manifest him self may gesse,
> Then either Turnus king or king Latinus list expresse.
> Such worke in Latium land there was.

> edoceat, multasque viro se adiungere gentis
> Dardanio et late Latio increbrescere nomen:
> quid struat his coeptis, quem, si fortuna sequatur
> euentum pugnae cupiat, manifestius ipsi
> quam Turno regi aut regi apparere Latino.
> Talia per Latium.[29]

The English translation offers an almost exact mirror of the Latin. Words appear in the same position in the lines. For example, in the third line, 'quid struat his coeptis' takes up precisely the same proportion of the Latin line as 'What these beginnings meane' does of the English. In the fifth line, the chiasmus 'Turno regi aut regi apparere Latino' is cleverly captured by 'either Turnus king or king Latinus list expresse'. This passage is thus an instance of how closely Phaer could adhere to Virgil. This proximity to the Latin is something that his contemporaries noticed. In *A Discourse of English Poetrie* (1586), William Webbe cursed accentual rhyming poetry as a 'rude kinde of verse' that was 'borrwed from the Barbarians'.[30] Webbe wanted to see English metre reformed until it was properly quantitative, 'a farre more learned manner of versifying'.[31] He saw Phaer as one of the leading figures who showed that English verse can ascend to the height of classical verse. The closeness of Phaer's fourteeners to dactylic hexameter, without seeming strained or unnatural, is thus one of the reasons why contemporaries viewed the translation as especially lofty. Using George Steiner's terminology, we could say that Phaer seeks for his translation to live 'inside' the source.[32] A transformed version of the medieval ballad metre surprisingly becomes an innovative approximation of the Latin hexameter in English.

This mixed approach, part medieval and part humanistic, is also apparent in the position Phaer takes towards the epic as a whole. Sometimes he comes across as an anachronist, conflating a mythical Rome and a fantastical Britain into one colourful present. 'Nymphae' (4.168) become 'the mountain fairies' and a gloss in Book 4 tells us about 'Field Nymphes otherwyse called fayeries'.[33] The countryside is peopled by 'Mermaides', 'lusty yonkers' and 'eger knightes', who roam through 'burgeis townes'.[34] The political structures of ancient Rome are curiously like those of Tudor Britain. There is a 'Mynster, court, & hall', and a couple of the courts even have their own 'parliaments'.[35] The gods have their churches: we encounter 'Apollos church' as well as 'Phebus church'.[36] However, for all these anachronisms, Phaer also displays a keen interest in the distinctiveness of ancient Roman culture. He instructs us in glosses about ancient funeral fires, the ancients' understanding of Aurora and the threat Hannibal posed to Rome.[37] He describes augury as an 'old superstition of divination by byrdes called augurium', and he seems to approve of the fact that 'Kinges that tyme were preestes'.[38] He even takes an interest in the way the ancients dined: 'Antiquity fedde upon beddes as the Turkes do yet.'[39]

Indeed, in spite of the persistent anachronisms, history plays a crucial part in Phaer's translation. Near the beginning of Book 2, a gloss informs us, 'The entent of this work is onelye to tell the beginninge of Rome.'[40] This translation is a poem about the origins of a noble Roman people and their aristocratic lines. In Book 5, Phaer adds a gloss to inform the reader that the competitors in the games for Anchises were 'Auncestors of certen the noblest men in Rome when he wrote thys booke'.[41] And as he does throughout his whole translation, he reinforces the high aristocratic importance of these characters by frequently adding titles such as 'sir', 'duke' and 'lord', as well as adjectives such as 'noble' and 'pure'.[42] In the heavily commented Book 6, Phaer does not include a single gloss from the point where Aeneas enters the underworld until he meets his father. At the prospect of the future nobility of Rome processing before Aeneas, however, Phaer becomes excited: 'Here Virgil taketh a wonderful occasion to discourse the posteritie of Eneas and to set furth the glory and nobilitie of Rome.'[43] Webbe describes the *Aeneid* as an epitome of 'that princelie part of Poetrie, wherein are displaied the noble actes and valiant exploits of puissant Captaines, expert souldiers, wise men, with famous reportes of auncient times'.[44] Phaer would have agreed, and his glorification of the ancient aristocracy would have added another factor to the perception of his translation's loftiness.

A correlating part of the historical dynamic of Phaer's translation is his interest in how the ancient times have reached down to the present. He notes that the Sibyl's 'cave yet remains' and that Averna is 'yet a terrible place to loke on'.[45] One can already find in Phaer the nascent interest in the material reality of the ancient world. This sort of interest would eventually come to fruition in travel narratives such as George Sandys's *Relation of a Journey* (1615), in which Sandys tells how he looked for remnants of the classical past while travelling through Italy. It is tempting to speculate that Phaer's Welshness contributed to his sense of continuity. Unfortunately such a connection must remain conjectural. As a highly learned, Oxford-educated man who lived most of his life in Wales, he would have been aware of the special place that Troy played in Tudor history. The Trojan heritage of Wales – the belief in its descent from the Trojan Brutus, as recounted in Geoffrey of Monmouth's *Historia regum Britanniae* – was a central part of the British nationalism of the Tudor era.[46] The prophecy of Cadwaladr predicted the Welsh reconquest of Britain. This prophecy was taken to refer to the Welsh heritage of Harri Tudor and made Welsh history relevant for the whole nation. But Phaer never alludes to this mythical history of Britain anywhere in his text, even when he highlights his own Welshness. For instance, at the end of every book Phaer reminds his readers that he was translating 'in foresta Kilgerran Southwallie'.[47] Or, to take another example, when Allecto is described in Book 7 as stirring people up like boys playing with a top, Phaer notes: 'This play is yet used in wales and the ball is called knappan.'[48] Humphrey Llwyd's description (and the Renaissance stereotype) of the Welsh as 'overmuch boastying of the Nobilitie of their stocke' might correspond to Phaer's high praise of the ancient Trojan and Roman nobility.[49] However, there can be no doubt that Phaer believed that the Roman nobility's heritage was still a vibrant part of the world in the middle of the sixteenth century and that this contributed to the emphasis on history throughout this translation. At the end of his summary of the *Aeneid*, he writes

> of [Aeneas'] issewe afterwarde proceded the greatest Princes of the worlde, by whom Rome was founded, that sometyme was ruler of the universall earth, and yet among all christen kyngdomes beareth no litle sway of auctoritie and dominion.[50]

Phaer thus read the *Aeneid* as a historical epic that told of the loftiest and most influential nobility to have walked the earth.

The great nobles of history were especially important for Phaer because he believed they could serve as a guide to the readers of his own time. His *Aeneid* provided the examples that the readers could imitate.

In addition to the nobles, a second group of individuals were also exemplars: these were the admirable pagan gods who become 'saints' in this translation. In a moment that perhaps displays a touch of Phaer's Catholicism, at 7.204, 'sponte sua' in the Latin prompts the remarkable translation, 'But uncompeld, our gods example old our freewills drawes.'[51] The readers have a choice: they are free to follow, or reject, the many examples of virtue that are offered in the epic. The role that the nobles and saints play – 'examples old' that draw men's wills – is representative of the larger didactic project that Phaer's translation pursues. In the letter to his readers, Phaer identifies two reasons he undertook his translation. The first is 'for defence of my countrey language', and the second is 'for honest recreation of you the nobilitie, gentelmen and Ladies, that studie not Latine'.[52] Phaer sees his translation as a substitute for readers who are not able to understand Virgil's Latin. The phrase 'honest recreation' combines the elements of delight and education, of *delectare* and *prodesse*. Here is an English *Aeneid* that will be able to move readers who otherwise would not be touched by Virgil's epic. In this way Phaer conceives the *utilitas* of his *Aeneid* translation.

As a substitute, however, Phaer's *Aeneid* is not able to recreate all of the original. Tudeau-Clayton has traced a 'hierarchy of privilege' in which there is a moral 'schoolboy's Virgil' and a more exclusive, esoteric 'learned man's Virgil'.[53] This latter Virgil is a master of natural philosophy and sometimes even of magic. It is precisely this esoteric Virgil that Phaer insists he is unable to translate into English:

> you know, there be many misticall secretes in this writer, whiche uttered in English, would shew litle pleasour, and in mine oppinion are better to be untouched, than to deminish the grace of the rest with tedyousnes or darknesse.[54]

The key locus for this sort of wisdom is Book 6 of the *Aeneid*. In the glosses to this book Phaer sometimes hints at knowledge hidden within the Latin: Virgil wraps 'Truth in darkness', the golden bough signifies 'wysdome that overcometh all thynges' and Aeneas is addressed as the 'Trojan duke of wisdome sage'.[55] But as noted above, Phaer makes no glosses from the point when Aeneas enters the underworld until he meets his father. Phaer leaves all of the 'misticall secretes' untouched.

Instead, he focuses on the moral and historical values that Tudeau-Clayton locates as part of the schoolboy's Virgil. He sees his audience as in need of guidance: 'some what I have in places omitted, somewhat have altred, & some thinge I have expounded, and all to the ease of inferior readers, for you that are learned, neede not to be instructed'.[56] To make the poem more accessible for less learned readers, the translation contains several simplifications. Some of these are geographical and cultural. The word 'Moor', for instance, is the English rendering of a wide range of Latin names: it translates 'Numidae', 'Poenorum', 'Maurusia [. . .] | gens', as well as 'Gaetulis'.[57] The phrase 'si te Karthaginis arces | Phoenissam Libycaeque aspectus detinet urbis' (4.347–8) becomes 'And you a Moore among the Moores rejoyce this town to see'.[58] Another type of simplification occurs in the underworld. Phaer has imagined Virgil's underworld as having only three important parts: Limbo, Hell and Paradise. 'Limbo' translates a range of Latin terms, including 'Stygio', 'Ditis', 'Orci', 'Acherontis' and 'Erebi'.[59] 'Hell' is generally the translation for 'Tartarus', which is rendered as 'Hell it self'.[60] 'Elysium' accordingly becomes paradise.[61] It seems that Phaer understood this map of the underworld in moral terms, and he occasionally even alters the Latin. For example, Virgil's Euryalus descends to 'Tartara' (9.496), but Phaer kindly amends the youth's destination to 'Limbo'.[62]

The purpose of these simplifications and alterations in Phaer's *Aeneid* was to facilitate access to the didactic core of the epic. In this translation, the central concern is pedagogic and moral rather than mystical or allegorical. Phaer generally follows the model promoted by Italian Renaissance humanism. As Craig Kallendorf has shown in his book, *In Praise of Aeneas*, this model is built upon the categories of epideictic rhetoric and views Aeneas as a rhetorical example of the good man being praised.[63] At the time when Phaer was writing in the mid-sixteenth century, the most commonly printed Renaissance commentary on Virgil was that of Jodocus Badius Ascensius. According to Badius, Virgil intended to put before Augustus the model of a perfect prince in the character of Aeneas. Badius writes:

> for Virgil knew that nothing is better for a republic than to have a prince who is merciful and prudent and brave and temperate and just and endowed with other virtues. Virgil depicted such a prince in Aeneas for Augustus to imitate, as Xenophon is said to have done in Cyrus, not as he was, but describing him as he ought to have been.[64]

Badius' Aeneas is a representation of how a good man should behave in all situations. Moreover, according to Badius, by creating this model figure of Aeneas, Virgil sought to outdo Homer, who treated the contemplative and the active lives separately in two different epics. Odysseus, on the one hand, was supposedly representative of the contemplative life, while Agamemnon and the Trojan War were representative of the active life. In the *Aeneid*, however, Virgil brought both of these lives together in the one person of Aeneas, who moves through both the contemplative life in the first half of the *Aeneid* and the active life in the second:

> For what Homer did in twenty-four books, our poet did in only six: seeing that, in the first six books he portrayed the *Odyssey* (that is the 'virum'), and in the following six he imitated the *Iliad* (that is the 'arma'). Just as it seems that Homer's intention was to unfold both the contemplative life, which is portrayed in Ulysses, and the active, which is expressed in the wisely waged Trojan war, so it was our poet's [Virgil's] intention to depict both lives: but Virgil depicts them for us in one man, which is more glorious.[65]

There is thus a fullness of character in Aeneas. This fullness is what allowed Sidney to claim that Aeneas represents 'so excellent a man [in] every way'.[66] Aeneas is, in fact, the prime example of what Sidney thought literature could offer: a perfect person, such as the real world could not produce, who would be able to act as a model for others to follow, and who, through praises heaped upon him, would spur his readers to follow his example. Likewise, Edmund Spenser, in 'The Letter to Ralegh', follows the same theory about the value of Virgil's Aeneas. And Spenser presents the same division that we saw in Badius: the *Odyssey* represents private virtues, the *Iliad* public virtues and Virgil's *Aeneid* has combined the two in the one character of Aeneas, whom Spenser hoped to imitate with King Arthur.

In Phaer's translation, this is the reading of the *Aeneid* that is offered for the noble English audience. Early in Book 1, when Aeneas makes his famous 'O socii' speech, Phaer adds a significant gloss: 'Under the name of Eneas is described in Virgill the part of a perfite wise man and valiant capteyn if ye marke it.'[67] We find here in a nutshell the whole humanist's *Aeneid*. Aeneas is presented as an absolute model in all facets of life, combining both the contemplative ('perfit wise man') and the active ('valiant captayne'). The reader is encouraged to 'marke it' and thus be moved by the rhetorical power towards a virtuous life. And virtue is another key concept behind Phaer's translation. Whereas other English translators will focus on the 'godliness' or the 'bravery' of Aeneas, in Phaer's *Aeneid* 'virtue' is the word that captures the hero's exceptional quality. Aeneas is the essence of the ideal English prince or courtier. At the opening of the poem, Aeneas is described by Virgil as 'insignem pietate' (1.10). Phaer rewrites these words as 'This noble prince of vertue milde',[68] a phrase that sets the programme for the hero. This is not the only time Phaer chooses a different word for 'pietas'. At the culmination of Book 6, 'pietate insignis' (403) becomes 'curteis prince', and when Anchises hails Aeneas for having reached him in Elysium through 'pietas' (6.688), Phaer translates, 'Thy vertue overcame this passage hard.'[69] The power of virtue in the face of fortune is one of the central beliefs of Renaissance humanism, and faith in this power is inscribed deeply into Phaer's translation.

On the day before his death, Thomas Phaer sent a translation of two and a half verses to William Wightman, the 'Recepuour [*sic*] of South Wales'.[70] These lines were the opening words of Hercules' lament over the deceased Pallas, and they are from a part of the *Aeneid* Phaer was unable to complete:

Stat sua cuiq*ue* dies, breve & irreparabile tempus
omnibus est vitæ: sed famam extendere factis,
Hoc virtutis opus.
Ech mans day stands prefixt, time short & swift wt cureles bretche
is lotted al mankind, but by their deedes their fame to stretche
That privilege vertue gives.[71]

Phaer chose his final words well: these verses are the best summation of his work as a translator of Virgil, as they combine nearly all the major elements of his translation. There is a close fidelity to the Latin and a mirroring of the structure of Virgil's lines. The theme is the bold belief that the Renaissance humanists had in the power of virtue to conquer fortune and win glory. But most significantly, these lines give us a much clearer conception of what precisely would make Phaer's *Aeneid* strike its readers as especially *lofty*.

Phaer's translation not only claims that the English language can mirror the Latin; it not only glorifies the British and Roman nobility. Phaer's translation also offers an especially high opinion of man. His Aeneas is the consummate hero of virtue, the *vir virtutis*. And it is this belief in virtue that leads to one of the most striking deviations. In Book 3, Virgil's Aeneas avoids the pass between Scylla and Charybdis at the warning of Helenus. In Phaer's translation, however, Aeneas sails right through:

But than again king Helenus commaundments did us stay,
To keepe betwene Charibdis gulfe, and Sylla myddle way.
Betwene them both we past with danger great.[72]

These three lines reveal a great deal about the difference between Phaer's conception of the epic hero and Virgil's ambiguous portrayal of Aeneas. Phaer was convinced in the powers of his Aeneas: the pass between Scylla and Charybdis could not harm his glorious hero.

Thomas Twyne and the 'Unperfect' *Aeneid*: Reverence, Continuity and Change

About a decade after Phaer's death, the London physician Thomas Twyne completed the remaining two and a half books of the *Aeneid*

Phaer had left unfinished. To the new publication, Twyne also contributed a translation of the *Vita Donati*, arguments for each book of the epic, and a translation of Maffeo Vegio's Book 13, which appeared in 1584. These paratextual contributions were printed in all four editions of the Phaer-Twyne *Aeneid* that appeared after 1584. Twyne's contribution to the central English Renaissance *Aeneid* was thus substantial. Nevertheless, he has remained in the shadow of his predecessor: most critics treat the Phaer-Twyne *Aeneid* solely as the work of Thomas Phaer, without distinguishing between the two translators. Only one attempt, by Steven Lally, has been made to treat the two translators' contributions separately. In the second portion of this chapter, I will explore Twyne's distinctive contribution to this central English Virgil.

In his critical edition of this translation, Lally builds a case that Twyne needs to be considered as a very different figure from Phaer. Whereas Phaer is portrayed by Lally as a populariser and medievalist, Twyne was the son of a prominent English classicist. Unlike Phaer, Twyne was 'more interested in the newfangled and innovative, than in the tradition-bound'.[73] While Lally admits that Twyne leaves 'Phaer's language almost completely untouched', he believed that Twyne attempted to bring Phaer's verse within 'the quantitative trend begun by Surrey'.[74] In order to do so, Twyne supposedly carried out a thorough orthographical and typographical reform, 'in order to shift the aesthetic focus away from accent and, instead, draw attention to the individual vowel length'.[75] The example of this Lally offers is the different 'e' sounds in the new version. In the 1573 *Aeneid*, one can find 'e', a ligature of 'ee' and a ligature of 'eé' distinguished from each other. Since the changes are introduced so thoroughly, Lally argues that we should credit Twyne with the changes. The result is an English line that is supposed to be closer to the classical, quantitative hexameter.[76] Lally concludes that Twyne should be considered a major contributor to the translation as it was read after 1573.

Lally's interest in Twyne's contribution to the final Phaer-Twyne *Aeneid* is well placed. His conclusions, however, are misleading. Lally does not show how these reforms would create a line in any way closer to the Latin hexameter or even to the English hexameters that were being written. More importantly, the 'orthographical reform' and the typographical changes might have had nothing to do with Twyne: it was probably the work of the printer, William How. How's poetic and prose texts from as early as 1569 use all of the different ligatures one finds in the 1573 and 1584 editions of the Phaer-Twyne *Aeneid*. These ligatures are even included in rather frivolous publications that show no sign of quantitative verse. Thus in 1570, How published a one page poem titled *A Mervaylous Straunge Deformed Swyne*.[77] The poem describes a pig from Belgium that appeared with monstrous features, and a picture of the incredible pig is also provided. The pig evidently prefigures the apocalypse, and thus demands the attention of readers (as I cannot reproduce the 'e' ligatures, I mark them here with italics):

> Come n*eé*re good Christians all,
> beholde a Monster rare:
> Whose Monstrous shape (no doubt) fortels
> Gods wrath we should beware.
> His wondrous works we ought not judge,
> as toyes and trifles vaine:
> Whither it be Childe or brutish Beast,
> forwarnings they are playne.
> As now, this mingled brutish Beast,
> Gods creature is we s*ee*:
> Although as straunge of shape and forme
> As possyblie may be.

The opening twelve lines, in ballad metre, display all three 'e' sounds that Twyne supposedly worked into Phaer's Virgil. To consider Twyne's Virgil translation, we clearly need another starting point.

Rather than beginning with the novelties of Twyne's work, it is more productive to begin with the similarities between him and Phaer. In this case, the closeness between the two is more remarkable than the divergences. Twyne does not seek to emulate Phaer, as he seems to have held Phaer's work in great reverence. For example, the two and a half lines Phaer translated before his death are incorporated seamlessly into Twyne's translation of Book 10. For another example, we can look at the glosses. It seems that Phaer also died before having been able to complete the glosses on Books 8 and 9, for there is only one in the 1562 edition. In Twyne's 1573 edition, however, new glosses are silently added around the one gloss by Phaer, which is preserved. Twyne even adds Latin notes at the end of each of the books he translated, stating where and when the translation was completed. These notes precisely echo those that Phaer had added to Books 1–9. Taken together, these three instances show how careful Twyne was to respect everything Phaer had done. But more than this, Twyne was also a sensitive reader of Phaer's poetry. He stays true to the style and concerns of his predecessor's translation. In the letter preceding the 1573 publication, Twyne writes, 'I have enterprised more ventrously then wisely, & with better courage then cunning to end that which he left unperfect. Not that I thinke my self comparable unto him in any thing that he tooke in hande.'[78] Even if Twyne's expression of modesty could be regarded as conventional, there is no reason to doubt that he really did have the highest respect for Phaer's achievements.

Twyne continued his translation in fourteeners, and he seems to have understood how Phaer used them as a medium for recreating the Latin. As did Phaer, Twyne recreates all of Virgil's half-lines in the English. And as did Phaer, Twyne generally places the English content as close as he can to the position that it had in the Latin line. Let us look at a simile from Book 11. The Latin of this simile has a complex syntax – one that is extremely difficult to recreate in English – but Twyne tackles the challenge with great dexterity:

> And lyke a woolfe, before the hatefull hunters him do chace,
> Unto the wast forlorne hilles forth hies himself a pace,
> When he some heardsman hath, or heckfer great of grease, and lim
> Devourd, and guiltie in hart of that foule fact, and deede full grim:
> His tremblinge tayle between his legges lets fall, and wooddes doth seeke.

> ac velut ille, prius quam tela inimica sequantur,
> continuo in montis sese avius abdidit altos
> occiso pastore lupus magnove iuvenco,
> conscius audacis facti, caudamque remulcens
> subiecit pavitantem utero silvasque petivit.[79]

Twyne's practice of translating Virgil's hexameters is almost identical to Phaer's style in the later books.

In his prefatory letter, Twyne states his belief that Phaer's primary purpose was 'to delight the nobilitie of this Realme'.[80] In Books 10–12, Twyne continued Phaer's focus on elements of nobility in Virgil's epic. Accordingly, we can find the same extensive expansion of titles that marked Phaer's verse. In Book 12, for example, there are a total of 62 titles in the English text (including Prince, King, Lord, Dame, Queen, Knight, Sir, Captain, Duke) and more than half of these (34) are additions by Twyne, with nothing in the Latin text prompting them. In Twyne's translation, everything is 'noble', from the dogs leading hunts to the hall a sparrow flies through.[81] Glosses point out the importance of nobility when they state that it is 'more honorable to be slayne by a noble conqueror'.[82] We find also, perhaps even more so than in Phaer's part, that the noble status of Aeneas is of special importance. Several times we find Aeneas' epithet 'pius' being translated as 'lord'.[83] In a gloss at the beginning of Book 11 that echoes Phaer's early gloss on Aeneas as 'a perfite wise man and valiant capteyn', Twyne writes that 'care over the dead [is] the part of a noble | Captaine and of a good man'.[84] This gloss is yet another sign of the careful continuity Twyne establishes between his work and Phaer's.

Along with nobility, another concept central to Phaer's translation was the humanist notion of 'virtue' and Twyne's translation stresses this concept as well. These two concepts were closely tied together in the Renaissance commonplace *virtus vera nobilitas*. While the debate about *vera nobilitas* could potentially have subversive (anti-hereditary) implications, in the Northern Renaissance this debate was typically resolved by insisting that the virtues are almost always displayed by the ruling classes.[85] Lawrence Humphrey's treatise on *The Nobles; or, Of Nobility* is one prominent example, defending the connection between nobility and virtue.[86] In Twyne's translation, the nobility and the virtue of Aeneas are two interconnected sides of the hero's excellence, just as they are in the work of Phaer. It is in this light that one should view Twyne's addition of Maffeo Vegio's Book 13 in 1584. Twyne writes that he was 'mooved with the worthines of the worke, and the neerenes of the argument, verse and stile unto *Virgil*, wherin as I judge, the writer hath declared himself an happie imitatour'.[87] It was not so much the 'neerenes of the argument' to Virgil that moved Twyne, however, as it was the nearness of the argument to Phaer's *Aeneid*. Vegio's Book 13 makes several alterations to the tone and language of Virgil's epic, but the most significant is that Aeneas becomes, in Michael Putnam's words, 'the emblem of Renaissance *virtù*, the combination of valor of body and excellence of mind which shapes the essence of the ideal Italian prince'.[88] Vegio read Virgil through the lens of epideictic rhetoric, and in Book 13 Aeneas becomes the paragon of Renaissance 'virtue'.[89] A similar transformation took place in Phaer, as Aeneas' chief quality was captured by the English word 'virtue'. While Twyne continues Phaer's interpretation of Aeneas in Books 11 and 12, it is primarily in Book 13 that this aspect comes to the forefront.

In Twyne's translation of Vegio, the Roman hero is 'Lord Aeneas farre excelling all in vertue bright', 'the *Trojan* prince of vertue most renowne', an epitome 'of wit and vertue rare'.[90] The Renaissance *vir virtutis* was capable of possessing god-like qualities, and the reward that was owed to such excellence was 'the tribute of honour, glory and praise'.[91] As we have seen, at the end of his life, Phaer had sent William Wightman verses which encapsulate this central belief about the *vir virtutis*: these verses declared that to great men 'by their deedes their fame to stretche | That privilege vertue gives'.[92] At the end of Vegio's Book 13, Aeneas is called up into the heavens to claim his eternal rewards. In the English translation, Venus declares to Jupiter that '*Aeneas* vertue longes to dwell above in lasting blis'.[93] At this moment, the final gloss Twyne adds to his translation of Vegio, and thus the final gloss in the whole epic, informs readers that 'verteous deedes make men immortal'.[94] It is remarkable how Twyne's final gloss corresponds to the message in the final verses translated by Phaer. Both Phaer and Twyne read the *Aeneid* as a poem celebrating the potential triumph of virtue, and it is this lofty belief that most clearly binds them together. Both would have approved of Jupiter's final words in Vegio's Book 13: 'Fulfilling eke the world with noble deedes of glory gay, | Those likewise will I to the skies advance.'[95]

The outlook on the *Aeneid* that Phaer and Twyne shared allowed the complete Phaer-Twyne *Aeneid* to be a coherent and (for their time) definitive translation of Virgil's epic. Twyne wanted the final product to read as a single, continuous enterprise. His effort was a success and helped to establish this translation as the one to emulate in England for the next fifty years. However, for all the care he took to blend his work with Phaer's, there are a couple of differences that come out upon a close study. These differences are by no means intrusive, but they are significant. Before moving on to look at Richard Stanyhurst's translation, I wish to draw attention to the most significant of the differences: the shift from Catholicism to Protestantism. This change points to the direction the English *Aeneid* would take in the seventeenth century.

Phaer was a committed Catholic and dedicated the first translation to Queen Mary, 'defendoure of the faithe'.[96] Although he did not set out to write a specifically Catholic translation, signs of his belief appear throughout. Burrow has pointed out that Phaer includes a Catholic gloss in Book 6: 'No grace [without] prayer'.[97] Similarly, Tudeau-Clayton has noted that Phaer also uses the word 'Limbo' in his descriptions of the underworld.[98] Other signs of Catholicism might include his references to pilgrims. When Dido travels between the 'delubra' of Carthage (4.66), offering sacrifices and prayers, Phaer renders these acts as her 'pilgrim dedes'.[99] In Book 5, an epic simile describes a 'viator' (5.275) who happens to wound a serpent while travelling by in a cart. Phaer translates this word with the phrase 'pylgrym passing by'.[100] Another sign is the occasional transformation of pagan gods into saints who bestow grace upon humans. Hercules' transition to heaven is the process of him becoming one of the blessed who can answer prayers: 'Alhayle undoubted child of god, new joy to saincts above | Come visit us w^{t} grace, & these thy gifts accept & love.'[101] One book later, the Berecyntian queen is portrayed as part of the same company. She is a 'lady sainct' with her 'queeres of spiritual wights', and she performs a 'marvel' when she rescues the Trojan ships from the fires of the Rutulians.[102] Even if they do not go to the heart of his translation, these Catholic touches can be found throughout Phaer's version.

In contrast, Twyne was not a Catholic or even sympathetic to Catholicism. He wrote two prophetic texts based on natural phenomena, and these texts can give us an idea of his religious beliefs. For example, Twyne was one of several people in England who wrote about the appearance of a comet in the sky on 11 November 1577. This comet is most famous because it led to Tycho Brahe's scientific observations that challenged Aristotelian physics.[103] However, Twyne used the apparition of the comet as a chance to speculate about international politics. In 1578, he published a tract with the title *Of Certain Wonderful Effects*. Considering the events in Flanders, Twyne interpreted the comet as a sign against the 'open enemies unto Jesus Christe in his members', and by this he meant the enemies of the 'refourmed states'.[104] The star moreover appeared in the house of women, which signified the 'inseparable conjunction & marriage, as it were, of our most true and naturall soveraigne Queene *Elizabeth*, with the holy Church and Gospel of Jesus Christ, indissolubly united'.[105] Twyne was a committed adherent to Elizabeth's religious and political policies.

It should thus come as no surprise that in Twyne's portion of the translation there are no Catholic references. This is perhaps the easiest way to distinguish between the two translators. Where the difference comes through most subtly, however, is in the gradual shift in qualities with which Aeneas is associated. While Twyne does not offer a distinctly Protestant reading of the *Aeneid*, we can already find in him hints of what would become the basis for the puritan John Vicars' translation of the epic. In Phaer, the key quality Aeneas possesses is 'virtue' or 'manfullness'. Twyne retains this reading, but we can see that another word is competing with 'virtue': this word is 'godliness'. In the argument Twyne prefixes to Book 1, he translates 'insignem pietate' as 'a man endued with singulare godlynesse',[106] and in the argument prefixed to Book 13 Twyne stresses that Turnus is 'not without deserved reproches for resisting the providence of the *Gods*'.[107] As we shall see in Chapter 5, a distinctly Protestant mode of translating the *Aeneid* opens up as soon as the outstanding quality of the hero becomes his adherence to God's providential plan.

Aeneas the Martyr: Richard Stanyhurst and the Lofty Irish Virgil

A couple of years before Twyne undertook his translation of Vegio's Book 13, the Anglo-Irish writer Richard Stanyhurst was at work on another Virgil translation in which 'loftiness' was yet again the central concern. This translation has become infamous in English literary history for what C. S. Lewis has described as its unique 'mixture of slang and pedantry'.[108] However, Stanyhurst's place in the history of Renaissance Virgil translators needs to be reconsidered. *The First Foure Bookes of Virgils Æneis* (originally published in Leiden in 1582) was the first English *Aeneid* to be undertaken not only under the weight of Virgil's reputation, but also under the shadow of the Phaer-Twyne's success. Three of the seven pages of the dedication are spent discussing the work's relation to its illustrious predecessor, and Stanyhurst confronts many of the same concerns as Phaer and Twyne. Like Phaer, Stanyhurst is interested in how one can best render the loftiness of Virgil's epic in the vernacular. But as I shall demonstrate, Stanyhurst translates with special, personal concerns in 1582. As a result, he undertakes his translation with an entirely different conception of what is most important in the epic, as well as what the proper English language is and sounds like. Stanyhurst's Virgil was the first of a new phase of Virgil translations, which isolated smaller units of the poem and suggestively challenged the position of the newly established, lofty British Virgil.

When Richard Stanyhurst completed his translation of Virgil in 1582, he was on the outside of English culture, as an exile who had just recently made his home in the Netherlands. While Phaer and Twyne led lives that were relatively untouched by tumult and controversy, Stanyhurst's life was every bit as dramatic as those of the Civil War translators such as Sir John Denham, Henry Vaughan or Abraham Cowley. And just as in the case of these later translators, Stanyhurst's personal experiences shaped the way in which he translated. To begin, we need to consider how and why Stanyhurst came to be an exile in the early 1580s and what was at stake in his writing during this period.

Stanyhurst was born to an Old English family that had flourished in Dublin since the late fourteenth century.[109] His family took great pride in their history of service to the English crown in Ireland. It is a testament to their status and success that in Richard's own lifetime his father James was named speaker of the Irish House of Commons on several important occasions.[110] Having grown up in Dublin, Richard had a great attachment to both the city and his family's history there: as his biographer Colm Lennon has noted, he signed every one of his works, until the very end of his life, 'Richard Stanyhurst, Dubliner'.[111] Stanyhurst even contributed two major works on the history of Ireland, both of which trace the crucial presence of Old English families in the Pale.[112] These works outline an illustrious, British history for Ireland: following Giraldus Cambrensis' *Expugnatio Hibernica*, Stanyhurst believed that Gurguntius, King of the Britons, had conquered Ireland and allowed others to settle there.[113] For Stanyhurst, the Old English families in the Pale, such as his own, had ancient and mighty roots.

As his immense histories of Ireland would suggest, Stanyhurst also had a formidable educational background. Having first studied in

Kilkenny at the grammar school of the Oxford-educated Peter White, Stanyhurst himself proceeded to Oxford in 1563.[114] At University College, he quickly made a name for himself as a prodigious young intellect by undertaking a full-scale study of Porphyry that was printed in 1570, when Stanyhurst was twenty-three.[115] This study, the *Harmonia*, was the first exposition of the Aristotelian logical system written in Britain and worked with many complicated Greek commentaries.[116] Something of the young Stanyhurst's reputation can be glimpsed in the many commendatory verses in the *Harmonia* by prominent figures such as Lawrence Humphrey. It is especially interesting that Thomas Twyne wrote one of these commendatory verses himself. Nobody has previously noted that there might have been a connection between these two translators, but it is possible that they were acquainted through their associations at Oxford. In his commendatory verse, Twyne writes admiringly of Stanyhurst's accomplishment: 'For all the volumes which the logicians wrote the learned Stanyhurst has compiled into one book.'[117] There is no further evidence regarding the relationship between these two translators, but Twyne's short poem shows that they must have moved in similar intellectual circles around the time when Twyne was translating the *Aeneid*. Another contributor of a commendatory poem, Edmund Campion, was to become a close friend of Stanyhurst's and a decisive influence in his life. In 1570, when Stanyhurst returned to his family's home in Dublin, Campion was there working on a history of Ireland. This was the first specifically Irish literary project that Stanyhurst was to become involved in. When the Catholic Campion had to flee from Ireland in May 1571, he left his work for the young scholar to complete.[118] This 'Historie of Irelande' was eventually to form a substantial part of Holinshed's *Chronicles*, in which it was published in 1577.

Until the early 1570s, it would have appeared that Stanyhurst's life was to take the course that his family had followed for generations in Dublin. Around 1570, however, his situation in Ireland began to change. After the arrival of Henry Sidney as Lord Deputy in 1565, the Elizabethan government increasingly supported a hardline attitude towards reforming Ireland – the programme generally advanced by the New English colonisers. This programme stood in contrast to the educational and humanistic reforms supported by most of the Old English Palesmen.[119] Centuries of intermingling and miscegenation between the Gaelic and the Old English had made them suspicious in the eyes of the New English colonisers; there were consequently fewer and fewer positions for the old families in the administration of the Pale.[120] Moreover, by the middle of the 1570s, most of Stanyhurst's closest ties to Dublin were being severed.[121] Perhaps Stanyhurst's most decisive connection was his friendship with the exiled Edmund Campion. Due to their friendship, it seems that the English government grew progressively suspicious of Stanyhurst himself.[122] This suspicion was probably not without reason, as sometime around the end of the 1570s Stanyhurst seems to have converted to Catholicism. In 1581, the year when Campion was executed in Tyburn, Stanyhurst fled to the Netherlands, where he received a pension from the Spanish government.[123] At first, he settled in the northern town of Leiden, where he completed his translation of Virgil in June 1582. Within a couple of years, however, he had moved into the Spanish-controlled south of the Netherlands, where he wrote his second major treatise on Ireland, the *De rebus in Hibernia gestis* (1584). While Stanyhurst's later life makes for exciting reading – he spent years investigating occult medicine at the Spanish court and serving as a court chaplain to the archducal couple in the Netherlands – for a study of his translation of Virgil, the key years are those between the publications of his two major works on Ireland: his contributions to 'The Historie of Irelande' in Holinshed's *Chronicles* of 1577, and the *De rebus in Hibernia gestis* of 1584.

As this brief overview of Stanyhurst's life has shown, the late 1570s and early 1580s were tumultuous years. It is not surprising therefore that Stanyhurst's views on Ireland changed over this period. His conversion to Catholicism, his falling out with the Elizabethan government and his exile to the Netherlands altered the tone in which Stanyhurst wrote about the Gaelic Irish. In 1577, as Florian Kläger states, Stanyhurst 'condemns the barbarous savageness of the Irish and is eager to distance himself and his Old English peers from it'.[124] In the *Chronicles*, Stanyhurst is largely in line with the Elizabethan government's policy towards Ireland, even if he stresses that the Old English should be valued above the New. In 1584, however, Stanyhurst's position towards the Gaels was somewhat less severe. It would not be until after the O'Neill rebellions in the 1590s that he would completely change his tone towards the Gaels and support them, but already in 1584 there are signs of softening. Lennon points to a passage in which Stanyhurst admits that the Gaelic do in fact have some civility: 'Although the Irish are averse to the urbanity and elegance of the English province, they do not conduct their lives, as is claimed, without any culture.'[125] His attitude towards the Gaelic Irish grew less straightforwardly dismissive over time.

However, what is most notable about Stanyhurst's view of Ireland during this period is his perception of the role that language has to play in the colonial venture. This perception is remarkably consistent across the two texts.[126] Since culture and language are inseparable, the true colonisation of a people comes when they submit to the language of their conquerors. Given this outlook, the distinction between English and Irish in Ireland was naturally of the greatest importance. The accusation that the English in the Pale spoke a garbled form of the language that had been corrupted by the Irish tongue was a serious charge to Stanyhurst: that would be tantamount to a betrayal of civility. In the *Chronicles*, he describes the linguistic drama within Ireland as follows:

> The inhabitants of the English pale haue beene in old time so much addicted to their ciuilitie, and so farre sequestered from barbarous sauagenesse, as their onelie mother toong was English. And trulie, so long as these impaled dwellers did sunder themselues as well in land as in language from the Irish: rudenesse was daie by daie in the countrie supplanted, ciuilitie ingrafted, good lawes established, loialtie obserued, rebellion suppressed, and in fine the coine of a yoong England was like to shoot in Ireland. But when their posteritie became not altogither so warie in keeping, as their ancestors were valiant in conquering, the Irish language was free dennized in the English pale: this canker tooke such deepe root, as the bodie that before was whole and sound, was by little and little festered, and in manner wholie putrified.[127]

Phaer had felt the need to defend the English language in comparison with Latin, but Stanyhurst focuses on the civility of the English tongue in comparison with the Gaelic. The English language was an essential part of the true civility in Ireland.

There is, however, one further wrinkle to Stanyhurst's argument. I have already noted how Tudeau-Clayton emphasises that in early translations which claim to be promoting 'English', one first needs to ask *whose* English is being promoted.[128] This is a crucial question for Stanyhurst because he did not consider all forms of English to be equal. Indeed, he believed the situation in Ireland – where the English had to form a tight-knit community with strong ties to the past – actually produced a form of English that was more authentic, despite the corruptions that the Gaelic language may have introduced. While the English speakers in England had mixed their tongue with other languages, the English speakers in the Pale had preserved 'the dregs of the old ancient Chaucer English'.[129] This belief is sketched out in the *Chronicles*, but it receives a much fuller treatment in *De rebus*, where Stanyhurst makes the claim for the superiority of his people's English more explicit:

> Those who live in the English province . . . are very far from this new and too-foreign magniloquence, collected thievishly from the languages of other nations. Rather, they preserve the uncorrupted antiquity of the English language. This language was the glory of the poet Chaucer – that which the ancient and noble poet (without doubt the Homer of the English) employed in his writings: he spoke English so that you would not believe that English could be more English.[130]

Ignoring the obvious historical fallacy (Chaucer's language contained many novelties, as Richard Verstegan understood in the early seventeenth century[131]), this passage reveals Stanyhurst's polemical pride in his own, unusual form of English. He carried this distinctive pride with him when he went into exile in the early 1580s.

This claim for the cultural superiority of the Palesmen's English raises obvious questions for Stanyhurst's eccentric translation. Stanyhurst's rendition of Books 1–4 of the *Aeneid* is the most infamous Virgil translation of the English Renaissance. Containing gems such as 'With chuffe chaffe winesops like a gourd downe droups to [the] growndward'[132] or 'Thus sayd: al in blubbring she floath, with clamorus howling | Thee place shee tinckled',[133] this version of the *Aeneid* was a target for mockery, even in the very decade when it appeared. Since then, there has been a wide range of attempted explanations. One mode of interpretation was put forward by Robert Southey in the nineteenth century, when he suggested that the translation could only have been a travesty of attempts at quantitative verse.[134] Around the turn of the twentieth century, several critics regarded the translation as primarily a product of Stanyhurst's metrical experimentation.[135] He was a part of the quantitative verse movement, and much of the awkward phrasing and convoluted word order in the translation is due to attempts at fitting the dactylic hexameter. More recently, with an eye on the political context of the poem, John Kerrigan has suggested that the peculiar diction of the translation is the result of Stanyhurst's dialect: he translated the *Aeneid* into 'an almost Joycean, neologizing Hiberno-English with no apparent anxiety about losing classical dignity'.[136] While there is much truth to both the metrical and dialectical claims, in what follows I will add a third consideration. For in addition to metre and dialect, the presence of the translation by Phaer and Twyne was one of the key factors that bent Stanyhurst's Virgil out of shape.

Stanyhurst's vexed relationship to the Phaer-Twyne translation is due in part to his closeness to it. His metrical innovations, for instance, should be seen as an extension of what Phaer and Twyne did with their fourteeners. Much like his predecessors, Stanyhurst recreates all of the half-lines in English, and he seeks for the English line to mirror the Latin precisely. We can compare the 'o lux Dardanidae' speech in Book 2:

> O star of al Trojans, of towne thee prosperus holder,
> What lets thee lingred? from what far countrie, syr Hector,
> Long loockt for coomst thow? so that after dangerus hazards,
> And divers burials of freends, of kinred, of oothers
> Wee tost now doe se thee. By what chaunce filthye thy visadge

Is thus disfigured? These wounds why mortal apeere they?
Hee little accoumpted this fond and vanitie childish,
But sigh upplucking from breast ful deepelye, thus answerd.

o lux Dardaniae, spes o fidissima Teucrum,
quae tantae tenuere morae? quibus Hector ab oris
exspectate venis? ut te post multa tuorum
funera, post varios hominumque urbisque labores
defessi aspicimus! quae causa indigna serenos
foedavit vultus? aut cur haec vulnera cerno?'
ille nihil, nec me quaerentem vana moratur,
sed graviter gemitus imo de pectore ducens.[137]

Stanyhurst's translation carries to completion the line of progressively classicising metrical developments in translations of the *Aeneid*. If each translator before him moved closer to the Latin metre, Stanyhurst made the final leap to recreate the hexameter. We can see how each of these eight lines follows the arrangement of the Latin. We can also see, for instance, how in the final line he has contorted the English far from the natural word-order in order to preserve this arrangement. Where the Phaer-Twyne could still pass as reasonable English, Stanyhurst's translation pushed the syntax beyond the breaking point.

Similarly, Stanyhurst's translation engages as liberally in anachronisms and additions as Phaer's does, but Stanyhurst uses them more provocatively. Since he was a highly educated and accomplished scholar, these anachronisms should not be taken as signs of ignorance. Rather, they purposefully leave impressions upon the text. For one stylistic example, Stanyhurst is prone to adding little metaphors in the English. He takes words in the Latin that are rather abstract and then renders them in English with more tangible, metaphorical phrases. We can note a few from Book 4. The phrase 'parva metu primo' (176) becomes 'First like a shrimp'; the verb 'volat' (184) becomes 'swallolike' [*sic*]; the angry Iarbas is described as 'accensus' (203), but Stanyhurst recreates this as 'wild as a marche hare'; and the famous phrase 'varium et mutabile semper | femina' (569–70) becomes 'a wind fane changabil huf puffe | Always is a woomman'.[138] In each case, more abstract Latin words are rendered in concrete images of shrimps, swallows, hares and windvanes. A steady stream of these in Stanyhurst's translation changes the texture of Virgil's poetry, which typically relies on a much smaller range of metaphors.

But the most significant type of modernisation in Stanyhurst is the introduction of Catholic allusions. He follows many of the methods we have seen Phaer employing. The gods in Stanyhurst's translation also frequently become saints. We can take three examples from the full range of the translation: in the opening passage the 'caelestibus' (1.11) are translated as 'Sayncts celestial'; when Aeneas sees the gods pulling down Troy, the 'numina magna deum' (2.623) become 'of Saincts foure deities did I see'; and in the fourth book, Dido 'gentis imagine capta' (4.84) becomes '(for sainct thee shrinecase adoring)'.[139] When worship is perceived as mistaken, Stanyhurst will depict it as pagan or even Jewish: the magician in Book 4, the 'Hesperidum templi custos' (4.484), is now the 'Sexten of *Hesperides* Sinagog'.[140] On the other hand, when the worship is perceived as sound, it is presented in Catholic terms: the 'domus' (1.168) of good nymphs becomes 'thee Nunry'.[141] In his letter to the reader, Stanyhurst claims that he delves deeper into his source than Phaer did:

> Moreover in some points of greatest price, where the matter, as it were, doth bleede, I was mooved to shunne *M. Phaers* interpretation, and cling more neere to the meaning of mine authour, in slicing the huske, and cracking the shell, to bestowe the kernell upon the wittie and inquisitive Reader.[142]

Having recently converted to Catholicism and having been exiled because of it, Stanyhurst would have believed that his more pervasive modernisations were one part of 'cracking the shell' of the hidden meanings in Virgil's *Aeneid*. Phaer was scratching the surface: Stanyhurst uncovers the kernel, revealing the hidden truths and the lasting relevance.

The most intriguing alterations in Stanyhurst's translation, however, are the ones that are especially autobiographical. In *Translation and the Poet's Life*, Paul Davis has argued that the act of translation was 'a natural medium of self-examination for the [Augustan] poets who practised it. It is no accident that Denham, Vaughan, Cowley, Dryden, and Pope all took up translating at moments of crisis or transformation in their lives.'[143] Davis's argument does not apply to many translators of Virgil before Denham. But in the case of Stanyhurst it is highly relevant. The first metaphor for translation Davis explores is that of 'exile'. With Stanyhurst, as we have seen, exile was a pressing reality: he had just left his home in Dublin for the Netherlands. It is therefore striking that in Stanyhurst's translation, the concept of Aeneas as a pilgrim and exile is more prevalent than in any other translation of Virgil into English. From the first page, Aeneas is 'lyke wandring pilgrim'.[144] His travels – 'peragro' (1.384) – make him 'lyke a poore pilgrim'.[145] The same phrasing repeats again and again, as Aeneas' 'errantem' (1.756) makes him 'lik pilgrim', and his 'exsilia' (2.780) becomes a 'pilgrimage'.[146] At the beginning of Book 3, the whole wanderings of Aeneas are described as 'foorth to run exiled, too seeke soom foren aventures'.[147]

Moreover, Stanyhurst is unique among English translators in also presenting Aeneas as a martyr: Virgil's hero is 'martyred in battayls, ere towne could stately be buylded'.[148] This notion of Aeneas stretches well beyond the scope of the Phaer-Twyne *Aeneid*, which only occasionally represents Aeneas as a pilgrim. But it makes sense for Stanyhurst in 1582. His exile to the Netherlands was on account of his Catholicism, and one year previously he would have learned that his close friend and mentor Edmund Campion had been hanged. Lennon has stated that there can be little doubt that 'the dead Campion remained an inspiration to him in the years which followed'.[149] There can be little doubt either that Campion was in Stanyhurst's mind as he translated. In the description of Sinon, Stanyhurst interjects one of his boldest anachronisms: 'In doubtful matters thus stands hee flatly resolved, | Or to cog, or certain for knaverie to purchas a Tyburne.'[150] Tyburn was the place in Middlesex where Campion was executed less than a year before. The nexus of ideas surrounding exile, pilgrimage and martyrdom was significant for Stanyhurst as he composed his Virgil translation. His particular reason for choosing Books 1–4 was that these books were the ones focused upon Aeneas' exile from his homeland. The topicality of Stanyhurst's translation was not simply pointing outwards, but rather it reflected upon the situation of the author himself in 1582. Stanyhurst's Aeneas is not, as he was for Phaer and Twyne, the *vir virtutis* and winner of glory; rather, he is an exile who martyrs himself for his religious cause. And it is because of this difference that Stanyhurst needed to find a new language and style for his Virgil.

These Catholic and biographical underpinnings of the translation should inform any critical approach, since they show that this is a work to be taken seriously: it is not a travesty. Stanyhurst never published a work that was not meant as a serious contribution to scholarship, history, medicine or politics. One thing that should have come out of the brief overview of his biography is how seriously most of his contemporaries took him, even if they were appalled by his translation. The conception of Aeneas as a martyr would have seemed for him a noble reading of Virgil's epic. So how then should one explain the eccentricities of his language in the translation? The explanation that it was primarily a question of the demands of the quantitative metre is not sufficient, since Stanyhurst's quantitative translations of the Psalms and of various epigrams display no eccentricities comparable to his Virgil translation.

The site of the greatest eccentricities is not a part of Stanyhurst's translation of Books 1–4. Rather it is a brief excerpt from Book 8 that he included in the appendix. The contemporary satirisers of Stanyhurst's Virgil focused their attention on this excerpt. The Latin passage is from Book 8.416–39 and describes Vulcan descending to his caverns under

Aetna. There, the fire-god tells his giants to stop their work and prepare the shield for Aeneas. Stanyhurst's rendition in English contains a great density of onomatopoeic phrases: 'tonant' (8.419) becomes 'Lowd dub a dub' and 'frapping rip rap'.[151] The word 'fornacibus' (8.421) creates 'from fornace flashye be whisking'.[152] The sound of Jove's thunderbolt becomes 'rownce robel hobble' and the single word 'sonitum' (8.431) becomes 'ruffe raffe roaring'.[153] The mixing of anger into Jupiter's weapons – 'miscebant operi flammisque sequacibus iras' (8.432) – is the source of the English phrase, 'With peale meale ramping, [with] thwick thwack sturdilye thundring'.[154] The density of curious phrases in this passage understandably prompted reactions from satirists. Thomas Nashe wrote four verses in imitation of Stanyhurst's translation:

> Then did he make heauens vault to rebound,
> with rounce robble hobble
> Of ruffe raffe roaring,
> with thwicke thwacke thurlerie bouncing.[155]

Nashe clearly built these lines out of Stanyhurst's Book 8 translation. Likewise, when Joseph Hall wrote his satire of Stanyhurst, he focused on precisely the same passage: 'If Jove speak English in a thund'ring cloud, | "Thwick thwack, and riff raff," roars he out aloud.'[156]

That both Nashe and Hall considered this passage as among the worst portions of Stanyhurst's translation is worth taking into consideration. What caused so great a density of eccentricities at this place? Fortunately, Stanyhurst gives us a hint, and he notes that he translated Vulcan's forge from Book 8 for a particular reason:

> The description of Liparen, expressed by *Virgil* in the eight booke of his *AEneis*, in which place, the *Poet* played, as it weare, his price, by advancing at ful thee loftines of his veyne: done into *English* by the translatour for his last farewel too the sayd *Virgil*.[157]

Stanyhurst considered this section in Book 8 to be the passage in which Virgil attempted to soar to his highest peak, a judgement that is often repeated in the history of Virgilian scholarship. This section is even quoted in Edmund Burke's treatise *On the Sublime*.[158] The 'loftines' here is precisely the same quality that Stanyhurst found in Phaer's diction and was one of his overriding concerns with the *Aeneid*. What is even more interesting, however, is that when one looks at the moments in Books 1–4 where Stanyhurst's English is most strained and unusual, they coincide with scenes that rise to a certain pitch: the mountain of Aeolus, Pyrrhus breaking into the palace of King Priam, the attack of the Harpies and Mount Aetna are the passages that have the densest use of Stanyhurst's extravagant vocabulary.[159] It was always the moments when Stanyhurst tried to rise up to the heights where he produced the most disastrous results.

Virgil was a daunting poet to live up to. His verse and its authority could exert an immense influence over translators, and Stanyhurst invested himself fully to live up to that challenge. According to Julius Caesar Scaliger, Virgil had raised style to the highest point of perfection: 'Indeed, through the study of a choicer nature and through judgement, Virgil raised the rude art that he received from Homer to the highest summit of perfection.'[160] But more than just Virgil, Stanyhurst had to deal with the challenge that the Phaer-Twyne *Aeneid* presented. Stanyhurst felt his translation could not come too close to that of Phaer. He tells us in the dedication that those who suggested Phaer's work made his task easier were wrong: Phaer 'hath rather doubled than defalckt ought of my paines, by reason that in conferring his translation with mine, I was forced, to weede out from my verses such choise wordes, as were forestalled by him'.[161] While early modern translators are generally content to borrow a great deal from their predecessors, Stanyhurst was wary of coming too close to Phaer. The word 'forestalled' suggests that he had arrived belatedly, when certain Virgilian territory was already occupied. One is tempted to read into Stanyhurst an early trace of Harold Bloom's 'anxiety of influence'.[162] The difficulty he faced seems to have been to live up to the heights of Virgil while writing an English distinguishable from the translation by Phaer and Twyne. For Stanyhurst, emulation was more problematic than it seems to have been for Humphrey.

What sort of English would be apt for Stanyhurst? The two satirists offered different interpretations as to how Stanyhurst mangled his diction. Joseph Hall was alive to the ambitions of this translation: 'Another scorns the homespun thread of rhymes, | Match'd with the lofty feet of elder times.'[163] But Hall rebukes what he believes was a neologising tendency in Stanyhurst's English: 'Fie on the forged mint that did create | New coins of words never articulate.'[164] This accusation would have shocked and offended Stanyhurst; in the *De rebus*, Stanyhurst attacks 'illi verborum opifices' ('those forgers of new words') who have introduced new corruptions into the English language. Instead, he believes that conservatism in language was the special quality of the Palesmen. James L. Rosier undertook a study of Stanyhurst's eccentric lexical usage in Holinshed's *Chronicles* and *The First Foure Bookes of Virgils Æneis*. The results of Rosier's study showed that, while some of Stanyhurst's words were drawn from Middle English (e.g. *giglot*, *busked*, *dusked*), most of them drew their vitality from the colloquial language: they were not literary innovations, but alterations of common words.

Rosier concludes that Stanyhurst 'finds the most expressive English to be that of the common speech'.[165] And thus it seems that Nashe's criticism of Stanyhurst's translation is closer to the mark: Nashe laments that the Irishman had 'recalled to life what euer hissed Barbarisme hath been buried this C. yeere'.[166] Contrary to Hall, Nashe accused Stanyhurst of digging up obsolete words that had the ring of barbarism. One can see how different their perspectives on the English language were. For Nashe, the language had been purified, refined and civilised over the previous century; for Stanyhurst, the language had been corrupted and had drifted away from its purer roots. Nashe's comment is closer to the mark than Hall's, but it is not quite precise either. Stanyhurst did not try to *revive* an old language. His lexical usage does not show signs that he attempted to restore 'an older word-stock', as Elyot and Puttenham sought to do.[167] Instead, as Rosier shows, the full force of Stanyhurst's language was colloquial: his reliance upon what he perceived as the Palesmen's common idiom makes sense once we remember that he believed the language that the Palesmen spoke still contained the proper 'dregs' of the English tongue. It was not to be found in innovation, but by listening to what had been around him all of his life before his exile.

Stanyhurst believed in the pure English language which 'Chauncerus vetus ac nobilis Poeta' had used. It is thus not coincidental that in the introduction to his translation, when he desires to praise Virgil in the highest possible terms, he does so by comparing him to Chaucer:

> But our *Virgil* not content with such meigre stuffe, doth labour in tylling, as it were a *Canterburie* tale, to ferret out the secretes of *Nature* . . . with eche decorum so duely observed, as in truth he hath in right purchased to himselfe the name of a surpassing Poet, the fame of an odde oratour, and the admiration of a profound philosopher.[168]

Stanyhurst's understanding of Chaucerian English was far from precise (as his claim that it was pure from foreign influences suggests). I imagine that Stanyhurst felt that the Palesmen's contemporary English idiom sounded much like Chaucer's did. Stanyhurst attempted to create an alternative form of loftiness in the English language, one that he felt would be closer to the source of the language. Exile and martyrdom are high and noble themes, and Stanyhurst needed a language that would be apt for his task. Whereas Phaer attempted to write Virgilian loftiness into the centre of the Tudor culture, Stanyhurst translated that loftiness into the British past and the Palesmen's present. For him, the lofty British Virgil needed to speak in a different tongue. His translation of Books 1–4 of the *Aeneid* was a very personal attempt to display that language.

The Highpoint of Humanist *Aeneids*

The translations by Phaer and Twyne mark the highpoint of the lofty, humanistic *Aeneid* in England. Stanyhurst's translation comes directly on their heels, but his translation already transitions us into another phase of Virgil reception – one in which translators focus on portions of the epic and offer readings that confidently (and provocatively) contradict the central humanistic perception of the epic which was by then commonplace. The Phaer-Twyne translation stands out in the English Renaissance because it presented the *Aeneid* in the broadest sense. It is one of the least topical translations that will be considered in this study. In the case of Phaer and Twyne, translating the *Aeneid* is best understood through Humphrey's simile of opening a treasure. In their vision, the *utilitas* of the *Aeneid* lies in its ability to present the most noble and lofty image of man to the nation. In its continuity throughout the period that I will study, the Phaer-Twyne also provides a foil against which the more topical readings of the poem stand out. Perhaps its presence also made them possible. But the new translations also reflect the shifting attitudes towards the *Aeneid*. Stanyhurst's translation was already more personal and quirky than any of the Virgil translations before his. Even if he is concerned with recreating a noble British Virgil, his reasons for translating the story of Aeneas, the pilgrim and martyr, display a new way of responding to the epic. His translation of Books 1–4 marks the end of one phase of *Aeneid* translations and the beginning of another phase that would take centre stage with the partial translations by Christopher Marlowe, an anonymous Elizabethan courtier, Sir John Harington and Sir William Mure.

Notes

1. Lally, 'Introduction', pp. xi–xii.
2. Ibid., p. xii.
3. In his 'Introduction', Lally shows places where Phaer borrows from Douglas and Surrey.
4. Nashe, *Works*, III, p. 319.
5. Googe, *Eglogs, Epytaphes, and Sonnettes*, sigs. E3^{v}–E4^{r}.
6. Puttenham, *The Art of English Poesy*, p. 149.
7. Webbe, *A Discourse of English Poetrie*, sigs. C3^{v}–C4^{r}.
8. Hall, *Ten Books of Homers Iliades*, sig. A2^{r}.
9. Stanyhurst, *The First Foure Bookes*, sig. A3^{r}. Throughout this chapter I quote from the 1583 London edition rather than the 1582 Leiden edition: the 1583 edition would have had a greater influence in England.

10. Webbe, *Discourse of English Poetrie*, sigs. E1^{r} and E3^{v}.
11. Nashe, *Works*, III, p. 319.
12. *OED*, 'Haughty, adj.', meanings 2 and 3.
13. Googe, *Eglogs, Epytaphes, and Sonnettes*, sig. E3^{r}.
14. Phaer, *Thomas Phaer and 'The Boke of Chyldren'*, p. 27.
15. Phaer, *The Kegiment* [*sic*], sig. a3^{v}.
16. Phaer, *Kegiment,* sig. a4^{v}.
17. Bowers, 'Thomas Phaer', p. 28; Lally, 'Introduction', pp. xiii–xviii.
18. Tudeau-Clayton, 'Richard Carew', p. 512.
19. Tudeau-Clayton, *Jonson, Shakespeare and Early Modern Virgil*, p. 37.
20. In Badius and others, *Universum poema*, fol. 124^{r}.
21. Greene, *The Light in Troy*, pp. 242–6.
22. Ibid., p. 33.
23. Phaer, *Seven*, sig. A1^{r}. Throughout this chapter I quote from the earliest possible edition of the translation by Phaer and Twyne. A modern edition of the combined text has been prepared by Steven Lally (Phaer and Twyne, *The 'Aeneid'*).
24. Phaer, *Seven*, sig. X3^{r}.
25. Bawcutt, *Gavin Douglas*, p. 137.
26. Sessions, *Henry Howard*, pp. 260, 272 and 281.
27. See the discussion in Rener, *Interpretatio*, pp. 207–8.
28. Surrey, *The 'Aeneid'*. Douglas, '*Aeneid'*.
29. Phaer, *Nyne*, sig. Aa1^{r}. *Aeneid,* 8.13–18.
30. Webbe, *Discourse of English Poetrie*, sigs. F1^{v}–F2^{r}.
31. Ibid., sig. F2^{v}. Webbe was writing at the height of the 1580s quantitative verse movement: Attridge, *Well-Weighed Syllables*, p. 105.
32. Steiner, *After Babel*, p. 327.
33. Phaer, *Seven*, sigs. I4^{r} and F3^{v}.
34. Ibid., sigs. A2^{v}, B3^{r}, U4^{r} and U4^{v}.
35. Ibid., sig. S4^{v}. For the 'parliaments' see sig. B2^{r} and Phaer, *Nyne*, sig. Ff3^{r}.
36. Phaer, *Seven*, sigs. P1^{v} and P2^{r}.
37. Ibid., sigs. K4^{v}, L2^{r} and L2^{v}.
38. Ibid., sigs. B2^{r} and F4^{r}.
39. Ibid., sig. I4^{v}.
40. Ibid., sig. A1^{v}.
41. Ibid., sig. M2^{r}.
42. See, for one example, the translation of 5.117–21 at Phaer, *Seven* (1558), sig. N2^{r}. For some other examples drawn from the whole length of this book: 'Hectorei socii' (5.190) becomes 'O lively laddes of noble kynd' (M3^{v}); 'pater optimus' (5.358) becomes 'The noble prince' (N1^{v}); 'pater' (5.461) becomes 'lord' (N3^{r}); 'maximus | . . . Aeneas' (5.530–1) becomes 'Eneas perelesse prince' (N4^{r}); and 'Aeneas' (5.850) becomes 'my lord and prince' (O4^{v}). Phaer also writes about their pure lineages: 'auncient stocks and undefilde' (N1^{r}).
43. Phaer, *Seven*, sig. R4r.
44. Webbe, *Discourse of English Poetrie*, sig. E1^{r}.
45. Phaer, *Seven*, sigs. P2^{r} and Q1^{r}.
46. See Schwyzer, *Literature, Nationalism, and Memory*, pp. 6–7.
47. Phaer, *Seven*, sig. C3^{r}.

48. Ibid., sig. T4^{v}.
49. Kerrigan, *Archipelagic English*, p. 120.
50. Phaer, *Seven*, sig. A4^{v}.
51. Ibid., sig. T1^{r}.
52. Ibid., sig. X2^{r}.
53. Tudeau-Clayton, *Jonson*, pp. 44–112.
54. Phaer, *Seven*, sig. X2^{v}.
55. Ibid., sigs. P3^{r}, P3^{v} and sig. R1^{v}. Cf. 'dux inclute Teucrum', *Aeneid* 6.562.
56. Phaer, *Seven*, sigs. X2^{v}–X3^{r}.
57. For the translation of 'Numidae' (4.41), see Phaer, *Seven*, sig. I2^{r}; of 'Poenorum' (4.134), sig. I3^{v}; of 'Maurusia . . . | gens' (4.206–7), sig. I4^{v}; and of 'Gaetulis' (5.51), sig. M1^{r}.
58. Phaer, *Seven*, sig. K2^{v}.
59. For the translation of 'Stygio' (6.252), see Phaer, *Seven*, sig. Q1^{r}; of 'Ditis' (6.269), sig. Q1^{r}; of 'Orci' (6.273), sig. Q1^{v}; of 'Acherontis' (6.295), sig. Q1^{v}; and of 'Erebi' (6.404), sig. Q3^{r}.
60. Phaer, *Seven*, sig. R1^{v}. Cf. *Aeneid* 6.577.
61. Phaer, *Seven*, sig. R1^{r}. Cf. *Aeneid* 6.542.
62. Phaer, *Nyne*, sig. Ee2^{r}.
63. Kallendorf, *In Praise of Aeneas*.
64. In Badius and others, *Universum poema*, fols. 123^{v}–124^{r}: 'quia enim novit nihil reip*ublicae* esse utilius q*uam* & clementem, & prudentem, & fortem, & te*m*peratum, & iustu*m*, & ceteris virtutibus præditum h*abe*re principem, talem in Ænea Augusto imitandu*m* depinxit forte, ut Xenophon de Cyro fecisse perhibetur, no*n* semper qualis fuit, sed qualem fuisse decuit perscribens.'
65. Ibid., fols. 123^{v}–124^{r}: 'na*m* quod ille vigenisquaternis libris: hoc poeta no*ste*r senis effecit, in sex si quide*m* prioribus libris Odyssea*m*, hoc est viru*m* expressit: in reliquis sex Iliada, hoc est arma co*n*secutus. Sicut ergo Homero p*ro*positum v*idetur*: ut, & vitam contemplativam quæ in Ulysse sign*ifi*cata est: & activam quæ in bello Troiano prude*n*ter gesto expressa est, explicet: ita & poetæ no*stro*, ut utra*m*que vitam: sed in uno (quod gloriosius est) ho*mine* nobis depingat.'
66. Sidney, *A Defence of Poetry*, p. 24.
67. Phaer, *Seven*, sig. A3^{v}.
68. Ibid., sig. A1^{r}.
69. Ibid., sigs. Q3^{r} and R3^{r}.
70. Ibid., sig. Gg3^{r}.
71. Ibid.
72. Ibid., sig. H4^{v}. Cf. *Aeneid* 3.684–6.
73. Lally, 'Introduction', p. xix.
74. Ibid., p. xxxii.
75. Ibid., p. xxxiii.
76. Ibid., p. xxxvii.
77. *A Mervaylous Straunge Deformed Swyne* (London, 1570).
78. Phaer and Twyne, *Whole*, sig. A2^{r}.
79. Ibid., sig. Kk2^{r}. *Aeneid* 11.809–13.
80. Phaer and Twyne, *Whole*, sig. A2^{r}.
81. Ibid., sigs. Nn2^{v} and Mm2^{v}.

82. Ibid., *Whole*, sig. Gg1r.
83. Ibid., *Whole*, sigs. Ll2r and Ll4r.
84. Ibid., *Whole*, sigs. Gg2v.
85. Skinner, *The Foundations of Modern Political Thought*, I, p. 238.
86. Humphrey, *The Nobles; or, Of Nobilitye*.
87. Phaer and Twyne, *The .xiii. Bookes*, p. [v]. This is Twyne's letter 'To the gentle and courteous *Readers*'.
88. Putnam, 'Introduction', p. xiii.
89. Kallendorf, *In Praise of Aeneas*, p. 127.
90. Phaer and Twyne, *The .xiii. Bookes*, sigs. V4v (cf. Vegio, 'Book 13', ll. 122–3), V7r and X1v.
91. Skinner, *The Foundations*, I, p. 99.
92. Phaer, *Nyne*, sig. Gg3r.
93. Phaer and Twyne, *The .xiii. Bookes*, sig. X3r. Cf. Vegio, 'Book 13', l. 605.
94. Phaer and Twyne, *The .xiii. Bookes*, sig. X3v.
95. Ibid., sig. X3v.
96. Phaer, *Seven*, sig. a2r.
97. Burrow, 'Virgil in English Translation', p. 21. Phaer, *Seven*, sig. P2r.
98. Tudeau-Clayton, 'Richard Carew', p. 508.
99. Phaer, *Seven*, sig. I2v.
100. Ibid., sig. M4v.
101. Phaer, *Nyne*, sig. Bb1r. Cf. *Aeneid* 13.301–2.
102. Phaer, *Nyne*, sig. Dd1r.
103. Geneva, *Astrology and the Seventeenth Century Mind*, p. 90; Christianson, 'Tycho Brahe's German Treatise', p. 119; Vanden Broecke, *The Limits of Influence*, pp. 212–14.
104. Twyne, *Of Certain Wonderful Effects*, sig. C3v.
105. Ibid., sig. B3r.
106. Phaer and Twyne, *Whole*, sig. A1r.
107. Phaer and Twyne, *The .xiii. Bookes*, sig. V2v.
108. Lewis, *English Literature in the Sixteenth Century*, p. 365.
109. Lennon, *Richard Stanihurst*, p. 15.
110. Ibid., p. 20.
111. Ibid., p. 24.
112. Stanyhurst wrote 'The Description of Irelande' and contributed to 'The Historie of Ireland' in Holinshed's *Chronicles*. See Holinshed, *Chronicles of England, Scotland, and Ireland*, VI; Stanyhurst, *De rebus in Hibernia gestis*.
113. Holinshed, *Chronicles*, VI; p. 77; Stanyhurst, *De rebus*, p. 58.
114. Lennon, *Richard Stanihurst*, pp. 24–6.
115. Ibid.
116. Sgarbi, *Aristotelian Tradition*, pp. 79–80.
117. Stanyhurst, *Harmonia*, sig. B1v: 'Omnia nam Logices conscripta volumina passim, | Contulit in librum Doctus Stanihurstius unum.'
118. Lennon, *Richard Stanihurst*, p. 33.
119. Ibid., pp. 29–30.
120. McCabe, *Spenser's Monstrous Regiment*, pp. 33–5.
121. Lennon, *Richard Stanihurst*, pp. 39–40. Richard's father, James, died in 1573, and Sir Christopher Barnewell, Richard's father-in-law, died in

1575. One year later, the son of the Earl of Kildare, Lord Garret, whom Stanyhurst had been tutoring, also passed away.

122. Lennon, *Richard Stanihurst*, p. 41.
123. Ibid., p. 41.
124. Kläger, *Forgone Nations*, p. 49.
125. Stanyhurst, *De rebus*, p. 31: 'Quamquam enim ab Anglicæ provinciæ urbanitate, & lautitia utcumque abhorrent; non tamen omni ab humanitate, sicut fertur exuti, vitam traducunt.' See Lennon, *Richard Stanihurst*, p. 89.
126. 'In Stanihurst's text one cannot separate origin and character from language used.' Hadfield, 'Briton and Scythian', pp. 404–5. See also: Kläger, *Forgone Nations*, p. 47; Lennon, *Richard Stanihurst*, pp. 79–81; and McCabe, *Spenser's Monstrous Regiment*, pp. 178–94.
127. Holinshed, *Chronicles*, VI, p. 4.
128. Tudeau-Clayton, 'Richard Carew', p. 512.
129. Holinshed, *Chronicles*, VI, p. 4.
130. Stanyhurst, *De rebus*, p. 28: 'qui in Anglica provincia habitant . . . vero a nova hac, & nimis peregrina magniloquentia, ex gentium exterarum linguis furacissime collecta, longius absunt: tame(n) incorruptam Anglicæ linguæ vetustatem servant. Chaunceri Poetæ laus. illam nimirum, quam Chauncerus vetus ac nobilis Poeta, & Anglorum sine dubio Homerus, in suis scriptis usurpavit: qui ita Anglice dixit, ut non ipsam Angliam magis crederes esse Anglicam.'
131. See the discussion in McCabe, *Spenser's Monstrous Regiment*, pp. 180–1.
132. Stanyhurst, *Æneis*, p. 59.
133. Ibid., p. 51.
134. Southey, *The Poetical Works*, p. 587.
135. See, for example, Saintsbury, *A History of Prosody*, II, p. 175.
136. Kerrigan, *Archipelagic English*, p. 67.
137. Stanyhurst, *Æneis*, pp. 28–9. *Aeneid* 2.281–8.
138. Stanyhurst, *Æneis*, pp. 67 (for the first three examples) and 78.
139. Ibid., pp. 1, 37 and 64.
140. Ibid., p. 75.
141. Ibid., p. 5.
142. Ibid., sig. A3^r.
143. Davis, *Translation and the Poet's Life*, p. 15
144. Stanyhurst, *Æneis*, p. 1.
145. Ibid., p. 11.
146. Ibid., pp. 21 and 42.
147. Ibid., p. 43.
148. Ibid., p. 1.
149. Lennon, *Richard Stanihurst*, p. 33.
150. Stanyhurst, *Æneis*, p. 23.
151. Ibid., p. 91.
152. Ibid.
153. Ibid.
154. Ibid.
155. Nashe, *Works*, III, p. 320.
156. Hall, *Works*, XII, pp. 166–7.

157. Stanyhurst, *Æneis*, p. 91.
158. Also, on the importance of this passage to Augustan translators, see Sowerby, *The Augustan Art of Poetry*, pp. 132–4.
159. Stanyhurst, *Æneis*. Aeolus (pp. 3–4): 'narrowlie whizling', 'terribil huzzing', 'flush flash' and 'tag rag'. Pyrrhus (pp. 33–4): 'crash swash', 'rip rap bouncing', 'topsyed turvie', 'shogging' and 'snorting'. The Harpies (pp. 48–9): 'ram'd cram'd garbage', 'gulligut', 'gaggling whirlerye' and 'coouie'. Aetna (p. 58): 'rufflerye rumboled', 'flash flame', 'coute snort', 'flash furie', 'pouke bugs' and 'rags iags'.
160. Scaliger, *Poetices*, IV, p. 46: 'Vergilius vero artem ab eo [Homero] rudem acceptam lectioris naturae studiis atque iudicio ad summum extulit fastigium perfectionis.'
161. Stanyhurst, *Æneis*, sigs. A2^{v}–A3^{r}.
162. Bloom, *The Anxiety of Influence*.
163. Hall, *Works*, XII, p. 166.
164. Ibid., p. 167.
165. Rosier, 'Richard Stanyhurst', p. 127.
166. Nashe, *Works*, III, p. 319.
167. Rosier, 'Richard Stanyhurst', p. 127.
168. Stanyhurst, *Æneis*, sigs. A2^{v}.

Chapter 2

'Sound this Angrie Message in Thine Eares': Sympathy and the Translations of the *Aeneid* in Marlowe's *Dido Queene of Carthage*

The following speech of Dido's, from the final scene of Marlowe's *Dido Queene of Carthage*, can illustrate the different layers of adaptation, imitation, translation and quotation of Virgil's *Aeneid* which run throughout the play:

DIDO. Now *Dido*, with these reliques burne thy selfe,
And make *Aeneas* famous through the world,
For perjurie and slaughter of a Queene:
Here lye the Sword that in the darksome Cave
He drew, and swore by to be true to me,
Thou shalt burne first, thy crime is worse then his;
Here lye the garment which I cloath'd him in,
When first he came on shoare, perish thou to:
These letters, lines, and perjurd papers all,
Shall burne to cinders in this pretious flame.
And now ye gods that guide the starrie frame,
And order all things at your high dispose,
Graunt, though the traytors land in *Italy*,
They may be still tormented with unrest,
And from mine ashes let a Conquerour rise,
That may revenge this treason to a Queene,
By plowing up his Countries with the Sword:
Betwixt this land and that be never league,
Littora littoribus contraria, fluctibus undas
Imprecor: arma armis: pugnent ipsique nepotes:
Live false *Aeneas*, truest *Dido* dyes,
Sic sic juvat ire sub umbras.

(5.1.292–313)[1]

We can find here instances of free invention: line 300, for example, has no parallel in *Aeneid* 4, where there is no mention of 'papers' from Aeneas. We can find here examples of imitation: Dido addressing the relics which Aeneas left behind as she is about to commit them to the flames (292–4) is an adaptation of her speech at *Aeneid* 4.651ff., but

Marlowe's rendition is only a very loose re-creation. In lines 306–8, we can find a direct translation of lines 625–7 from *Aeneid* 4, where Dido pleads for an avenger to arise from her ashes. And in the Latin at the end of this passage, we can find exact quotations of the original lines 628–9 and 660 of Virgil's epic. As this speech of Dido's illustrates *in nuce*, Marlowe's play moves freely between different levels of engagement with the *Aeneid*. Although the majority of the play is free adaptation, which cannot be pinned down to any specific lines in Virgil's Latin, certain passages in Marlowe's drama are demonstrably translations from Virgil. Roma Gill has considered the entirety of *Dido* as an example of the Renaissance category of translation called 'paraphrase', but her account tends to brush over the different layers within the drama.[2]

Although the categories of imitation and translation were held in close proximity to each other by most Renaissance theorists, they were typically considered distinguishable. Lawrence Humphrey offers the clearest theoretical discussion of this distinction from the English Renaissance in the *Interpretatio linguarum* (1559). Humphrey was keenly aware of the complications of categorising translation and considers what different acts the Latin word *interpretatio* can describe.[3] Nevertheless, as I have shown in the introduction, he is insistent that there is a real distinction that should be made between translation and imitation. He often characterises this distinction as the difference between being an *interpres* and a *scriptor*. In Humphrey's account, one of the problems of excessive freedom in translation is that the boundaries between these two roles will be transgressed. The translator who works too freely behaves 'as if there were no difference between being a writer and a translator'.[4] Humphrey explains:

> For a writer is free to say what he wants, and in what order, and with whatever words, as long as they are of an approved kind; but the translator has a limit fixed before his eyes and boundaries beyond which he cannot wander, if he wants to render the meaning of the author faithfully and to fulfil his duty.[5]

Valerie Worth and Glyn P. Norton have noted that early modern French theorists also make this clear distinction; Worth writes that Du Bellay, Sebillet and Peletier, 'even if recognizing the close relationship between translation and imitation, nevertheless conceive of translation as a separate and identifiable category'.[6] Marlowe's *Dido* could arguably be considered as 'translation', though its status as such varies throughout, and only select portions of the text strive to maintain a high degree of fidelity to Virgil's Latin. Marlowe's tragedy jumps back and forth over the boundaries that Renaissance writers established between *scriptor* and *interpres*, often blurring the obvious demarcations.

Studies of *Dido* have so far overwhelmingly focused on those instances where Marlowe moves the furthest away from Virgil: critics look towards the places where Marlowe can be seen as intentionally 'subverting' Virgilian authority, where he can be seen to be marking out his difference. Such a principle underlies studies such as those by Emma Buckley, Roma Gill, Malcom Kelsall and Clare R. Kinney, as well as Mary E. Smith's book on this play, '*Love Kindling Fire*'.[7] For Smith, 'the differences between Marlowe and Virgil are more significant than the similarities'.[8] Recently, many critics, such as Patrick Cheney, Clifford Weber and Deanne Williams, have also speculated about the contemporary political relevance of the drama.[9] In this chapter, however, the focus is on another side of Marlowe's tragedy. I am interested primarily in those moments where we can say that Marlowe moves *closest* to Virgil's Latin: those moments that can be identified as translation proper.

Such a study of the direct translations in *Dido* can, I argue, establish three new insights into the play. First, the translations, far from being negligible additions, are fundamental to the play's structure. Translations both open and bring to a close the plot of *Dido*, and they are organised to highlight the violence inherent in the Virgilian gods' interactions with men. Second, contrary to previous critical wisdom, I will show that Marlowe closely engages with both the English tradition of Virgil translation and currents of Renaissance commentaries on the *Aeneid*. *Dido* needs to be considered within such a context and not simply in light of Marlowe's later works. Such a context, furthermore, can help us identify what makes Marlowe's response to Virgil unique in the English Renaissance. Marlowe alone presents translations of the poem stripped of the sympathetic narrative voice of the epic. In all other sixteenth-century Dido dramas, this voice is reincorporated through the inclusion of choruses; in all other translations, it is inherent in the Virgilian narrative. In contrast, Marlowe isolates the divine imperatives of Virgil's gods and lays them out for the reader with the greatest conceivable force.

Marlowe's *Dido* and the Renaissance *Aeneid*

At the end of the introduction to her critical edition of *Dido*, Roma Gill states that Marlowe's play does not engage with the translations or commentaries that were prevalent in his time:

> Marlowe ignored other English translations of the *Aeneid* that would have been available in print to him, and he seems to have had no need of a commentary on the Latin, such as the one he used when translating Lucan.[10]

In the case of Marlowe, we do not possess the copy of Virgil he owned, and there is no clear indication to point towards a specific edition. The question of how best to contextualise Marlowe's translation within a broader reception of Virgil in Renaissance England has thus proved challenging. However, in spite of Gill's statement, there are some signs that Marlowe's reading does engage with at least a couple of prominent aspects of both the English translation tradition and Renaissance commentaries on the *Aeneid*.

One particularly revealing interpolation by Marlowe – and one that has not received sufficient attention – comes at the end of Act 3. Dido and Aeneas have been driven together by the storm, and just before they leave the stage to enter the cave, Aeneas exclaims to Dido:

AENEAS. If that your majestie can looke so lowe,
As my despised worths, that shun all praise,
With this my hand I give to you my heart,
And vow by all the Gods of Hospitalitie,
By heaven and earth, and my faire brothers bowe,
By *Paphos*, *Capys*, and the purple Sea,
From whence my radiant mother did descend,
And by this Sword that saved me from the Greekes,
Never to leave these newe upreared walles,
While *Dido* lives and rules in *Junos* towne,
Never to like or love any but her.

(3.4.41–51)

This elaborate declaration by Aeneas has no parallel in the Latin: Virgil tiptoes very cautiously around the issue of what was or was not said by Aeneas. He leaves the reader to imagine what sort of pledges of love or faith Aeneas may have offered to Dido. All we are explicitly told is that *she* 'coniugium vocat' (4.172) ('calls it marriage'). So why does Marlowe add this declaration? The proper context for reading this interpolation is found within the English tradition of Virgil translation. The silence of Aeneas in the Virgilian version of this episode led to one of the major points of disputation regarding the quality of Aeneas' character. This crux became a focal point, in the two centuries before Marlowe, in the work of Geoffrey Chaucer and Gavin Douglas.

As has been demonstrated by Christopher Baswell, Chaucer's reading of the *Aeneid* is rich and complex. Confronting the varied and conflicting readings of Virgil available in late medieval England (pedagogical and allegorical responses, an Ovidian counter-tradition and medieval romances), Chaucer revels in the hermeneutic discrepancies. In *The House of Fame* and *The Legend of Good Women*, he makes Dido into the 'center of an unresolved hermeneutic dialogue between literary traditions'.[11] Chaucer tends to view the *Aeneid* from one angle at one moment, but then to switch to another angle a moment later, constantly asking questions as to where the real poetic authority is to be located. In 'The Legend of Dido', this agonistic treatment of the different traditions is evident from the very beginning:

Glorye and honour, Virgil Mantoan,
Be to thy name! and I shal, as I can,
Folwe thy lanterne, as thow gost byforn,
How Eneas to Dido was forsworn.
In thyn Eneyde and Naso wol I take
The tenor, and the grete effectes make.[12]

Here Chaucer begins by honouring the name of Virgil and claiming that he will follow him, by using the image that Dante uses of Statius following Virgil. However, even by the fourth line Chaucer has veered away from Virgil's lantern towards the romance tradition, and in the fifth line Ovid interjects. Moreover, Chaucer all the while assertively speaks in his own voice, as if he will arbitrate for himself between the different versions. Hence he feels free to add in the non-Virgilian detail that 'Eneas to Dido was forsworn'. There are two points about this statement that are remarkable: first, it represents a sort of hermeneutic levelling, in which Virgil's text is not exclusively privileged and other details can be added from outside; second, it undercuts the epideictic reading of the *Aeneid* that was already favoured in the fourteenth century, especially among Italian authors. If the *Aeneid* is seen as the epitome of epideictic rhetoric, then Aeneas cannot be touched with blame.[13]

Gavin Douglas completed his manuscript translation of the *Aeneid* in 1513, by which time the epideictic reading of Virgil had become standard. Douglas thus pointedly objects to Chaucer's 'Legend of Dido'. As an early Scottish humanist, Douglas includes with his translation poetic commentaries claiming that his work returns to the original purity of Virgil's text: 'Ry*ch*t so am I to Virgillis text ybund.'[14] He writes for an aristocratic audience ('At the request of a lord of renown | Of ancistry nobill and illustir baroun')[15] and attempts to show that Aeneas possesses 'eu*er*y vertu belangand a nobill man'.[16] In his prologue to Book 1, Douglas comments very shrewdly on Chaucer's 'Legend of Dido':

My mastir Chauser gretly Virgill offendit.
All *th*och I be tobald hym to repreif,
He was fer baldar, cert*is* by hys leif,
Sayand he followit Virgillis lantern toforn,
Quhou Eneas to Dydo was forsworn.
Was he forsworn? *Th*an Eneas was fals –

> *Th*at he admittis and callys hym traytour als.
> Thus, wenyng allane Ene to haue reprevit,
> He haß gretly *the* prynce of poet*is* grevit.
> For, as said is, Virgill dyd diligens,
> But spot of cryme, reproch, or ony offens,
> Eneas for to loif and magnyfy,
> And gif he grant*is* hym maynsworn fowlely,
> *Th*an all hys cuyr *and* crafty engyne gais quyte.[17]

To challenge Aeneas' actions in Book 4 of the *Aeneid* is not only to challenge his behaviour at that moment, but to undercut an entire model for reading the poem. Likewise, in the Phaer-Twyne translation, which as we have seen was the dominant English version of the *Aeneid* available when Marlowe was writing his play, Aeneas is a perfect and wise man: an early gloss tells us, 'Under the name of Eneas is described in Virgill the part of a perfite wise man and valiant capteyn if ye marke it.'[18] If any point was a crux for disputing this claim, however, it was Aeneas' love-affair with Dido.

With its elaborate declaration of love by Aeneas, Marlowe's *Dido* of course falls on the side of Chaucerian freedom and works against the humanist response of Douglas. Inserting such a declaration into the play is a firm repudiation of the epideictic version of Virgil. Instead of the clear, humanistic model of reading Virgil, Marlowe was drawn closer to the hermeneutic intermingling of the Chaucerian model. Like Chaucer, Marlowe is interested in probing the authority of the Virgilian text by setting it alongside other possibilities. As Dido herself states, 'For many tales goe of that Cities fall, | And scarcely doe agree upon one poynt' (2.1.108–9). As Emma Buckley has recently stressed, *Dido* is a play that is aware of conflicting versions of the very story that it is telling.[19] However, what has not been sufficiently taken into account, and what is made clear by looking at this passage in light of Douglas, is that a specifically epideictic conception of the *Aeneid* is at stake.

The second major issue in Renaissance responses to the *Aeneid* that shapes Marlowe's drama pertains to the oratorical qualities of the epic. As an example, we can begin again with a particular oddity of this play: in *Dido*, Aeneas is presented time and again as being a brilliant orator. Dido asks her sister, 'Speakes not *Aeneas* like a Conqueror?' (4.4.93). And whereas Virgil's Dido exclaims about Aeneas, 'quem sese ore ferens, quam forti pectore et armis!' (4.11) ('How noble is his mien! How brave in heart and feats of arms!'), Marlowe's Dido translates, 'Is not *Aeneas* faire and beautifull? . . . Is he not *eloquent in all his speech*?' (3.1.63–5; my italics) With a similar enthusiasm for the epic's oratory, Gavin Douglas had written about Virgil's 'flude of eloquens',[20] and indeed it was probably from Douglas's translation, which was printed in London in 1553, that Marlowe took the idea of Dido being captured by Aeneas' speech rather than his face. At this very point Douglas's Dido had exclaimed, 'Quhou wyß in speche and in his co*m*monyng | He schawys hym self.'[21] Regarding Aeneas' speeches in Book 4 of the *Aeneid*, modern scholars could hardly react more differently. Feeney, for instance, writes about the 'taciturnity' of Aeneas in the face of Dido's rhetorical flourishes.[22] However, in Marlowe's translation, both Aeneas and Dido are consummate rhetoricians. One part of this transformation is the incorporation of Aeneas the storyteller into the drama. In the *Aeneid*, 'Aeneas the storyteller' displays a deft command of language and rhetoric, but this storyteller exists in two books only.[23] Today, these books are often treated as separable (as for instance Feeney does in his essay) from the general characteristics of Aeneas as a taciturn man elsewhere in the epic. Marlowe makes no divisions and creates a consistently loquacious and eloquent hero.

Marlowe's fascination with the rhetorical side of characters in the *Aeneid* is a distinctive part of the Renaissance reception of Virgil. The rediscovery and first printing of Tiberius Claudius Donatus' commentary in 1488 marks one of the key points in the transition from the medieval to the Renaissance *Aeneid*. Donatus became the second most printed commentary from 1469 to 1599, second only to Servius.[24] In Donatus' commentary, Virgil's primary skill is that he is the greatest of all orators. Donatus believed that the essential quality of Virgil's writing was its oratorical strength. His commentary thus concentrates on this quality in every book of the *Aeneid*.[25] At the beginning of the commentary, Donatus states, 'if you attend correctly to the poems of Virgil and fittingly grasp their spirit, you will find in the poet the greatest rhetorician, and from this fact you will understand that it is not grammarians, but rather the chief orators who ought to teach Virgil.'[26] Virgil displays the 'fullest art of speaking',[27] and this oratorical capacity comes through in the speeches of all the characters in the epic. Thus Juno's persuasive speech to Aeolus in Book 1 is praised in no uncertain terms: 'if one examines this point rather attentively and diligently, one will find nothing which one will not marvel at; for it is wholly filled with the art and subtlety of speaking'.[28] Gods and men have remarkable powers of speech. It was this Renaissance tradition of reading the *Aeneid* as a fount of oratory that influenced Douglas and Marlowe when they write of the extraordinary eloquence of Virgil's characters.

How Marlowe ultimately treats the powers of speech in the *Aeneid*, however, is greatly different from the standard, moral tradition, which subsumes all of the epic's rhetorical grandeur under the category of *laudativum*. In Marlovian drama in general, power and rhetoric are closely tied together. As Harry Levin writes:

> Driven by an impetus towards infinity and faced with the limitations of the stage, the basic convention of Marlovian drama is to take the word for the deed . . . Magniloquence does duty for magnificence . . . Hence the hero is a consummate rhetorician and, conversely, weakness is represented as speechlessness.[29]

Levin was writing here specifically about *Tamburlaine*, most likely composed shortly after *Dido*, but the statement seems true of the earlier play as well. In an epideictic conception of rhetoric, the power of language is fundamentally benevolent and will sway an audience towards the good. In Marlowe, however, this is not necessarily the case; in fact, it is rarely the case. Even in this early play, we can witness the dramatist exploring for what ends of deception and coercion language can be used. Stephen Greenblatt has argued that Marlowe's conception of rhetoric is essentially Gorgian, which is to say that deception is the very essence of its practice.[30] When we consider the translations from Virgil below, we shall see how deception and coercion are two common themes in Marlowe's reception of Virgil.

What seems to have fascinated Marlowe about the *Aeneid* are thus two different facets. One is the sheer rhetorical power embodied in the speeches in the epic. Marlowe found himself in a position where highlighting this aspect of the *Aeneid* was aided by the cast he was writing for: the primary asset of a child actor was his voice, which would be highly trained in elocution.[31] This connection between the casting of children and the rhetorical aspects of Marlowe's *Dido* has been recognised astutely by Jackson I. Cope, who argued that with their training, 'the sweet singing boys were ideally prepared to declaim complex verse'.[32] Such a cast gave Marlowe a chance to foreground elaborate speeches. The second is the status of Virgilian authority: how the different hermeneutic strands of the Renaissance reception of Virgil can be placed against each other.

Patrick Cheney has argued that for Marlowe, Virgil and Spenser remain 'largely monolithic' poets, who represent first and foremost a writing of nationhood.[33] In Cheney's account, Marlowe then opposes this with a poetics of counter-nationhood, modelled upon Ovid (and, as he has argued more recently, the Lucanian sublime).[34] Opposition or subversion, however, is too simple a model for Marlowe's engagement with the *Aeneid*. There were distinctive qualities associated with the Renaissance Virgil by which he was fascinated. These qualities must be brought into any consideration of the translations within the play.

Translations of the *Aeneid* in *Dido*

In *Dido*, translations from the *Aeneid* are found almost exclusively in Acts 1 and 5. Acts 2, 3 and 4 together only include a handful of lines that show a direct reliance upon the Latin. Translations thus provide a framework within which Marlowe invents much of his own material for the central acts. While source study can often become a rather dry and unrewarding pursuit, in the case of *Dido* it reveals much about the basic structure of the play and provides insights into the method of composition. In this section, I will trace all of the key instances in the drama where Marlowe is conspicuously translating Virgil. As we shall see, there is a pattern and a common significance to those moments when Marlowe moves himself closest to Virgil, where he translates rather than freely adapts.

Act 1 famously begins with Jupiter dandling Ganymede upon his knee. This opening, which is pure Marlovian invention, serves to call into question the ethical value of the god who is overseeing the universe, as critics have frequently remarked. Judith Weil has convincingly argued that this opening sets up an ironic analogy for the audience, who will later see Dido dandling Cupid upon her knee, and even later the old nurse dandling Cupid as well. The audience will then perceive that *eros* seems to be guiding this whole Marlovian cosmos, and that justice and pleasure are not being distributed fairly.[35] The opening scene of the play thus emphasises the *unernst* aspect of the classical gods – an aspect which is hinted at in Virgil but never so clearly foregrounded. Perhaps Marlowe was responding to these hints in the original,[36] but Virgil is never so overtly provocative as Marlowe is at the beginning of his play. Marlowe portrays Jupiter handing over all control to Ganymede: 'Sit on my knee, and call for thy content, | Controule proud Fate, and cut the thred of time' (1.1.28–9). Erotic indulgence is thus the first note that is sounded in *Dido*.

The Jupiter of Act 1 scene 1 is not, however, simply the god of Marlovian *eros*. Remarkably, later in the same scene, when Venus pleads with the king of the gods to save her son, he responds in lines that directly imitate and translate Virgil's Latin. After a free and provocative beginning, when Marlowe came to Jupiter's prophecy, he evidently put the text of Virgil in front of him as he wrote. The beginning and end of Jupiter's speech, for instance, clearly translate into English *Aeneid* 1.257–8 and 272–4. The careful reproduction of the Latinate adjectives and proper names calls attention to the source text. 'Parce metu, Cytherea' literally becomes 'Content thee *Cytherea* in thy care' (1.1.82), and 'Hic iam ter centum totos regnabitur annos | gente sub Hectorea' becomes 'Thus in stoute *Hectors* race three hundred yeares' (1.1.104). For a moment, Virgil's authorial presence appears within Marlowe's drama. Given how different the initial Marlovian presentation of Jupiter is, the return to the Virgilian Jupiter so swiftly is perhaps meant to surprise an audience; but it also establishes early on that Marlowe is not always writing freely, away from Virgil's epic. He keeps his copy of Virgil at hand, as it were, and consults it on occasion. Marlowe takes care to integrate translation here, and the importance of this early moment in the narrative should not be underestimated. It is the one moment that sets out the providential course that the epic, or drama, will need to take: Jupiter prophesies that Aeneas will eventually land in Italy and that he shall found the Roman race. Aeneas' political mission will thus overrule his affection for Dido and Carthage. And Marlowe spells it out in authoritative tones, in the Virgilian voice. According to Donatus, the phrase 'parce metu, Cytherea' is part of Jupiter taking on the 'character of a king, not of a father', and it is remarkable how quickly the king of gods can secure peace when he wishes: 'How quickly he relieves the mind of the grieving one!'[37] The secure, divine providential framework is thus looming in the background of *Dido*, even if the opening suggested another direction. The spectator is thus left to wonder how the Marlovian Jupiter and the Virgilian Jupiter should ultimately fit together.

The most extended sequence of translation in Act 1, scene 1, however, does not come until later, during the encounter between Venus and Aeneas (187–202). The goddess, disguised as a Tyrian huntress/maid, confronts her son and informs him that he has landed in Libya, that Carthage is near and that his ships have not been lost in the storm. This sequence covers nearly seventy lines and is the most sustained instance of translation in *Dido*. It includes translations of *Aeneid* 1.321–3, 326–34, 335–41, 369–70, 378–3, 384–5, 390–1 and 407–9. Marlowe renders a few lines, then leaps forward, renders a few more lines, and then leaps forward again. The only major omission (341–69) is Venus' account of Dido's past. As the longest section of translation, this sequence provides an opportunity to observe Marlowe's practice as a translator:

O, dea certe –
an Phoebi soror? an nympharum sanguinis una? –
sis felix, nostrumque leves, quaecumque, laborem,
et, quo sub caelo tandem, quibus orbis in oris
iactemur, doceas. Ignari hominumque locorumque
erramus, vento huc vastis et fluctibus acti:
multa tibi ante aras nostra cadet hostia dextra.

Marlowe translates:

> Thou art a Goddesse that delud'st our eyes,
> And shrowdes thy beautie in this borrowd shape:
> But whether thou the Sunnes bright Sister be,
> Or one of chast *Dianas* fellow Nimphs,
> Live happie in the height of all content,
> And lighten our extreames with this one boone,
> As to instruct us under what good heaven
> We breathe as now, and what this world is calde,
> On which by tempests furie we are cast,
> Tell us, O, tell us that are ignorant,
> And this right hand shall make thy Altars crack
> With mountaine heapes of milke white Sacrifize.[38]

As much if not more than Phaer and Stanyhurst, Marlowe is careful to render each part of the Latin into English. But unlike his predecessors, he does not attempt to create a roughly equivalent number of English lines. Marlowe breaks away from the stylistic trends we saw in Chapter 1. Instead, he domesticates more freely and even adds his own flourishes. Thus the line 'And shrowdes thy beautie in this borrowd shape' is unnecessary and only contributes to the poetic quality of the English version. Such freedom allows Marlowe's translation to be, it seems to me, much more successful as a piece of poetry. This type of freedom is all the more striking when viewed in comparison with the *Aeneid* translations that directly preceded Marlowe. George Steiner included Marlowe's translation of Ovid's *Amores* 2.10 as an example of what he called 'transfiguration': the rare instance where a translator produces a work of art greater than his source text.[39] This is perhaps an excessive tribute, but by comparing his translations of the *Aeneid* with those of Phaer and Stanyhurst, we can see how novel his brilliance as a translator was in the 1580s.

Along with Marlowe's translation of this sequence between Venus and Aeneas, and his translations from the prophecy of Jupiter, the one other substantial translation in Act 1 is in scene 2 and is taken from the speech of Ilioneus to Dido at *Aeneid* 1.522–41. In Marlowe's play, however, the speech is split into three different parts and given to three different speakers: Ilioneus, Cloanthus and Sergestus (1.2.4–47). Together, these three instances of translation – Jupiter's prophecy, the Venus and Aeneas dialogue, and the speeches to Dido – make up a significant portion of Act 1. What, if anything, do they hold in common? In the case of the first two, it is clear that they both involve the relations between gods and men. These are moments where the gods determine the course the Trojans will have to take. The third instance, the speech of Ilioneus, does not as clearly fit in, but we should note that the centre point (and the bulk) of this brief translation is the declaration to Dido that the Trojans are seeking out 'Hesperia'. It thus once again pertains to the fated mission of Aeneas and his men. What Marlowe does in Act 1 of his play is to present a series of translations from the *Aeneid* intermingled with his own provocative inventions. The translations set a predominantly Virgilian tone near the outset, and the characters are placed in the context of the Virgilian mission destined for them by the gods.

The translation from Act 1, scene 2 is the last extended piece of translation for almost three full acts. Given how much translation there is in scene 1, one might be surprised to see how far Marlowe travels from his source. The lack of translation in the central acts is striking in itself. It is not simply a matter of there not having been opportunities to include translations. The 160 line account of the fall of Troy in Act 2 surely provided numerous opportunities to translate passages from the *Aeneid*. But Marlowe avoids direct translation, and, as J. B. Steane writes, Marlowe's 'version of the story is virtually independent of its source'.[40] Instead of translating Virgil, Marlowe uses the opportunity to engage in Lucanian hyperbole and horrors:

> AENEAS Yong infants swimming in their parents bloud,
> Headles carkasses piled up in heapes,
> Virgins halfe dead dragged by their golden haire,
> And with maine force flung on a ring of pikes.
> (2.1.193–6)

Likewise, Act 3, scene 2 would seem to present many obvious opportunities for translation. In this scene Juno and Venus discuss the happenings at Carthage and debate what course events may take. This is clearly built upon *Aeneid* 4.90–128. But Marlowe again avoids letting the dramatic speeches move too close to Virgil, who is held at arm's length. Instead, the language of this passage blends into the occasionally exalted, often playful, amorous lyricism that pervades the central act. With one very brief possible exception, the central acts avoid engaging the *Aeneid* directly. Indeed, it is as if the Virgilian narrative is temporarily forgotten. And I would argue that this is precisely the effect that Marlowe would have wanted the central acts to have upon their audience: they open up a space in which the Virgilian original fades into the background. The re-emergence of the original towards the end of the play is thus made all the more dramatic.

In *Aeneid* 4, Iarbas' invocation marks a turning point. His complaint to Jupiter leads the narrative up to heaven, where the king of the gods acknowledges the prayer, and then sends Mercury down to earth to tell Aeneas he must leave Carthage. It is the starting point of the god's intervention that leads towards the final tragedy of Aeneas' departure. And it is entirely fitting with Marlowe's practice of Virgil translation in this drama that this speech should begin the move back towards the Latin source. Much like the speech by Jupiter at the beginning of the play, Iarbas' invocation of the gods in Act 4, scene 2 is not fully a translation, but Marlowe has put the Latin in front of him once again.[41] The structure of the speech precisely mirrors the structure of Virgil's: there is an invocation of Jupiter at the beginning, a switch to a complaint about Dido just short of half-way through (again at the beginning of a line) and then a plea for justice, the due reward for his piety, at the end of the plea. Several of the lines within this invocation are also close translations: 'cui litus arandum | cuique loci leges dedimus' (4.212–13), for instance, becomes 'With whom we did devide both lawes and land' (4.2.14), and 'femina, quae nostris errans in finibus' (4.211) becomes 'The woman that . . . straying in our borders up and downe' (4.2.11–12). Iarbas' invocation hints at the return of the Virgilian voice which is to come in Act 5, and it effectively does so by subtly re-incorporating translation from the *Aeneid* at the most ominous of moments.

At the beginning of Act 5, Marlowe's Aeneas has decided that he will stay in Carthage. He and his fellow Trojans are debating what to name their city, and they appear to be perfectly happy in their current state: 'Triumph, my mates', exclaims Aeneas, 'our travels are at end. | Here will *Aeneas* build a statelier *Troy*' (5.1.1–2). The drama appears to have reached an elated stasis, where the characters are existing in a seemingly endless state of lyrical pleasure. Shortly before, Dido had remarked, 'If he forsake me not, I never dye, | For in his lookes I see eternitie, | And heele make me immortall with a kisse' (4.4.121–3). Act 4 ends on such an elated note, and Act 5 begins with a subsequent and satisfied calm. But this ends when Mercury descends upon Carthage. And when he presents Jupiter's message that Aeneas must leave, Marlowe reverts, for the first time since Act 1, into an extended, direct translation.[42] As I have shown, the translations in Act 1 focused on the gods and their relations with men, and the fate to which they have destined Aeneas. The same is true in Act 5, where this declaration by Mercury turns the drama on its head. In Renaissance commentaries, the vehemence of this speech by Mercury is given special emphasis. The speech is described by Donatus as an emphatic 'obiurgatio' ('rebuke').[43] Two of the most influential Renaissance commentaries in circulation in the sixteenth century, Cristoforo Landino's and Jodocus Badius Ascensius', both likewise emphasise the vehement tone. They illustrate how Virgil rhetorically stresses the gravity of Mercury's command. For instance,

Landino begins by describing Jupiter's command as 'an oration full of indignation'.[44] And as Badius notes, Jupiter's power is highlighted to emphasise both the authority of the command and the fear it should instil: 'The king of gods: by the authority of this person he makes the rebuke even graver, and he describes Jupiter's power so that Aeneas' fear will be greater.'[45] Marlowe's tragedy picks up all its momentum from this point – there is no turning back. The Virgilian voice, which had largely been forgotten since the first act, returns with a vengeance here at the beginning of Act 5.

J. B. Steane has argued that Act 5 is an artistic failure because it moves much closer to Virgil. It seems he took this as a sign that it was a rushed effort. He supposes that Marlowe did not invest himself so thoroughly in the final sequence of events as he did earlier in the play, and the direct quotations from the Latin are the epitomes of this lack of artistic engagement:

> But his being content merely to quote Virgil shows him not to be taken up, involved in the material, as he had been in Aeneas' narrative. The impression throughout is that he is in too much of a hurry: doing a job, no more.[46]

Steane, as do others, places far too much value on Marlovian independence in *Dido*. The instances of closeness to Virgil are just as integral to the drama's structure. And if Steane condemns Act 5 on these principles, he would have to condemn Act 1 as well, which contains as much Virgilian material. Instead, it is more fruitful to see the incorporation of translations and quotations as a structural device which Marlowe utilises to frame his play and, most importantly, to contrast with the free, lyrical invention that predominates in the central acts. The carefully controlled translations of the Latin that pile up in Act 5 are selected from all parts of Book 4 of the *Aeneid*, and they create the impression of a narrative that is collapsing towards its closure after it seemed to reach towards infinity at the end of Act 4.

The text of Virgil, which appears through the translations, intrudes when the play first sets out its providential vision, and then again when it drives towards its realisation. There are three ways that suggest themselves for interpreting this frame. On the one hand, we could perhaps say that Marlowe is, even at this early stage in his career, reluctant to write his own tragic endings. Prolonged tragic conclusions were not his strength, and so he modestly left the task of bringing *Dido* to an end to Virgil, an author more skilled in this area – so Roma Gill has argued.[47] Similarly, a drama such as *Tamburlaine* invests very little in the tragic demise of the title character. In Harry Levin's formulation, Marlowe writes about the rise and fall of heroes, but his emphasis is entirely upon the rise.[48] Following another line of argument, we could see this frame of translations as evidence of the joint authorship of the play. The title page of the 1594 printing of *Dido* states that it was 'Written by Christopher Marlowe, and *Thomas Nash. Gent.*'. (The italicised part is in a smaller type-size and is placed a line below.) One could argue that the closer adherence to the source text in Acts 1 and 5 has something to do with the two distinct authors at work. The shift from more Virgilian parts to the freer central acts could be a sign of a change in authorship, as Brian Vickers has recently argued is the case with the Latinist George Peele's role in *Titus Andronicus*.[49] This solution, however, has a couple of problems. The first is that critics of this play have not reached any sort of conclusion as to what part Nashe might have written. The vast majority of critics treat *Dido* solely as Marlowe's play, and Don Cameron Allen's judgement may be taken as typical: Nashe's 'share, if I may use the touchstone of my intuition, was certainly inconsequential'.[50] Almost all critics agree that Marlowe's voice seems to be at work throughout the whole drama, including the translations.[51] Moreover, the initial audience would have viewed the play as an artistic unity. The approach I am taking is to consider it as such. This way, it can be viewed as a carefully crafted whole, and these translations play an important part within this whole.

Marlowe found a narrative violence in Virgil's epic that he brings in at carefully planned moments of his drama. This narrative violence is found above all in the arbitrary strength of the gods and their power over men. The translations thus act as rhetorical interventions, which ultimately drive the drama towards its tragic conclusion. A learned audience member could have recognised these moments. The protagonists are allowed to dabble in Ovidian lyricism throughout much of the play. It is a world in which Dido can ask, 'What more then Delian musicke doe I heare, | That calles my soule from forth his living seate, | To move unto the measures of delight'? (3.4.52–4). When the Virgilian passages appear in the fifth act, however, they spur on moments of recognition, in which the characters, as it were, are forced to remember the epic space they are supposed to inhabit: the lyrical and romance figures of the central acts suddenly find themselves within a different universe. It becomes a world in which imperial matters impose themselves with the powerful rhetorical gestures of the Virgilian original.

Colin Burrow and David Quint have written about the different ways that Virgilian epic creates meaning through narrative order. Burrow writes, 'This history of Virgil's influence suggests that the imaginative drive of the *Aeneid* lies in its digressions, in the way vagrant desires are stunned and discarded. This makes it a powerfully perverse poem: its energy lies in what it asserts to be irrelevances.'[52] In a similar vein, David Quint has commented:

> Virgil's poem attached political meaning to narrative form itself. To the victors belong epic, with its linear teleology; to the losers belongs romance, with its random or circular wandering. Put another way, the victors experience history as a coherent, end-directed story told by their own power.[53]

Pity, in the case of Burrow's study, and resistance to empire, in the case of Quint's, threaten to protract teleological missions interminably, but Virgilian narrative turns these impulses back. In *Dido*, Marlowe is interested in exactly this sort of rhetorical violence that can pull a narrative back onto its course. He has little faith in the grand scheme: Marlowe highlights the capricious aspects of his king of the gods. But he nonetheless preserves power for the gods. It is a power that, in this play, leads towards an ending, whereas in his later plays, when his heroes assume such rhetorical gestures *against* the gods, it will create a movement towards a sort of narrative infinity. The sequence of translations from the *Aeneid* in *Dido* are carefully chosen to highlight the Virgilian energy that can tragically impose an ending upon what appears to be an interminable moment of amorous bliss.

Dramatic and Epic Voices in *Dido*

Marlowe's adaptation of Book 4 of the *Aeneid* allowed him to pick and choose, down to the individual line, what portion of Virgil's epic he would translate. This is a freedom not available to most translators of the *Aeneid* in the sixteenth century and it sets Marlowe apart. Furthermore, Marlowe not only translates between Latin and English; he also performs a generic translation, from epic into drama. Having considered the instances where Marlowe translates lines from Virgil's epic, we are in a position to consider how these specific instances of translation are excerpted and transplanted into the dramatic form. For this discussion, modern classicists provide a useful starting point: the so-called 'dramatic' and 'epic' qualities of the *Aeneid* and their interrelations are an important part of contemporary Virgilian criticism. It is frequently noted, moreover, that Book 4 of the *Aeneid* borrows many elements from the tradition of Greek tragedy.[54] It should thus not be surprising that *Aeneid* 4 lends itself to being adapted into a drama: it contains traces of the dramatic genre within itself already. This is surely a part of the reason why the episode was adapted so frequently for the stage. In the sixteenth century alone, for instance, there are important

Dido plays written in Italy by Alessandro Pazzi (*Dido in Cartagine*, 1524), Giambattista Giraldi-Cinthio (*Didone*, 1543) and Lodovico Dolce (*Didone*, 1547), in France by Étienne Jodelle (*Didon se sacrifant*, between 1552 and 1563) and in England by Edward Halliwell (*Dido*, lost, but performed before the Queen in 1564), William Gager (*Dido*, 1583) and Christopher Marlowe.

In an essay which has recently been published in English in the collection *The Poetry of Pathos*, Gian Biagio Conte provides an overview of what he calls the 'Virgilian paradox': the incorporation of drama into epic.[55] Conte builds upon a long tradition of German scholarship that has influenced many twentieth-century English Virgilians, most notably Brooks Otis. This tradition began by interpreting a contrast between Homer and Virgil. Richard Heinze, in his seminal work of 1903, argued that in Homeric narrative there is a single point of view that transcends the authorial persona to merge with objective reality. (In traditional Roman epic – Ennius, Naevius – this single point of view will be identified with a grand political and historical design, in which all personal truths are subsumed.) In contrast, Virgil created a new form of epic by making two great changes. These are described by using a specific terminology which I shall borrow. First, it was argued that Virgil narrated in a highly sentimental tone. One line commonly quoted to illustrate this is his imitation of *Iliad* 6.244 at *Aeneid* 2.503, during the fall of Troy. Where Homer writes, referring to the rooms of the children of Priam, 'fifty chambers of polished stone', Virgil, with a sense of the tragic loss at Troy, laments, 'quinquaginta illi thalami spes tanta nepotum' ('those fifty bedchambers – such great hope of grandchildren'). Homeric objectivity is transformed into Virgilian pathos. This narrative pathos has been termed *sympatheia*. Second, Virgil creates an empathetic relationship between his narrator and his different characters. In doing so, he reaches out time and again towards the different characters' own perspectives. This has been called *empatheia*. As Conte argues, this second quality comes from the Virgilian incorporation of drama. The Virgilian characters are not subsumed under a single objective lens. Rather, Virgil's new epic attempts to create a texture that is essentially 'polycentric', allowing the characters their own, unreconciled, tragic sensibilities.[56] Conte states: 'Virgilian *empatheia* is not just a pose of the narrative surface to generate pathos, but rather a bold appropriation of the fractured and confrontational language of drama.'[57]

This multiplication of fractured points of view within the epic threatens to undermine any objective overview. One of the most distinctive marks of Virgilian epic is that it is constantly in danger of collapsing into tragedy; it exists on the brink of having its epic status – its claim to portray a teleological and meaningful vision for Rome – break down under the weight of countless individual tragedies which cry out in their own voices. What acts against this disintegration of the poem into a cacophonous mixture of perspectives is the overarching perspective and sympathy of the omniscient narrator: he suffers along with the characters, but always supports a comprehensive view of the epic's direction. In Conte's account, the Virgilian texture is thus one full of competing, subjective voices, but it is held together, however precariously, by the narrator's *sympathetic* persona. Moreover, the competing, tragic voices become strongest at those moments of the narrative where Virgil has drawn the most from Greek drama. This is witnessed above all in the episode of Dido and Aeneas.

Can any of this modern criticism on the *Aeneid*, built upon distinctions first made by German Romantics, be applied to Renaissance dramatic adaptations of Virgil? The task may seem at best precarious and at worst completely anachronistic. However, there is a way that this analysis of 'epic' and 'dramatic' elements within the *Aeneid* can be an illuminating lens for Renaissance Dido dramas. It becomes apparent by looking at a collection of Renaissance Dido tragedies that many of the playwrights were aware that there are dangers in adapting *Aeneid* 4 into drama, and that the primary danger is the loss of a sympathetic, overarching, moral perspective. Thus in almost all previous Dido dramas – including those by Pazzi, Giraldi-Cinthio, Dolce, Jodelle and Gager – we find extensive choruses. These choruses, combined with other new inventions, usually act to pre-empt the disintegration of epic into tragic subjectivity. Don Cameron Allen, who has provided an overview of these early Dido dramas in his essay, 'Marlowe's *Dido* and the Tradition', has noted that Giraldi's, Dolce's and Jodelle's plays 'unite in defending Aeneas' desertion of Dido', even if they emphasise different points.[58] In Dolce's play, for instance, honour is the central theme. In the case of men, this honour appears in duty, and in the case of women, in chastity. Aeneas maintains his honour; Dido loses hers. The result is a play that uses Virgil, in Craig Kallendorf's words, to 'reinforce the traditional, patriarchal hierarchy in Renaissance Venice'.[59] In this play, the chorus has an important function, especially in the final act. During the last moments of the drama, as news of Dido's death is received, the chorus provides a voice that is both sympathetic to Dido's plight – 'O caduca beltade, | Come misera, come | Picciol momento ti consuma, e perde' ('O fleeting beauty, how wreteched; what a brief moment consumes and wastes you') – and nevertheless emphasises the divine purpose: 'Ch' ogni cosa mortal governa il Cielo' ('Heaven governs every mortal thing').[60] This perspective is what critics have associated with the sympathetic voice of the epic narrator in the *Aeneid*.

Another example we can look at to see how these choruses can incorporate the 'epic' quality into the dramatic texture is William Gager's *Dido*. Produced for Prince Albertus Alasco's visit to Christ Church, Oxford in May 1583, Gager's *Dido* appeals to its specific, noble audience.[61] For this discussion, the most important aspect of the drama is the change of perspective rendered by the chorus. In Gager's *Dido*, the chorus turns the drama into a civil event: it becomes the downfall of a city, viewed from the perspective of the citizens. In the first chorus of the play, Dido is presented as the greatest of all princesses, at times nobler even than Aeneas; by the end, however, the chorus is mourning the fall from grace of their queen. Gager's chorus and epilogue thus treat Dido sympathetically, even while incorporating her into a larger, overreaching view of history: 'sed Elisa fato Tyria miserando occubat' ('Tyrian Elisa came to a piteous end').[62] Once again, the chorus finishes a play by restoring the sympathetic epic voice that holds together the tragic subjectivity.

A different approach to this problem is taken in Ben Jonson's *Poetaster*. This play does not contain an extended narrative from the *Aeneid*. But, as many critics have noted, Jonson makes a clear parallel between the fates of Ovid and Julia and of Dido and Aeneas.[63] Caesar's judgement against the young lovers raises many of the issues that are raised by the Virgilian gods when they command Aeneas to leave Carthage. In *Poetaster*, unlike most Renaissance Dido dramas, there is no chorus to reinstate the transcendent narrator's sympathetic voice. But this is not a problem because Virgil himself steps in to fulfil this role, along with Caesar Augustus. Jonson makes Virgil stand 'at the absolute centre (with Augustus) of a circle of being/truth'.[64] Jonson removes the two major problems that Marlowe's play raises. Ovid's fate is justified, since Augustus and Virgil pronounce it from a position of unimpeachable authority. Horace describes Virgil as 'bearing the nature, and similitude | Of a right heauenly bodie: most seuere | In fashion, and collection of himselfe, | And then as cleare and confident, as IOVE'.[65] And even though Caesar's pronouncement against Ovid is stern in Act 4, in Act 5 Caesar is portrayed having much greater sympathy for Ovid and Julia.[66] While he may not be as generous as Horace, he too laments that he must pass a stern judgement and is 'grieved to reprove':

CAESAR. We, that haue conquer'd still, to saue the conquer'd,
And lou'd to make inflictions feard, not felt;
Grieu'd to reproue, and ioyfull to reward;
More proud of reconcilement, then reuenge;
Resume into the late state of our loue.[67]

Echoing Anchises' pronouncements in Book 6 of the *Aeneid*, these words display the compassion of Jonson's virtuous Augustus and thus restore the balance of sympathy and divine justice that Marlowe's play calls into question.

In the most extended study of Renaissance Dido drama to date, Barbara Bono charts a growth towards a greater romantic freedom as the Virgilian dilemma is retold again and again in the Renaissance.[68] Bono's overview of these Dido dramas, however, seems to underestimate what is decisively new about Marlowe's *Dido*. According to Bono, Marlowe is 'profoundly subversive' and treats his subject amorally, but she also believes that Marlowe makes the love between Dido and Aeneas merely 'a shallow idealization'.[69] Consequently, the whole play is predominantly trivial. This seems to me to avoid the significant innovations that Marlowe makes. The most significant of these is that he has avoided any hint of re-incorporating sympathetic epic elements into his play. Unlike all of his predecessors, there is no chorus in Marlowe. There is likewise no sustained attempt to justify Aeneas along the lines of epideictic rhetoric. While the whole scope of Trojan history is portrayed in his drama, there is no unifying voice that can sympathise with the characters. The result is a play that dramatises the 'polycentric' aspect of Virgil's *Aeneid* more emphatically than any that had come before. The gods become simply other voices (even if all-powerful ones) within the story. Instead of a narrator who can relate sympathetically to the suffering, all we have is the fickle gods imposing their will. The frame of translations from Virgil that we saw above is thus imposed all the more inexplicably.

By eliminating all traces of Virgil's sympathetic epic narrator, the polycentric voices are laid bare in all their individuality. In a short piece in *Notes and Queries*, Lucy Potter has recently claimed that Marlowe was not simply pitting an Ovidian perspective against a Virgilian perspective, but rather that he was finding tragic elements within Virgil's epic itself.[70] The above exploration of translations of the *Aeneid* in *Dido* can offer, I argue, further evidence of Potter's claim. Drawing on the immense rhetorical strength that was associated with the epic in the Renaissance, Marlowe incorporates translations of the Virgilian original to emphasise those moments where Virgil dismisses the errant desires of his characters. This thwarting of the heroes' desires is, of course, inherent to Virgil's epic, although Marlowe's presentation of these moments without the sympathetic narrative-voice of the *Aeneid* makes them even more poignant than they are in the original. These stark moments of translation, moreover, provide the structure within which Marlowe's free inventions are built.

After the rather literal and moralistic Phaer-Twyne *Aeneid*, Marlowe's dramatic translations were among the first to appear in England, and they could hardly present a more different reading of the epic. Marlowe's *Dido* deserves a special place in any history of English Renaissance translations of the *Aeneid* because of how creatively he uses direct translations from the Latin to frame the play. Breaking away from the humanistic translations of Douglas, Surrey, Phaer and Twyne, Marlowe found a means to bring out the most violent and coercive side of the Renaissance Virgil. For this reason, this play should be regarded as the one, and only, extensive example of a *pessimistic* reading of Virgil's epic from the English Renaissance.

Notes

1. All quotations from *Dido* are taken from Roma Gill's edition: Marlowe, *Complete Works of Christopher Marlowe*, I, pp. 125–74.
2. Gill, 'Marlowe and the Art of Translation', p. 332.
3. See Humphrey, *Interpretatio*, p. 3.
4. Ibid., p. 23: 'quasi interesset nihil inter scriptorem & interpretem'.
5. Ibid., pp. 23–4: 'Scriptor enim liber est, ut dicat quae velit, & quo ordine, ac quibuscunque verbis, modo probatis: interpres praefixam habet ob oculos metam, & terminos extra quos evagari non potest, si autoris sensum reddere fideliter, si officio suo satis velit facere.'
6. Worth, *Practising Translation*, p. 3. Also see Norton, *Ideology and Language of Translation*, p. 197: 'imitation in the Renaissance is considered a process altogether distinct from translation'.
7. See Buckley, '"Live false Aeneas!"'; Gill, 'Marlowe's Virgil'; Kelsall, *Christopher Marlowe*, pp. 34–46; Kinney, 'Epic Transgression'.
8. Smith, *'Love Kindling Fire'*, p. 101.
9. Cheney, *Marlowe's Republican Authorship*, pp. 78–96; Weber, 'Intimations of Dido and Cleopatra'; Williams, 'Dido, Queen of England', pp. 31–59.
10. Gill, 'General Introduction', p. 120.
11. Baswell, *Virgil in Medieval England*, p. 268.
12. Chaucer, 'The Legend of Dido', ll. 924–9. I quote from 'Text F' of *The Legend of Good Women*, in *The Riverside Chaucer*, p. 608.
13. Kallendorf, *In Praise of Aeneas*.
14. Douglas, *Virgil's 'Aeneid'*, II, p. 11, l. 299.
15. Ibid., p. 5, ll. 83–4.
16. Ibid., p. 12, l. 325.
17. Ibid., pp. 14–15, ll. 410–23.
18. Phaer, *Seven*, sig. A3^{v}.
19. Buckley, '"Live false Aeneas!"', pp. 130–1.
20. Douglas, *Virgil's 'Aeneid'*, II, p. 11, l. 310.
21. Ibid., p. 155, ll. 21–2.
22. Feeney, 'The Taciturnity of Aeneas'.

23. For Aeneas' use of rhetoric in Book 2, see: Nisbett, '*Aeneas Imperator*'.
24. Wilson-Okamura, *Virgil in the Renaissance*, pp. 31–2.
25. Comparetti, *Vergil in the Middle Ages*, p. 61.
26. Donatus, *Donati in libros duodecim Aeneidos*, sig. A3^{v}: 'si maronis carmina competenter attenderis, & eorum mentem congrue comprehenderis, invenies in poeta rethorem summum, atq*ue* inde intelleges virgilium non grammaticos, sed oratores praecipuos tradere debuisse.'
27. Ibid., sig. A3^{v}: 'artem plenissimam dicendi'.
28. Ibid., sig. A7^{v}: 'hunc locu*m* si quis attentius, diligentiusq*ue* discutiat, nihil q*uod* no*n* miretur inveniet. est *enim* arte & subtilitate dicentis admodu*m* satiatus.'
29. Levin, *Christopher Marlowe*, pp. 62–3.
30. Greenblatt, *Renaissance Self-Fashioning*, p. 215.
31. Gill, 'Marlowe and the Art of Translation', p. 334.
32. Cope, 'Marlowe's *Dido* and the Titillating Children', p. 317.
33. Cheney, *Marlowe's Counterfeit Profession*, p. 15.
34. Ibid., p. 82.
35. Weil, *Christopher Marlowe*, pp. 18–19.
36. Lyne, *Further Voices*, p. 85.
37. Donatus, *Donati in libros duodecim Aeneidos*, sig. B6^{v}: 'personam regis, non patris' and 'Quam cito mærentis animum solvit!'
38. *Dido*, 1.1.187–202.
39. Steiner, *After Babel*, p. 423.
40. Steane, *Marlowe*, p. 41.
41. *Dido* 4.2.4–22. Cf. *Aeneid* 4.206–18.
42. *Dido* 5.1.26–41. Cf. *Aeneid* 4.265–70.
43. Donatus, *Donati in libros duodecim Aeneidos*, sig. L5^{v}.
44. I quote Landino's commentary from the Venice, 1499 edition of Virgil 'with five commentaries': *Publii Virgilii Maronis opera cum commentariis*, fol. 189^{v}: 'or*atio* plena i*n*dignatio*n*is'.
45. I quote Badius' commentary from the Venice, 1558 edition of the 'universum poema' Virgil: *P. Vergilii Maronis, poetæ Mantuani, universum poema*, fol. 209^{r}: 'Ipse deum[:] Huius personæ auctoritate, graviorem facit suam obiurgatione*m* & ut maior sit metus, potestatem ipsius describit.'
46. Steane, *Marlowe*, pp. 48–9.
47. Gill, 'Marlowe and the Art of Translation', p. 336: 'I prefer to think that in retaining some of Vergil's lines Marlowe is betraying a quality not usually attributed to him – modesty. And, of course, an appreciation of the great beauty of those particular lines.'
48. Levin, *Christopher Marlowe: The Overreacher*, p. 43.
49. Vickers, *Shakespeare, Co-Author*, pp. 148–243.
50. Allen, 'Marlowe's *Dido* and the Tradition', p. 64.
51. As Mary E. Smith argues, in the translations of Virgil 'the translator of Ovid and Lucan can be seen at work' ('*Love Kindling Fire*', p. 111).
52. Burrow, *Epic Romance*, p. 46.
53. Quint, *Epic and Empire*, p. 9.
54. For an introduction, see Hardie, 'Virgil and Tragedy'. See also, Panoussi, *Greek Tragedy in Vergil's 'Aeneid'*.
55. Conte, 'The Virgilian Paradox'.

56. Ibid., p. 33.
57. Ibid., p. 55.
58. Allen, 'Marlowe's *Dido* and the Tradition', p. 64.
59. Kallendorf, *Virgil and the Myth of Venice*, p. 200. See also Lucas, 'Didon: Trois réécritures tragiques', pp. 593–604.
60. Dolce, *Didone*, fols. 39^{v} and 42^{v}. On these lines, see Terpening, *Lodovico Dolce*, pp. 121–2 and 125–6. I quote Terpening's English translations.
61. Boas, *University Drama in the Tudor Age*, p. 189.
62. The Latin and the English translation are from: Gager, *Complete Works*, I, pp. 342–3 ('Epilogus', l. 1252).
63. See, for instance, Erskine-Hill, *The Augustan Idea*, p. 120; Moul, *Jonson, Horace, and the Classical Tradition*, p. 158; Tudeau-Clayton, *Jonson, Shakespeare, and the Early Modern Virgil*, pp. 162–3.
64. Tudeau-Clayton, *Jonson, Shakespeare, and the Early Modern Virgil*, p. 158.
65. *Poetaster* 5.1.104–7. Jonson, *Poetaster*, pp. 292–3.
66. Erskine-Hill, *The Augustan Idea*, p. 117.
67. *Poetaster* 5.1.1–5. Jonson, *Poetaster*, p. 289.
68. Bono, *Literary Transvaluation*, p. 4.
69. Ibid., p. 130.
70. Potter, 'Marlowe's *Dido*: Virgilian or Ovidian?', pp. 540–4.

Chapter 3

Courteous Virgil: The Manuscript Translations of an Anonymous Poet, Sir John Harington and Sir William Mure of Rowallan

In recent years, manuscript translations have been gaining greater attention. They reveal a different side of reception history than is apparent in printed texts. As Henry Woudhuysen has demonstrated, early modern England was not only a print culture, 'it was also a manuscript culture'.[1] There were many reasons a text might be copied and circulated exclusively by hand: the subject-matter might be overtly seditious or delicately private.[2] In 2011, the first exploration of a range of English manuscript translations appeared in Stuart Gillespie's book, *English Translation and Classical Reception*. In the history of English Renaissance translations of the *Aeneid*, manuscript circulation plays a crucial role. The translation by Gavin Douglas, for example, had an extensive life in manuscript before it was printed posthumously in 1553, as is attested by the five surviving manuscripts. The translation by Henry Howard, Earl of Surrey and Sir John Denham's rendition of Books 2–6 of the *Aeneid* likewise existed in manuscript long before entering print.[3] Yet whereas these translations were eventually printed, several substantial English translations never entered print in any form during the Renaissance. These include the anonymous translation discovered at Castle Ashby in 1977 (now BL Add. MS 60283), the version of Book 6 Harington presented to King James and Prince Henry in 1604 and Sir William Mure's rendition of Books 1 and 4 in the Edinburgh University Library. These translations naturally invite a consideration of the distinctive potentialities in manuscript translations of the *Aeneid*. In the case of these three texts, we will see that two of them have more light-hearted reasons for their existence in manuscript, but a high degree of exclusivity is a vital part of all of them. Moreover, they all treat Virgil's epic with a freedom that is rare in printed translations. Indeed, all three translators would have fallen under Humphrey's censure for their lack of faith to Virgil's Latin and for their often mischievous ethics. In the first section of this chapter, I will offer the first reading of the anonymous translation of

Book 4 from the British Library, establishing for it a place within the history of Virgil translations and shedding more light on the author. In the second section, I will focus on how the Augustinian reading of Virgil in the commentary Harington attached to his translation would have influenced the young prince's reading of Book 6. In the final section, I will then look at a free and creative translation of the story of Dido and Aeneas which was composed by Sir William Mure as an amatory poem in the early years of the seventeenth century.

An Anonymous Manuscript Translation and Dido's Passionate Complaint

On 5 July 1978, a collection of Renaissance manuscripts came up for sale at Christie's in London. These manuscripts had been discovered less than a year before, tucked away 'in the back of an old drawer' at Castle Ashby.[4] Most of the manuscript collection consisted of works by Cosmo Manuche, but a previously unknown translation of Book 4 of Virgil's *Aeneid* was also found in the back of that drawer.[5] The scholar who was responsible for the discovery, William P. Williams, promptly hailed the new translation as 'an important addition to the corpus of Renaissance English poetry'.[6] In spite of Williams's initial excitement, however, interest in this new Book 4 manuscript has been slow to follow suit. In the 1980s, it enjoyed a brief moment of fame, when it became the subject of contention as to whether or not it was the work of Sir John Harington. But the debate was effectively concluded in 1989 when Simon Cauchi persuasively argued that it was not by Elizabeth's witty godson.[7] Since that time, interest in the anonymous Book 4 seems to have disappeared completely, while Harington's manuscript translation of Book 6 has been the focus of a new edition and some studies.[8]

It is useful to begin by surveying the reasons for the initial attributions to Harington.[9] The manuscript was first attributed to Harington in the Christie's Catalogue entry.[10] It was argued that the manuscript was written in the Harington household style. The provenance was traced through William Lord Compton, who was a friend of Harington's and an early owner of Castle Ashby; Cosmo Manuche was the 'protégé' of Lord Compton's grandson, James Compton. Moreover, it was argued that the translation showed signs of Harington's characteristic 'waggishness' and that the stanza form of the translation – sestets rhyming ababcc – emerged from Harington's experience in translating Ariosto. All in all, the catalogue stated that this translation of Book 4 was a 'distinguished addition to the corpus of Elizabethan-Jacobean verse'.

'We believe', it continued, 'that the cumulative weight of the evidence . . . puts the attribution to Harington beyond reasonable doubt.' Two years later, in 1980, Peter Beal endorsed this attribution in his *Index of English Literary Manuscripts*. But Beal rested even more of his judgement on the style of the writing itself: the translation, he averred, is 'so characteristic of Harington that it is difficult to believe that it could have been written by anyone else'. In particular, he considered the stanza as 'an experimental variation of the *ottava rima*', and thus the stanza was part of Harington's fascination with Italian culture.[11]

A slightly different account, however, was offered by William P. Williams. For him, the evidence also began with the penmanship: 'the style and use of secretary and italic fit patterns found in other Harington manuscripts, both autograph and scribal'.[12] But Williams's account differed on two key points. First, he supplied a new provenance. He surmised that the manuscript came to Castle Ashby with Bishop Percy (1729–1811) in the eighteenth century. Bishop Percy had made notes about the Manuche manuscripts with which the Book 4 was eventually found, and it was his notes that led to the discovery. Williams thus suggests that Percy could have borrowed the Virgil manuscript from the Haringtons (Percy was known to have borrowed from them) and then left it at Castle Ashby by mistake (as he evidently lost at least one manuscript). Furthermore, in regard to the style of the translation itself, Williams suggests a different reason as to why the translator opted for stanzas of six lines: the stanza form of the Book 4 is the 'Venus and Adonis' stanza, and Williams believed that Harington found it appropriate for the story of Dido and Aeneas.

The assumption that the translation was the work of Harington stood through most of the 1980s, until several dissenting voices changed the opinion. D. H. Craig first raised objections in a footnote in his book on Harington in 1985.[13] In his 1989 DPhil dissertation, Colin Burrow argued on stylistic grounds that the translation could not be by Harington.[14] Harington's verse typically uses full feminine rhymes with unstressed supernumerary final syllables, whereas in the *Aeneid* 4 the feminine endings are usually counted as part of the ten-syllable line. Moreover, these feminine endings often carry the rhyme. Even when the preceding syllables do not match, the translator will rhyme '-ed' with '-ed'. As Burrow argues, this is something that Harington never does. Simon Cauchi's 1989 article then made the full case against Harington's authorship. He wrote against every point that had been made in favour of the attribution. Regarding the penmanship, he stated that 'the Harington "household" hand argues no closer relationship than contemporaneousness'.[15] The two possible provenances were merely suggestive and, even if one were true, it would not determine that Harington was the author, as Harington and his scribes were responsible for copying works by many other poets.[16] Furthermore, Harington, who was in the habit of frequent self-referencing, makes no mention of a translation of Book 4 elsewhere in his writing. Cauchi's analysis of the style of the translation also suggested that Harington's authorship was not probable. Put simply, Harington condenses whereas the anonymous translator expands. The only common ground Cauchi allowed is that the anonymous translator and Harington share an interest in amatory poetry. Cauchi's conclusion was that the translation was 'the work of an inexperienced versifier, but reasonably competent Latinist, who had recently been reading Spenser', and that the only part Harington may have contributed was the two-line envoy.[17] Cauchi's argument has been accepted by scholars since.[18]

But as a consequence, since 1989, no new attention has been given to the manuscript from Castle Ashby. The questions thus remain as to who wrote it, when and why. There are indeed many ostensibly striking similarities between Harington and the anonymous translator. BL Add. MS 60283 and Harington's Book 6 are two of only three translations of the *Aeneid* into stanzas before the Civil War. Is this to be attributed to an Italianate influence upon both? Or to Spenser's influence? There is also the fact that neither of them was ever set in print. In the case of Harington's gift to the king and prince, one reason would seem to be the exclusive status of the book as gift. But what about the manuscript of Book 4? The answers to these questions – as far as it is possible to answer them – must be inferred from a careful study of the text itself.

The most determinative quality of this anonymous translation is the freedom it takes with its source. Indeed, the text is one of the freest extended translations from the *Aeneid* in the English Renaissance. This approach may be partly due to the demands of translating into a stanza form. But this only accounts for a portion of the freedom, as neither Harington, nor Fanshawe later, is so liberal with the source text. Where Harington translated the 901 lines of Book 6 into 1,072 lines of *ottava rima*, this Book 4 uses 1,022 lines to render only 705 lines of Latin. We can look at the first relatively self-contained stanza to see how this translator works:

Nor day, nor night, slepe ceaz'd her carefull eyes
Love's fiery vigor scornes dull slepes arrest
Ingraven in her hart *Æneas* lyes
For they that love (*Iove* knowes) doe seldome rest
    But when the morrow Sunne disclos'd his beames
    And Pheebus light daunc'd on the wavering streames.
(13–18)

This stanza translates *Aeneid* 4.4–7:

> haerent infixi pectore vultus
> verbaque, nec placidam membris dat cura quietem.
> Postera Phoebea lustrabat lampade terras
> umentemque Aurora polo dimoverat umbram.

Lines of Virgil's Latin appear in English in a reversed order: line 13 translates line 5 of the Latin, whereas line 15 translates line 4. This sort of inversion is common, and suggests that the translator approached the Latin more or less in blocks of text from which he chose details; he did not aim to translate everything. Here, one rather important detail – the 'verbaque' – is left out, but that is a relatively small omission compared to others. Lines 13 and 15 notably alternate with lines that have no immediate source in the Latin: 'Love's fiery vigor scornes dull slepes arrest' and 'For they that love (*Iove* knowes) doe seldome rest'. These lines add even more stress than there already is in Virgil to the powerful presence of love at the beginning of Book 4. Even when the translator renders the final two lines fairly faithfully, he still playfully elaborates 'umentemque . . . umbram' into 'daunc'd on the wavering streames'.

This freedom of the translator can be seen clearly in the treatment of Virgil's similes, as the translator wilfully trespasses over the boundaries of the comparisons. The author will raid a simile for information that is then applied directly to the narrative, while the simile itself is drastically shortened. To take one example, we can consider the simile in which Aeneas is compared to Apollo as he comes out for the hunt (4.142–50):

> infert se socium Aeneas atque agmina iungit.
> qualis ubi hibernam Lyciam Xanthique fluenta
> deserit ac Delum maternam invisit Apollo
> instauratque choros, mixtique altaria circum
> Cretesque Dryopesque fremunt pictique Agathyrsi;
> ipse iugis Cynthi graditur mollique fluentem
> fronde premit crinem fingens atque implicat auro,
> tela sonant umeris: haud illo segnior ibat
> Aeneas.

In the manuscript, this simile becomes:

> Next to the Quene *Æneas* tooke his place
> Whose haire with linckes of gold was plaited rounde
> (least they should overshade his comely face)
> And at his back a glittering Quiver bounde
> Like as *Apollo* when he goes to see
> *Delos* the place of his Nativitie.
>
> (217–22)

The nine-line simile comparing Aeneas to Apollo is reduced to two lines, while details from Apollo's description are applied to Aeneas. Thus Aeneas is now decked out with gold and glitter. The fact that it is possible for the translator to shift the material around in this manner perhaps says something about the Virgilian similes themselves. The details of the similes in Virgil often contribute new narrative information. In order to slide seamlessly into them, Virgil often lets the language of the simile intrude into the narrative surrounding it, or vice versa. R. O. A. M. Lyne has termed this phenomenon in Virgil a simile 'trespass', and this technique serves to illustrate how closely the main narrative and the simile are bound together.[19] The anonymous translator of Book 4 liberally makes use of this close connection, and we could perhaps call what he does at such moments a translator's 'trespass'.[20]

When all the various freedoms the translator takes with the original are considered, it becomes clear that this translation could not have been intended for a pedagogic purpose. Most of the English Renaissance translations of the *Aeneid* boast their usefulness for young students attempting to read the Latin. Gavin Douglas writes in the 'Dyrectioun of his Buik' that his translation is a 'neidfull wark' for children and students learning to read the original. Douglas therefore proudly declares, 'Thank me *th*arfor, mast*er*is of gra*m*mar sculys.'[21] Thomas Phaer, although it is not his main purpose, has an eye on young readers: he asks for the good will of those 'such as be teachers of children . . . though everye verse aunswere not to your expectation'.[22] Sir John Harington says that his translation of *Aeneid* 6 was initially undertaken 'for the benefyt of myne own chylde' who was then learning to read Virgil.[23] More democratically, John Vicars states that he translates for 'especially the common good and publick utility, which I hoped might accrew to young schollars and grammaticall *Tyroes*'.[24] The history of translation of the *Aeneid* in early modern England is closely associated with education. This is also true of translations of the *Eclogues* and *Georgics*. Abraham Fleming translated 'for the benefite of young learners of the latine tongue',[25] and John Brinsley's translations from the *Eclogues* and *Georgics* were carried out 'principally for causing Schollers to study of themselves'.[26] Moreover, where education is not a concern, translations often nevertheless stress their proximity to the Latin by printing it *en face*: the translations by Sir Dudley Digges and Sir Thomas Wroth are examples. The Book 4 from Castle Ashby, however, is an exception from the trend of fidelity in Virgil translations. This translation would be quite useless, and often very misleading, for someone attempting to learn the Latin. It does not purport to offer a means of access to the great master-teacher Virgil.

At the beginning of the translation, there is one stanza that is not a translation at all, but rather serves as an introduction to this poem's focus:

> Now Cupides quickning shaftes had mov'd desire
> And raging love within her breast remaynes
> Poore *Dido's* hart's inflam'd, loves furious fier
> Consumes her bloud and yet her bloud maintaines
>   Her Cruell enemy O fatall love
>   That findes soe fitt a place, soe prone to move.
>
> (1–6)

The story of how 'loves furious fier' consumes Dido is the primary interest of this translator. The two interpolations we looked at in the early stanza above also aimed one's attention towards the force of Dido's love, which is described in this opening stanza as 'raging', 'furious', 'cruell' and 'fatall'. The translator later makes it clear that Aeneas is also deeply touched. This Aeneas is a man torn apart by the conflicting pulls of love and country. As Burrow notes in his thesis, the curt Latin sentence 'hic amor, haec patria est' (4.347), which is Aeneas' final declaration to Dido that he must now reside in Italy, is mistakenly translated as an exclamation of the dilemma that confronts the hero: 'Love will's me stay, my Country biddes me goe' (493).[27] And just after the oak simile, the translator gives us a peek into Aeneas' tormented state of mind: 'feare and care within his breast | Remain'd till at the length from out it broke | And in his Countenaunce showed how little rest | He had within' (626–9). But just as Aeneas does not appear in the introductory stanza, so, I would argue, his plight is secondary to Dido's passion throughout this poem.

In the opening half of the book especially, Dido's passion is represented with greater erotic explicitness than in any other English Renaissance *Aeneid*. Dido's tears, which in Virgil merely well up in her eyes – 'sic effata sinum lacrimis implevit obortis' (4.30) – are suggestively portrayed as streaming down over her breasts:[28]

> Thus having spoke the teares so fast distil'd
> From her bright eyes: as that they watered
> Her Ivory Paps and her white breast was fil'd
> With floudes of teares.
>
> (49–52)

Whereas Virgil's Anna encourages Dido by asking her 'nec dulcis natos Veneris nec praemia noris?' (4.33; 'will you know not sweet children or love's rewards?'), this translator's Anna is rather more direct, asking

'Nor will you know fair *Venus* swete delight?' (57) And it seems that her plan to delay Aeneas – in Virgil, simply 'indulge hospitio' (4.51) – involves luring him with such pleasures: 'Then finde delayes | And whilst on swete delightes hee's surfetting | Tell him the surging Billow roughly playes' (86–8). In Anna's words, even the dangerous sea becomes erotically charged. Before long, Dido has determined:

> All her desire was but to yeild him pleasure
> Now she besought, desir'd, beseech'd, and praide
> That whilst her tender armes his neck enroulde
> Once more she wisht his woefull tale was told.
> (129–32)[29]

At this point in Virgil, she is merely hanging onto his story: 'pendetque iterum narrantis ab ore' (4.79). All these examples are drawn from the first 150 lines of the translation, and one could continue citing examples all the way through, even though there are naturally fewer in the second half. The general tone can neatly be summarised in a line which the translator adds in the English: 'No sight her lustful love could satisfie' (142).

Alongside this heightened eroticism is a greatly elaborated element of melodrama. It comes through in a typically colourful use of adjectives and, more prominently, in expansions. The ground is 'palecheekt' (121), Dido's tears are 'Christall' (578) and night has a 'sable vaile' (740). When Dido faints at the end of one of her speeches, Virgil writes 'suscipiunt famulae conlapsaque membra | marmoreo referunt thalamo stratisque reponunt' (4.391–2; 'Her maids support her, carry her swooning form to her marble bower, and lay her on her bed'). These two lines are translated into five:

> At length she faintly fell vpon the earth
> And panting there a while she lay for breath
>
> When straite her Ladyes rann and vp they rais'd
> The Quene, and on a bedd of Ivory
> They layed her.
> (551–5)

The scene, which has a great deal of pathos already in Virgil, is turned into a yet more sensational spectacle.

Simon Cauchi suggested that the interest in the amorous sides of poetry is something shared by Sir John Harington and the anonymous translator.[30] But it is also instructive to consider how Harington and this translator differ in their treatments of these elements. The glosses alongside the translation are a fitting place to compare their attitudes as

Harington invests so much in his. Jason Scott-Warren has stated that Harington's standard technique when dealing with erotic (or seditious) material is analogous to a 'crossing-out which leaves the text beneath it visible and draws attention to it, the self-correction which ensures that no one misses the indiscretion'.[31] In his translations, the process of 'crossing out' the indiscretion is often effected through the addition of a strong moral framework. Harington delights in the imperfections of human nature and the potential for mischievous pleasures, but there are distinct moral limits.[32] Thus his Ariosto, as Burrow writes, 'moves with less amorous sympathy than its original', and Harington uses the glosses to pursue a serious vision of aristocratic nobility and virtue.[33] In both his Virgil and his Ariosto, the preponderance of notes is moral.[34] The notes in this translation of Book 4, however, make no attempt towards a moral interpretation. They are all very curt and offer only basic glosses on mythological figures or geographical details. I can find no evidence that the author consulted (or would have needed to consult) Servius or another commentator. For example, he will gloss Saturnia as 'Iuno the daughter of Saturn' (152) or Aulis as 'A Promontory in Grece' (597). Again, we see that the text serves no educational or moral purpose. The glosses serve only to make sure that any reader could follow the story of Dido's passionate love affair with Aeneas.

There is one other significant set of images that contributes substantially to this translator's distinctive take on Dido's story. This set of images one might term 'courtly'. The word 'court' itself appears frequently in the translation, as the events are imagined as taking place at Dido's court and Iarbas resides in his own court. In the descriptions of the hunt, the translator seems to display an affection for processions of horses which are not specified in Virgil: 'troopes of horse vpon the plaines are laide', for instance, is an addition to the Latin (compare 4.117–18), and there are several more gratuitous references to horsemen.[35] The images of banqueting and feasting are likewise exaggerated. And perhaps the most curious examples of this courtly dynamic are in the occasional signs of class disdain. Take this description of Fama:

her exclamations
Sounde in every strete, and ioyfully
Vnto each vulger eare she published
That faire Quene *Dido* now was married

Vnto *Æneas* sprung of high descent
From out the royall bloud of *Troians* race.
(273–8)

In Virgil, Aeneas is described as being 'Troiano sanguine cretum' (4.191). The translator has built upon this little phrase a sharp contrast between the vulgar ears in the streets to whom Fama speaks and the royal blood of Aeneas, whom she harms by condemning. Furthermore, the use of the word 'publishing' in connection with Fama's cruel defamation of the royal lovers could be a hint of the author's own view of printing literature in general and of why this translation was never put into print. While there has been debate over whether there ever was such a thing as 'the stigma of print' in Elizabethan England, it is tempting to point to a trace of it here.

On this more speculative note, I would like to suggest a new context for the composition of this translation. So far, as we saw earlier, the two main suggestions have been either Harington or an inexperienced versifier with some knowledge of Spenser. A much more likely context, however, would be the court poets of the 1580s and 1590s. The style and concerns of the translation would fit perfectly with a writer who had been reading the poetry of courtiers such as the Earl of Oxford, Sir Edward Dyer and Arthur Gorges. Steven May's study *The Elizabethan Courtier Poets* carefully follows the rise of a new lyricism in the 1570s under the influence of Oxford and Dyer. Instead of functional, occasional pieces, these courtier poets developed a poetry of 'extravagant rhetoric and passionate stances assumed . . . for the amusement of the queen and her courtiers – the direct, functional nature of earlier courtier verse has given way here to a poetics which is to an important degree fictional'.[36] Theirs was a poetry, moreover, that had 'no positive example or ethical instruction'.[37] They also had an interest in the amorous side of Dido's story. One of Sir Arthur Gorges's longest poems is a translation of Joachim du Bellay's *Complainte de Didon à Enée, prinse d'Ovide*, and he also translated Du Bellay's *Sur la statue Didon, prins d'Ausone*, a paraphrase of Pseudo-Ausonius' Epigram 118.[38] While the manuscript translation of Book 4 has a very different style from Gorges's, its amorous account of Dido would have been appreciated in the same literary circles.

Furthermore, the popularity of the six-line, ababcc stanza among these writers is striking. Beal's suggestion that the translator adapted this stanza from *ottava rima* seems unlikely. Instead, as Williams initially suggested, this was a stanza used frequently for love poems during the Elizabethan era, most famously in Spenser's *Shepheardes Calender* and Shakespeare's *Venus and Adonis*. It was an especially popular metre among the courtier poets as well. Essex wrote in this metre (including his lengthy love complaint, 'The Passion of a Discontented Mind') as did the Earl of Oxford, Edward Dyer, Sir Arthur Gorges, Fulke Greville, Sir

Thomas Heneage, the Earl of Arundel, Sir Henry Lee and Lord Strange. Sir John Harington used the metre as well, but he did so only rarely.[39] The use of this metre for a translation of Book 4 of the *Aeneid* aligns it with the lovers' complaints being written by other late Elizabethans and presents it as a self-sufficient portion of the *Aeneid*, independent of the epic as a whole.

Whoever copied BL Add. MS 60283 was probably not the original author, as there are a couple of curious copying mistakes. The most telling example is at line 719, where the word 'solace' should have been 'place', as is demonstrated by similar phrasing at line 928; the hand from which this manuscript was copied most likely had an elaborate flourish on the *p*. Among the manuscripts that the Harington family copied or had copied, there are many unpublished poems.[40] And there are excerpts from at least one other translation of the *Aeneid* among the Harington manuscripts: BL Add. MS 36529 contains Books 1–3 of Phaer's translation of the *Aeneid* as well as Chaloner's translation of Ovid.[41] It seems very likely Harington played a part in the transcription of the Book 4 manuscript. While this must of course remain speculative, if it was by a courtier, Harington could certainly have had access to it, given his status as a courtier himself. Plausible provenances that would trace the poem from Harington to Castle Ashby have already been suggested. The context would thus fit very neatly, if this translation were indeed by a courtier during the late 1580s or the 1590s. A more precise guess about the author is extremely difficult, as we only know the names of a very small number of the courtier poets and their styles are difficult to distinguish.[42] Moreover, their writing was often diffused through extensive, complex networks of manuscript circulation. But whoever the anonymous translator was, this poet was interested in Book 4 of the *Aeneid* as a quintessential lover's complaint. The resulting translation is unique among the early modern English translations of the *Aeneid* and it deserves to take its place in the history of English Virgils.

Virgil Corrected: Sir John Harington and Book 6 of the *Aeneid*

Like BL MS 60283, the translation of Book 6 of the *Aeneid* by Sir John Harington exists in only one manuscript.[43] Harington's purpose in translating Virgil, however, could hardly be more different. This translation, the author declares in a dedication to King James, was intended as an educational tool for young scholars. Harington prepared manuscript copies for his own son, for Robert Cecil's son and for Prince Henry, the heir to the throne.[44] The unique copy that still exists was presented as a gift to the young prince in 1604, and the parchment binding bearing the royal arms of James I suggests that it did indeed find its way into the royal library. For this special copy, Harington prepared an English commentary to accompany the translation, which was thus 'amplyfyed for the vse of the Peerles Prince yor Maties heyr'.[45] In scholarship to date, Harington's version of Book 6 has been viewed politically as a work glorifying the new stability and imperial ambitions of the Stuart dynasty.[46] It is seen as a bid by Harington to secure patronage and to flatter the new royals.[47] However, the translation and commentary by Harington are far from being a straightforward encomium and the current critical responses dull the political implications of Harington's Augustinian Virgil. In his introduction to Harington's epigrams, Gerard Kilroy has pointed to the oddity of surrounding 'a poem that prophesies the future of Rome with a commentary drawn largely from a text that reflects on the fall of Rome, St Augustine's *De civitate Dei*'.[48] Taking seriously Kilroy's stress on the ironic nature of Harington's commentary, I shall argue two points. First, while it is true that the commentary and translation were prepared at different times, the Augustinian commentary can in fact serve as a guide to much of the translation itself: the opinions expressed about Virgil in the commentary shape Harington's verse as well. And second, the suspicious view Harington takes in the commentary is the most determinative factor for both the poetic shape and the politic relevance of his translation.

As a text composed with the declared aim that the young prince's 'mynde [may be] encyted to good and vertuows practyses', Harington's Book 6 fits within the mirror-for-princes genre. As Quentin Skinner has documented, this genre was very popular among northern humanists. Guillaume Budé, Jacob Wimpfeling, Johann Sturm and Erasmus are just some of the prominent figures who wrote such texts. These humanists were inspired by their belief in the vital connection between good learning and virtuous government.[49] In the case of Harington's Book 6, however, one precedent in this genre has special significance: King James's *Basilikon Doron*, which the king wrote in manuscript in 1598 and had printed in 1603. The *Basilikon Doron* purports to be the king's private advice to his eldest son and heir, and it is contained within a Virgilian wrapping. At the beginning of the work, an introductory poem states that the message is, 'reward the iust, be steadfast, true, and plaine, | Represse the proude, maintayning aye the right'. This echoes the advice Anchises gives his son at *Aeneid* 6.852–3.[50] James moreover concludes the text by quoting at length Anchises' famous advice in the Latin.[51] More impressionistically, one can also discern a distinctly

Virgilian ring to the general tone of the work, which tells Henry that '*ye are rather borne to* onus, *then* honos'.[52] A translation of Book 6 was thus an appropriate gift for Prince Henry, and Harington evidently had the *Basilikon Doron* in mind when composing the commentary. When he reaches the passage that James quotes, Harington comments, 'thear cannot bee a worthyer testimony of the estimacion of this booke of vergill then that a learned King wryting to his deerest sonne makes choyse of this passage for his conclusyon.'[53] Harington's manuscript translation of Book 6 should, in the first place, be read as a response to the use of Virgil in James's *Basilikon Doron.*

If Harington's translation is read as an educational tool in the mirror-for-princes genre, the question that follows is, what are the virtues Harington believed a young prince requires? The fullest answer can be found in the seventh chapter of *A Tract on the Succession to the Crown* (1602). In this work, Harington measures James against the pattern of a prince offered in the *Catalogus gloriæ mundi* of Barthélemy de Chasseneux and vows to take revenge on anyone who interferes with James's succession. While the list of virtues is taken over from the French author, Harington's commentary reveals the relative importance he places on each of Chasseneux's ten qualities (truth, justice, piety, affability, liberality, magnanimity, wisdom, chastity, fortitude and fidelity). Some of these virtues, such as affability or liberality, receive hardly a mention. In contrast, the greatest emphasis is placed upon the first and last of them, truth and fidelity, which Harington considers to be closely linked: truth 'may seame all one with the last'.[54] In the discussion of truth, Harington cites the *Basilikon Doron* (which he evidently read before it was printed in 1603) and stresses the immense wisdom of King James. It is his learning in human and especially divine affairs, Harington remarks, that make James fit to reign:

> how studious he hath bene thereof from his youth, his rare learning testified by those have conferred with him, as well as his wrytinges make proof, so as his constancie in truthe both humane and divine, give him a right as well to succeed hir Ma^{tye} in her worde semper eadem, as in his scepter whensoever she shall leave it.[55]

Harington has no trace of the Machiavellian counsellor; he insists here, as elsewhere, that knowledge of truth and fidelity to it are crucial for any fit ruler.

A king should possess these specific virtues because of the power that an example exerts over its audience. In the epigrams, Harington frequently insists that it lies within the power of a nation's ruler to redeem its faults: 'We do but poynt out vices and detect them | 'Tis you great

Prince, that one day must correct them',[56] or 'Might some new officer mend old disorder, | Yes, one good Stewart might set all in order'.[57] There are several ways in which a king can influence the populace, but one of the most central is by way of example. In the commentary to Book 6, Harington provides his clearest statement of this belief:

> yt ys an admirable thinge thowgh wee see yt dayly in the camp how moche the example of the commawnder encorageth a sowldyer, for long marches or for distresse of vittell or any payn which otherwyse they wowld be redy to mutyn yf they wear put vnto yt.[58]

The role that humanists believed Aeneas could play for readers – inciting them to virtue and turning them away from vice – is closely paralleled by the role that a king plays for the people. It is thus crucial that truth and fidelity are presented from the top. Not surprisingly, these two qualities are of especial importance in the gift that Harington presents for the education of the young prince.

Harington's translation of Book 6 shows many signs that he felt Virgil's narrative could function, at least in part, in an epideictic manner. At the two poles of virtue and vice in this work are the figures of Numa and Tantalus. Although Virgil makes no mention of Tantalus' kingship, Harington quietly introduces the word 'king' in stanza 89 to accentuate the role Tantalus plays as a ruler and *negative* precedent for Henry. Moreover, Harington informs the future king that 'the cheefe morall of w[ch] fable ys that neyther the state of Kings nor theyr ritches can keep them from torments eyther in this world or the next, yf they bee tyrannows and vngodly'.[59] With Numa, by contrast, Harington points out a ruler who invested his kingdom with religion and fidelity. In Virgil, Anchises shows Numa to his son as follows:

> Quis procul ille autem ramis insignis olivae
> sacra ferens? nosco crinis incanaque menta
> regis Romani primam qui legibus urbem
> fundabit.
>
> (6.808–11)

> (But who is he apart, crowned with sprays of olive, offering sacrifice? Ah, I recognise the hoary hair and beard of that king of Rome who will make the infant city secure on a basis of laws.)

However, in Harington's version Numa is portrayed in different clothing: ''Tis Numa (now I know) a Roman Kinge, | Attyrd halfe lyke a preest, hee makes to cease | All bloody warrs, and zeal and Iustys spring | whearby his howse and empyre doth encrease.'[60] Harington makes much more explicit this king's piety in order to stress the positive aspects of Numa as an example. He portrays this 'Roman Kinge' in sacred garments, increasing empire through his adherence to religion and truth. In the commentary Harington explains why Numa was so important:

> This was the fyrst that planted a rellygion in Roome wch thowgh yt was but according to the rytes of the Pagans, and consequently erroneus yet yt did breed him moche honor and his peeple great peace. for a relligiows prince winneth the harts of the subiects incredybly, especially of those that are relligiowsly enclynd.[61]

The commentary here reinforces the tone of Harington's translation. Between the figures of Tantalus and Numa, Harington's Book 6 offers a full spectrum of didactic examples for his royal audience, from kingly virtue to follow to tyrannical vice to avoid. That said, there are aspects to this translation that do not sit so well with an epideictic reading. These become apparent when we look into how Harington brings Ariosto into the translation.

One of the unique aspects of Harington's Book 6 is that it renders Virgil into Ariosto's stanza form, the *ottava rima*. The only other translator of Virgil in sixteenth- or seventeenth-century England to use this metre was Edmund Spenser in *Virgils Gnat*. It was a rare choice to pick this metre in England. And as Daniel Javitch has shown, the *ottava rima* was not even the established verse-form for translating Virgil in Italy.[62] Lodovico Dolce, Vincentio Menni, Aldobrandi Cerretani and Giovanni dell'Anguillara all published partial translations of the *Aeneid* in *ottava rima*, but of these only Dolce's immense transformation of the *Iliad* and *Aeneid* was reprinted (1571, 1572).[63] Much like in England where the Phaer-Twyne rendition of Virgil in a close approximation of the Latin metre became the standard, by the late sixteenth century Annibale Caro's *Aeneid* in *verso sciolto* had become the Italian standard. After it was first printed in 1581, Caro's *Aeneid* was reprinted time and time again.[64] While several critics have pointed to the uniqueness of Harington's metre in English, none has followed through in exploring the full implications of this unusual choice.

In the introduction to his edition of Book 6, Cauchi has argued that Harington's use of this verse-form puts him in line with other English writers who were using *ottava rima* for quasi-heroic poetry: the Countess of Pembroke, Samuel Daniel, Michael Drayton and Edward Fairfax.[65] Cauchi further argues that there was no other convincing alternative for Harington. I do not believe, however, that this argument sufficiently explains Harington's choice. Harington used a wide range of metres in his writing and was aware of previous English translations of Virgil (and of other classical poets) that did not use *ottava rima*. For example, he cites Phaer in his commentary and borrows from him in several places.[66] In the early seventeenth century, fourteeners were still being used in new translations of the *Iliad* (Chapman 1611) and the *Aeneid* (Wroth 1620). More importantly, Cauchi's argument does not sufficiently take into account the pervasive role that Ariosto plays in Harington's commentary as well. Harington evidently had Ariosto in his mind when he was working on his Virgil translation. I argue that he associated *ottava rima* with the broader *materia ariosteca*. Indeed, the role that Ariosto plays within his commentary on the *Aeneid* is striking. If one goes over every instance where Harington cites Ariosto (and the only author he cites more often is Augustine), a very clear pattern emerges. In most cases, Harington compares Virgil and Ariosto, and in almost every case where he does so he deems Ariosto the better poet. Thus one finds Harington explaining that 'ariosto in my conceyt doth moch better fayn', Ariosto is 'more Ingenuows', 'the place Aryosto discrybes ys far more sutable for a paradyce' and 'Ariosto makes a more gentle applycacion'.[67] The reason Ariosto's modern epic is superior to Virgil's is because Ariosto had access to Christian truth, and this access to truth allowed his epic to better the pagan's attempt at mapping the cosmos.

In the introduction to his translation of the *Orlando Furioso* in 1591, Harington had claimed that 'whatsoever is praiseworthy in Vergill' can be found in Ariosto, and that Ariosto even surpassed Virgil because his epic contained 'infinit places full of Christen exhortation, doctrine, and example'.[68] The second part of Harington's 'Briefe Apologie of Poetrie', in which he defends Ariosto by contrasting him with Virgil, is often taken more rhetorically than it should be. Based on the commentary to Book 6, it would appear that Harington truly considered Ariosto the greater moral poet. The initial publication of the *Orlando Furioso* sparked lengthy debates in Italy over its status as an epic poem. For one example, Giovambattista Giraldi, in his 1554 *Discorsi*, argued that the ancient classics could no longer satisfy the modern age and change was needed: Ariosto fulfilled this need for change.[69] G. B. Pigna, on the other hand, in his 1554 *I romanzi*, argued that Ariosto really conformed to the Latin classics and was thus worthy of the same dignity.[70] Another line of defence was taken by Clemente Valvassori in the preface to his 1553 edition of Ariosto, where he argued that Ariosto's knowledge of Christian doctrine allowed him to surpass Virgil as a poet. This third line of defence was the argument Harington adopted in 1591.[71] In 1604, we find Harington repeating it again. In the case of King Tantalus, who represents the negative pole of vice in this translation, we can find a perfect example of Ariosto's superiority. In this instance, Harington says that the example of Tantalus is parallel to the story of Senapo in

Ariosto, but that Senapo is a better model because 'hee fayns that vppon his repentawnce hee was restored by a duke of England'.[72] Ariosto's epic contains the full scope of the Christian drama, and Harington's comments point Henry towards Ariosto, whom he is to consult for better teaching.

Sometimes Virgil was so far from Christian truth that the Italian was at pains to correct him and to produce a Christian imitation. Here is Harington describing how Ariosto dealt with Virgil on the transmigration of souls:

> Heer he enters into a matter that breeds great questyon among the deepest dyvins, and thearfore no marvell yf a Poet wryte extravagantly and far from trewth in yt. Ariosto being a Christian and as some thinke a kynd of Chyrch man (a Dean or at least a Deacon) yet making ye lyke ficcion to this hee brings in the princes of the howse of Estee to appeer thear before they wear born wch ys more probably ficcion then this Pithagorean error of Transmigration of sowls owt of one body into an other wch ys against all skripture doctors & fathers.[73]

While modern accounts tend to focus on the light-hearted and lively imitations in the *Orlando Furioso*, Harington's Ariosto was a very moral 'kynd of Chyrch man'. Harington seems not to have been drawn towards the fantastic elements in the Italian epic. D. H. Craig writes about the *Orlando Furioso* translation as a 'blunting' of the original. Likewise Colin Burrow writes of its 'toughness'.[74] Harington's Ariosto was an upright poet, and even when he would write 'ficcion', at least his fictions did not contain grave errors like Virgil's. The Pythagorean belief in the transmigration of souls was one of those. Another such liability, as we shall see, was Virgil's belief in the permanence of Rome's greatness. In contrast, Ariosto understood how transitory Roman glory really was.[75]

Given Harington's reading of Ariosto and the Italian's role in the commentary as a corrective presence, Harington's translation of Virgil into Ariosto's metre is not merely a playful, Italianate response to the *Aeneid*. Rather, it was an attempt at modernising the epic and contrasting it with something better. Harington states that he translated only Book 6 because he found the translation 'so hard and so harsh for owr Englysh verse'.[76] It seems that transforming Virgil into *ottava rima* was more difficult than he expected. But this verse-form was an essential part of the work. Whereas with their 'fourteeners' Phaer and Twyne tried reverently to live inside the space of the Latin, in Harington's translation it is the *Aeneid* that must adapt to the advances of Christian epic. Harington did not feel the duty towards Virgil that Humphrey's ideal translator should. The Ariostean stanza can be seen as a part of his Christian emulation of both earlier translations and Virgil's epic itself.

And we can see this emulation repeated in Harington's many references to Augustine, who had become an important theologian for him the year before he translated Virgil.

In 1604 when Harington composed the manuscript for Prince Henry, he had just experienced the most tumultuous year of his life. In the decade prior, he had made several egregious mistakes. Publishing *The Metamorphosis of Ajax* in 1596 was a grossly misplaced bid to gain attention at court. His participation in Essex's debacle in Ireland (as well as receiving a knighthood from it) did not help his case in 1601. In May 1603, Harington's fortunes reached their lowest point. Having offered surety for his uncle, Thomas Markham, Harington was arrested for debt when Markham's son-in-law, Sir John Skinner, was unable to pay back 4,000 pounds.[77] Harington quickly found himself locked up in the Gate-House Prison. While his few months' stay was shorter than expected, Harington spent much of his time in prison reading the Bible and St Augustine, and this reading made a significant impact on his Virgil. Given that he composed his *Aeneid* commentary within a year afterwards, it should not surprise us that Augustine is the most quoted authority in the commentary. And much like Ariosto, Augustine plays a corrective role, remedying the errors of Virgil.

In the dedicatory epistle to King James, Harington gives us an important hint as to how he read his Augustine. He writes:

> I betooke my selfe cheefly to reeding, sometyme of his word that made the world, somtyme of his worke, that distinguisheth the Cyttesens of the Cytty of god, from the Citesens of the world, I mean Snt Awgustins excellent booke *De Civitate dei.* wch I read wth an old comment writt thearon by an Englysh man many ages since.[78]

Here Harington gives us two key facts. The first is that he primarily read the *City of God*. The second is that he was almost certainly working from an edition with the commentary by the fourteenth-century Oxford Dominicans Nicholas Trevet (*c*.1258–*c*.1335) and Thomas Waleys (*c*.1318–49).[79] Trevet had composed a commentary on all twenty-two books of the *City of God*. Waleys had then compiled a more extensive one on the first ten books that was usually printed along with the commentary by Trevet on the final twelve. In the first major printed edition of the complete works of St Augustine, the Amerbach edition (1505–6), the Trevet and Waleys commentary on the *City of God* was included, so it was widely available in the sixteenth century.[80] Reading the *City of God* along with this commentary, however, was not a simple process. In fact, Waleys's commentary is often at odds with Augustine's response to the pagan classics.

In the *City of God*, Augustine took a polemical stance against the *Aeneid*. Whereas several of his contemporaries, such as Macrobius and Servius, found in the epic a universal text, and he himself in earlier works such as the *Confessions* was moved by Virgilian pathos, the late Augustine read the *Aeneid* as the history of an earthly city fundamentally opposed to divine providence.[81] Virgil's pagan gods were associated with demons that shaped the course of Roman history and needed firm repudiation. Harington quotes Augustine to this end in *The Metamorphosis of Ajax*:

> of all which S. Augustin writes most divinely, to overthrow their divinitie; and therefore I referre the learned and studious reader, to his fourth and sixt bookes *de Civitate Dei*, where the originall, and vanitie of all these Gods and Goddesses is more largely discoursed.[82]

In the *City of God*, Augustine also followed Sallust's account of the causes of Rome's decline. *Libido dominandi* and desire for earthly glory overtook the virtue of the people, and the state eventually collapsed.[83] In Book 5, chapter 18 of the *City of God*, for example, Augustine quotes Virgil's praise of Brutus in 6.820–3 of the *Aeneid* as an example of the actions of the Romans carried out because of their vain 'libertas et cupiditas laudis humanae' ('freedom and desire for human praise').[84]

In the edition Harington was reading, however, a different perspective on the value of Virgil and ancient Rome was provided by the commentators. Waleys's commentary (which covered the first ten books of the *City of God* – the crucial portion for Augustine's views on the *Aeneid*) is first and foremost an attempt to accommodate the classics to Christian teaching.[85] The commentary thus works as a corrective to Augustine's zeal and defends the value of the pagan classics. Thus when Harington read about Virgil in his copy of Augustine, he encountered two conflicting voices: one attempting to discredit Virgil's demonic gods and the history of Rome; the other, the voice in the margins, encouraging greater respect for all that Virgil could teach and for the ways the pagans could illuminate Christian ethics.[86]

These two attitudes towards Virgil can both be located in Harington's translation and commentary on Book 6. The two voices frequently coexist tensely in Harington's work, and it seems that he never systematically reconciled them. On the one hand, the accommodating view of the classical poets can be seen in his admiring remarks on how far the pagans reached via the 'light of nature'. The seventeenth-century manuscript copy of the commentary by itself was given the title 'The Light of Nature in Heathens', which is indeed one major strand of Harington's text.[87] For example, when dealing with topics such as murder and funeral customs, Harington concludes that pagan philosophy was in accordance with Scripture:

> yt ys worth the observing how evn by the lyghte of nature the Pagans thowght the very place prophand and polluted whear any murder was committed, and this cryme of murder ys so odiows that the skrypture calleth yt a sin crying for vengawnce.[88]

In regard to funeral customs, Christians may even have learned from the practice of the pagans: 'yt may bee in soch indifferent things the Christians did not skorn to take example of the Iews and evn of the Pagans, as for example lamps and tapers'.[89] More significantly, however, Harington also allows that the pagans come close to touching on various essential matters of the Christian faith. He judges that the pagan fates are not so unlike Christian predestination: '*The fates*, wear vnderstood by the Pagans the gods decress not vnlyke to that wch Christians call a predestinacion.'[90] Harington even allows that the pagans are sometimes superior to certain types of Christians (his usual target being the puritans):

> It ys admirable to see how thease heathn Poets did rove at the misteryes of owr fayth & namly in this y^t^ ever they fayn the sonns of Iupiter to discend into Hell to do some rare exployt. as yf yt wear a proper work for ye sonne of god to descend into hell shall not thease pagans at ye last day condemne owr purytans.[91]

All of these moments of reconciling Christianity and the pagan light of nature can be said to be conducted in the manner of Waleys's commentary.

A more severe judgement upon the value of pagan philosophy, however, also comes through in Harington's Book 6. It is at these moments that we find the more direct influence of Augustine. The sacrifice to Pluto, for example, Harington declares as 'all meerly prophane', and the notion that souls are not allowed to pass an underworld river 'ys an opinion cleerly disproved by the skrypture'.[92] The pagan paradise is a 'poor description of a Paradyce or place of blisse, wch fayls evn in the fyrst glory wch showld bee the lyght'.[93] Much like Augustine, Harington exhibits lofty contempt for the Pythagorean doctrine of the transmigration of souls: 'this absurd Pithagoryan opinion ys long since reiected in the Christen churche'.[94] And for the purposes of considering the political investment of this translation of Book 6, the most interesting case is how Harington portrays the Roman Empire. On this topic, much like Augustine, he follows Sallust in stressing that the collapse of Rome came from internal, moral weaknesses:

> *Imperial Room.* how greatly Roome hath floryshed both in arms and pietye many trew storyes witnes, but in later ages yt hath so decayd in both and evn in snt augustins tyme for the fyrst being taken and sackt by the goths.[95]

Wrapping Virgil's account of the glorious progression of Rome with a commentary focused upon the fall of the Roman Empire leaves the reader poised between two visions of history. In Denis Feeney's account of the culmination of Book 6 of the *Aeneid*, what is at stake is not so much a religious revelation as 'an image of the nature of Rome and the political process'.[96] At a time when Rome was feeling its way through the integration of Augustus' special role within the old system of republican government, at a time when the state was moving towards a monarchy, the revelation of Anchises to Aeneas was a topical exploration of the hopes and fears of the Roman state. Critics such as Philip Hardie and Karl Galinsky have highlighted the fragility of this moment, especially as it is embodied in the figure of Marcellus.[97] The death of Marcellus prompts one of the most revealing comments in Harington's text. In Harington's eyes, the death of the heir to Augustus is already one stage in the gradual erosion of faith in the Roman Empire. The Roman political system was built upon humans and was thus unstable: it would have to give way to Christ.[98]

Several critics have read Harington's gift to King James and Prince Henry as a direct encomium of the new Stuart dynasty and the stability it would bring. This may have been the general message of the panegyrists in 1603 when James rose to the throne, and certainly the *Aeneid* was used to this purpose. However, Harington's translation and commentary are much more subtle. Instead of glorifying the new prince and an eternal line of succession, this version of Book 6 promotes caution. Poets sang the highest praises of Rome, but Rome fell nonetheless when it lost track of its basic virtues. The translation comes across more as a cautionary tale against hubris, and it suggests that any political state is liable to fall. Panegyrists used Virgil's poetry to reinforce ideals of political stability and James himself used the *Aeneid* in *Basilikon Doron* for this purpose. But Harington's Augustinian response to Virgilian politics claims that the only genuine stability is to be found in Christ.

As should be clear by now, Harington was not the type of Renaissance reader who saw Virgil as a universal poet, a divine poet or even the prince of poets. He did not treat Virgil with the reverence of Vida or Scaliger, or of Phaer or Stanyhurst. But when the *Aeneid* is not treated as a book of the gravest wisdom and highest art, it leaves space for a more light-hearted encounter. Harington states in his commentary, 'Poets so myx the trewth wth fables & storyes with allegoryes that no great heed ys to be taken of them.'[99] The less reverent approach Harington takes towards Virgil is responsible for many of the charming details and asides in this translation. These little additions are often incorporated to bring the Virgilian narrative up to Harington's own time. In the translation, for instance, he describes the underworld for his English readers as 'dull as winter nights with vs or duller | that show some shapes, but yet can Iudg no culler'.[100] And where Virgil explains the ancient cause for a place's name, Harington revels in the tradition of storytelling: '(so dwellers thear the story do recownt) | and call yt to this day Misenus mownt'.[101]

Whenever the Virgilian narrative touches upon a story that seems fabulous, Harington is likely to make an aside about the probability of such an event actually happening. Commentators often attribute this trait to Harington's desire to explain away or reduce the fantastical elements of poetry.[102] In the *Aeneid* commentary, however, what takes place is more akin to what Raphael Lyne has pointed out in the Ovidian commentary by George Sandys some two decades later:

> The phrase 'not only of old' is central in the commentary's approach, treating the *Metamorphoses* as a miscellany of marvels and curiosities, and extending that into the contemporary world; treating the *Metamorphoses* as a compendium of stories, and extending that too.[103]

Unlike most of the English Renaissance translators, Harington treats Virgil's text with great suspicion. This suspicion is the impetus behind the most creative parts of Harington's work. He constantly tests the ancient source's credibility, and whenever it pleases him he uses this as a springboard for his own marvellous storytelling. Occasionally the connection to the Virgilian text becomes extremely thin, as in his retelling of a bad pun on Scylla and Charybdis: '*Incidit in Sillam cupiens vitare charibdin.* wch a cuntry preacher thinking to apply one day on occasyo*n* by a lytle lapsus linguæ sayd *Incidi in Ancillam cupiens vitare Charibdim*' ('I fell into the slave girl while trying to avoid Charybdis').[104] At other times he seems purposely to avoid the seriousness of the subject, such as when he suggests that Aeneas' 'insomnia' was caused by indigestion![105]

Harington uses marvels in Virgil's poem to tell modern stories that touch upon similar subjects. As in George Sandys, the myth of Orpheus and Eurydice prompts a retelling of the tale of a German man whose wife returned from death.[106] The death of Misenus and the need for burying him is the starting point for Harington's account of how fish in Ireland will leave the area around the coast where a murder has been committed.[107] Caeneus' sex change might have seemed incredible 'yf the lyke wear not veryfyed in owr tyme'.[108] Perhaps the most revealing of these stories is his tale inspired by Virgil's account of the Pythagorean transmigration of souls. Harington begins this story by stating: 'In favor of wch opinion I never hard more then one tale, and y^{t} was of a madman in my Cownty and thearfore yt wear a madnes to geve moche credyt to yt. but thus I herd yt told by one that wowld take yt discortesy not to bee beleevd.'[109] He goes on to tell a lengthy and comical story in which souls transmigrate. On the next page of the commentary, however, Harington describes the Pythagorean doctrine as absurd and the preface to this story, describing the original storyteller's madness, suggests Harington did not believe this tale at all. The explanation for its inclusion is that Harington simply found the story amusing. Virgil's Book 6 offered him a collection of marvels which gave him a chance to tell his own collection of witty tales.

Harington's Virgil is doubtless at times serious, when it acts as a warning to the young prince that his rule will be a much more fragile entity than it may at first appear. Its existence only in manuscript allowed it to address its lofty audience with this important lesson. But Harington also shares with the other major manuscript translators of this period a freedom from the Renaissance tradition of Virgilian reverence. The belief that much in Virgil is wrong or misleading allows him to emulate both Virgil and other translators of the *Aeneid*, and also to take a more light-hearted approach to the epic. Harington thus became a predecessor for later storyteller translators such as George Sandys, who would treat Ovid with a similar narrative spirit.

Virgil Interrupted: Sir William Mure's 'Dido and Æneas'

The third translation considered in this chapter exists in a single manuscript in the Edinburgh University Library.[110] This translation of Books 1 and 4 of the *Aeneid* was the work of a young Scottish poet, Sir William Mure of Rowallan, and was composed around the year 1614. The manuscript translation was edited and printed in 1898, when it was published alongside the rest of Mure's work in a fine edition by William Tough for the Scottish Text Society.[111] In spite of this publication, however, Mure's text has not been studied since. Instead, it has suffered the fate of most early modern manuscript translations and fallen into oblivion. But Mure's 'Dido and Æneas' deserves to take its place alongside the anonymous British Library manuscript and Harington's Book 6 in the history of English Virgils. Like these earlier works, Mure's 'Dido and Æneas' can broaden our perception of what early modern English Virgil could be. Mure takes extensive liberties with the original, to the extent that his poem is the freest translation from Virgil's epic during the English Renaissance. Mure's unique and ambitious take on the *Aeneid* supplements the more conservative approaches taken by the translators who published their work in print during the same period.

There are many similarities between Mure's translation and the anonymous text from the British Library. They are both focused on Dido's story, they both use the six-line, ababcc stanza of the lover's complaint and they both take freedoms with the original. But the liberties Mure takes are in fact closer to the sort of freedom that Marlowe assumes in *Dido Queene of Carthage*. Mure varies between original writing, adaptation and direct translation, although he comes closer to exact translation as he progresses through the three books of his poem. His Book 1 is a reworking of Aeneas' story up until the beginning of Book 4 and is the freest part of the translation. In this book, Mure begins with an introduction (1.1–36) and then a summary of the action of *Aeneid* 2 and 3 (1.37–132). By offering this brief summary before he begins translating *Aeneid* 1, Mure transforms the structure of the narrative into a chronological account. When he starts translating, he moves without regard to sequence, rarely rendering a large section of Virgil in the order of the original. The first five stanzas (1.133–62) offer versions of *Aeneid* 1.34–6, 8–11, 19–21, 15–18 and 26–9 respectively. These stanzas are then followed by an interpolation both attacking and defending women (1.163–86), before he continues translating again, this time from *Aeneid* 1.37–41. Mure's second book, however, offers a much more consistent translation of lines 1–449 of *Aeneid* 4. In this book, Mure translates almost every line of the original in the proper order, but he allows himself to insert his own material. These additions add up to forty-two complete stanzas. In Book 3, Mure then translates the remainder of *Aeneid* 4, with only a few variations from the original and three additional stanzas of his own invention. The three books of Mure's translation thus display three different approaches to adapting or translating the *Aeneid*.

The translation is easy to position in Mure's life since he himself presents it as the work of his youth. In the introduction to the poem, he gives an indication of his age, writing of 'myn infant muse | (To twyse two lustres scarce of ȝeirs attained)' (1.7–8). Since a 'lustre' is a five-year period, this would mean that Mure was about twenty years old and dates the translation to around 1614. This dating means that the translation was a part of Mure's early, amatory phase of poetry, which lasted from 1611 until 1617. Mure was the nephew of the prominent Jacobean court poet, Alexander Montgomerie, and his early writing displays a debt to the poetry of his great uncle. During these years, Mure wrote in the 'Castalian manner', mostly composing lyric poetry to be performed in Scottish manor houses.[112] In a work from 1617 dedicated to Prince Charles, he expressed pride in his poetic ancestry: 'Machles Montgomery in his native tounge, | In former tymes to thy Great Syre hath sung, | And often ravischt his harmonious ear.'[113] Throughout these early years, Mure imitated his uncle's Petrarchan imagery, building especially on Montgomerie's emphasis on the cruelty of Cupid and the subsequent martyrdom of the lover.

However, there are a couple of crucial differences between Mure and Montgomerie. For instance, Mure's early poetry does not have the political undertones that his great uncle's did.[114] This difference is largely because Mure did not write as part of a royal court, as Montgomerie had. Rather, Mure wrote quietly at his estates near Kilmarnock and showed little political involvement until late in his life.[115] Furthermore, unlike his great uncle, Mure did not publish in print any of his love poetry, and this is true of his translation of the *Aeneid* as well. The reason for this seems to be that around 1617 Mure underwent a change of heart. In that year, he appears to have stopped writing altogether. He remained silent for over a decade until 1628, when he reappeared as the author of severe, religious, metaphysical poetry. In much of this new verse, he laments his earlier writing and presents himself in the guise of the 'sinner, longing for redemption'.[116] At the beginning of his *Doomesday, Containing Hells Horrour and Heavens Happinesse*, which was printed in 1628, Mure aspires to a 'second flight' and declares 'Giue place | Eare-charming fancies, Artes disgrace, | affoording false delight'.[117] In *Fancies Farewell*, printed at the same time, he laments how

> Love's false delight and beautees blazing beame
> Too long benighted haue my dazled eyes.
> By Youth misled, I too too much did prise
> Deceaving shads, toyes worthy no esteame.[118]

The 'lovelie layes' and 'wantone Muse' he was so proud about in his youth became something he repented for relentlessly in his later work.[119]

In spite of this later turn against the translation, however, Mure's 'Dido and Æneas' was an ambitious project when he undertook it. It has also been highly regarded by the few critics who have read it. Lindsay has described the translation as Mure's 'best purely literary achievement', Spiller thought it 'a very competent reworking' of Virgil and Tough considered it the 'happiest and most successful of all Mure's poetical attempts'.[120] The poet himself considered it as an important step in his literary career. Despite his modest accomplishments, Mure always presented himself as a career poet with a Muse presiding over his writing. The most common metaphors he used to describe his ambitions were those of climbing and flight. At the beginning of the Virgil translation, he writes:

> But ravisht with a vehement desyre,
> Those paths to trace which ȝeilds ane endles name,
> By the, to climb Parnassus I aspyre,
> And by thy feathers to impen my fame:
> Nothing asham'd thir colours to display,
> Vnder thy conduct as my first assay.
> (1.19–24)

Translating the *Aeneid* was a way for Mure to elevate his love poetry onto a grander level. In this regard, his use of Virgil translation to serve his own poetic ambitions is unique in the English Renaissance. No other poet so explicitly uses Virgil translation as part of a personal literary career. And no other poet suggests that translation in particular was suited to an ambitious young poet because it would allow for a safe fledging. Despite its epic scale and reputation as a mature work, the *Aeneid* here contributes to the early stages of a poet's development: by isolating a specific part of the epic, a young poet could raise amatory verse onto a grander, more ambitious level. The *Aeneid* was not always a poem for the end of a career; Mure used it to announce a beginning.

Mure's pride in his own poetic lineage and his personal ambitions for glory may explain why he felt so free to change and adapt the epic. Like the other two translators in this chapter, he did not feel a weighty obligation to honour Virgil and stay true to him. In this way, Mure shares very little in common with Gavin Douglas, the previous Scottish translator of the *Aeneid*, who declares his faithfulness to the master: 'Ry*ch*t so am I to Virgillis text ybund.'[121] In this context, Mure's choice of metaphors for the act of translation is revealing. He focuses on the translator's active role. In one metaphor, Mure presents himself as a performer, playing the part of Virgil behind a mask: 'That (mask'd with Maro) sweetly I may sing, | And warble foorth this Hero's changing state, | Eliza's love, and last, her tragick fate' (34–6). These lines give Mure the status of active collaborator and were perhaps prompted by the fact that much of his poetry was written to be sung at manor houses.[122] The other metaphor Mure chooses is that of Theseus following Ariadne's thread out of the labyrinth: 'Path'd wayes I trace, as Theseus in his neid, | Conducted by a loyall virgin's threid' (5–6). In the first stanza of the translation, Mure thus presents himself as the hero, while Virgil is displaced into the role of the lover offering vital advice. These bold metaphors fit the invasive approach that Mure would take in his translation. Lawrence Humphrey had argued that to translate too freely was unethical because it meant a translator pursued his or her own glory instead of serving the text and its causes.[123] Mure seems to have had exactly that in mind. He expresses a 'vehement desyre' for his own 'endles name' from the outset. Such a declaration is unique among the early English translators of Virgil.

The early modern *Aeneid* suited Mure's free and expansive approach because it was commonly remarked that Virgilian writing was refined and minimalistic. It contained many mysteries that could be explored and gaps that could be filled. Wilson-Okamura has sketched this early modern tradition of reading Virgil's style in *Virgil in the Renaissance*.[124] According to Tasso, for instance, Virgil always leaves things out, which creates the mystery and fascination of his writing.[125] When Mure composed his translation, he had recently been a student, probably at the University of Glasgow. He was certainly brought up with a rigorous classical education, writing neo-Latin poetry from a young age.[126] Mure was thus in a position to draw on the creative approaches to the classics that were present in Renaissance education.[127] For one example, he relies upon noting comparable moments across Virgil's *oeuvre* – a method of comparison he would have learned from Renaissance commentaries. For instance, when he comes to the bee simile at *Aeneid* 1.430–6, he expands it with material drawn from the *Georgics*. Thus 'Assail'd by stormes, some litle stones do beir, | And ballast thus do contrepoyze the winde' (1.499–500) is actually a translation of *Georgics* 4.194–6: 'et saepe lapillos, | ut cumbae instabiles fluctu iactante saburram, | tollunt, his sese per inania nubila librant.' Later on in the same simile, at 1.507–10, he offers a translation of *Georgics* 4.165–9. Mure often eruditely slides in material from elsewhere in Virgil's *oeuvre*.

The places where Mure expanded to greatest effect, however, were more provocative. He seems to have a knack for enlarging those passages where Virgil was most honoured for having treated sensitive matter with chasteness and brevity. At these moments, Mure delights in adding the material that Virgil left unsaid; wherever Virgil veiled a delicate subject with what Aulus Gellius described as 'verecunda quadam translatione verborum' ('a modest paraphrase'), Mure took the opportunity to paint the fullest picture.[128] The most notable such addition is the scene where Dido and Aeneas arrive at the same cave in Book 4. Virgil's careful avoidance of describing what happened in the cave was a commonplace in the Renaissance for illustrating his ethical maturity. In the highly influential *De arte poetica*, Vida writes about how Virgil tactfully treats the scene by not saying too much:

> Finally, if you find yourself faced with an episode whose telling would bring even a faint blush [to the cheeks of] the virgin chorus of the Muses, conceal it,

> and either glide by it with a light touch only, or turn your narrative elsewhere and put fictitious material in its place. If the omnipotent father is to shake all heaven with his thunder, let Dido and the prince of Troy take shelter in the same cave; but modesty must take care to add nothing further. For it will suffice if primal Earth and the witnessing Air give the signal of the marriage, and the Nymphs keen on the peaks of the hills.[129]

Similarly, in an influential commentary on the *Aeneid* that was printed two years before Mure composed his translation, de la Cerda takes the cave episode as an illustration for how chastely Virgil could handle amatory subjects:

> SPELUNCAM DIDO, &C.: Truly you may call him 'parthenian', that is, maidenly Virgil, since he treated these loves so chastely. He left the shameful matter only to suspicions.[130]

Mure did not share this opinion. Instead, he saw Virgil's silence as an occasion to add a piece of his own poetry, giving all the details of Aeneas' wooing of Dido.

I will quote the cave scene at length, because it both demonstrates how Mure slides in and out of translation and illustrates the character of his poem. It is useful also to draw a comparison here with the addition that we saw Marlowe make at this point in his play. This section begins with a stanza translating *Aeneid* 4.165–8 and ends with a stanza translating lines 4.169–72. In between, Mure breaks Virgil's silence:

> One cave, whil all the tempest dark do shield,
> The Trojane Duke and Dido both contained.
> Prodigiows presages sad earth did ȝeeld,
> With them when Juno in the cave convein'd.
> The guilty air gave light; the fire did glance;
> And montaine Faryes did bewaile the chance.
>
> Looke! how a Comet, whose bright flamming haire
> Brings tidings sad of dearth, or death of kings,
> Drawes all men's eyes to gaze amidst the aire,
> Conjecturing thereby of future things;
> So, whil at first, the Princes beauty shin'd,
> Æneas wond'ring ravish't was in minde.
>
> Her pure vnborrowed blush, her native white,
> The piercing rayes of her victoriows eyes,
> Bred in his soule such singulare delight,
> And did his senses suddainely supprise,
> In such a sort, that of all sense denude,
> He long a lifles, senseless statue stoode.
>
> But soone her looks, of pow'r t'awaken death,
> And ravish with amazement hardest hearts,

Reviv'd him frome his traunse, recal'd his breath,
And to his sleeping senses life empartes;
Who instantly confines, within his armes,
His sweetest Siren, who his fancie charmes.

Sie now how honour, love, and modesty,
With diverse colours dye her blushing cheeks!
When, (lay'd aside respect of majesty),
The fort to render, proud Æneas seeks.
And whil, (desire rul'd by the blinded boy,)
Loves sweet-stolne sport he labours to enjoy.

With faint repulses and denialls sweet,
Lo! how she shrinking, strives his sutes to shune;
But he now offers force, now doth entreate,
And still persewes, till last the prise is wonne.
The jemme enjoy'd, which women hold so deare,
And honour prostrate, blushing did reteare.

Can words, can vowes, can feeble hands resist,
With hote desire whil ȝowthfull blood doth boyle?
Though she repine, do his assaults desist?
Small glory is a ȝeelded foe to foyle.
Women must still deny and use defences,
Till charming Cupid lull a sleep the senses.

This wrought to sin, anone she waxeth bold,
And mutually her mate doth entertaine;
Loe! how her strict embraces him enfold,
Whil as they issue from the cave againe,
Nothing asham'd to come in open sight,
Thus vse in sinning soone maks sin seame light.

This disemall day did Didoes death begin;
This day of all her sorrowes was the source:
Now neither fame she cares, nor shame, nor sin,
Nor more devises any secrete cowrse
To cloake her love; but mariage this she thinks,
And at this foule offence, (effronted), winks.
(2.295–348)

Mure interrupts Virgil to offer a remarkable account of the wooing of Dido. It is helpful to compare this episode with the scene Marlowe adds at this point in *Dido*. In Marlowe, the brief addition in Act 3 is made to show Aeneas swearing to the gods his love for Dido, thus proving himself false. Marlowe's interpolation leads, in turn, to a pessimistic analysis of Virgilian rhetorical power and the role of force in the providential epic. However, Mure is not concerned with the gods (aside from Cupid) or with providence. He even omits the grand description of Aeneas' providential mission in *Aeneid* 1 with which Marlowe opens his drama. Moreover, Mure is not particularly concerned with the falsity or power of Aeneas' rhetoric at this stage. In fact, his Aeneas comes across as rather awkward, and Mure even makes it clear that Dido invents the notion that they are married. Nevertheless, as in Marlowe's account, one immediately sees that Mure's Aeneas is no impeccable hero. The primary fault of this Aeneas is his lasciviousness and his callousness as a lover. After being frozen without speech, he 'assaults' Dido 'with hote desire whil ȝowthfull blood doth boyle'. Aeneas is overwhelmed by Cupid's force and then treats the love as a sort of game: 'Loves sweet-stolne sport he labours to enjoy.' All the while he seems oblivious to the implications of his 'assault'. The nature of this attack becomes more tragic as the translation continues. Mure shows that Aeneas is a passionate lover, but a lover without pity. In Mure's early poetry, his standard pose is that of the helpless enamoured who has been hopelessly wounded by a woman; his love is not reciprocated but he nevertheless dedicates himself to his cruel beloved until death.[131] In this translation, Dido comes to play that part: she is wounded by Aeneas and is hopelessly subjected to Cupid while Aeneas transforms into the cruel lover.

It will therefore come as no surprise that most of Mure's additions are related specifically to the behaviour and emotional experiences of Dido and Aeneas. The only exception to this rule is his rewriting of Mercury's journey from heaven (2.445–68). Otherwise, all of the additions provide us with greater insight into the passions that Dido and Aeneas (but especially Dido) endure. Mure's main interpolations include a description of Dido being ensnared by Cupid and being unable to sleep at the end of Book 1 (aside from brief translations from *Aeneid* 1.715–22, all of 1.955–1008 are new). This passage is important because, for Mure, sight plays a pivotal role in love. Words can often fail a lover, but sight is always there to help: 'But whill she speaks, her speach confus'd doth faill . . . With looks anone she doth anew assaill, | Dumb oratours perswading more then words' (2.139–42). Early in Book 2, Mure offers original descriptions of Dido dreaming of Aeneas (2.7–18) and her internal battle between love and honour (2.43–60). He then doubles the length of her first speech condemning Aeneas (with lines 2.589–660 replacing *Aeneid* 4.307–9) and gives her several stanzas to tell young maidens not to be deceived by pitiless men (2.769–98). Each of these interpolations adds to the representation of Dido's emotional upheaval. These additions come to a climax in Book 3, when Mure adds stanzas in order to describe what Dido sees when Aeneas' fleet departs (3.235–40), to renew Dido's expression of rage against Aeneas (3.253–8) and to add a flourish at the end of Dido's final speech (3.379–84). In contrast, the only interpolations relating to Aeneas are a description of his first sight of Dido at 1.583–654, a brief presentation of his dilemma at 2.516–40 and a condemnation of his refusal to pity her at 2.847–58. The quantity and nature of Mure's inventions has the effect of shifting the balance of the poem so much more of the narrative is concentrated upon Dido.

The newly arranged poem also calls out explicitly for the reader's pity while condemning Aeneas' callousness. If most early modern translations of the *Aeneid* focus on the piety and religious virtues of Aeneas, Mure's translation is a prime example from the English Renaissance where pity, rather than piety, is the key concept by which characters are judged.[132] Mure seems to have felt Book 4 of the *Aeneid* explores a sort of crisis of compassion. At 2.769–98, Dido spends several stanzas warning maidens how pity can lead them astray. These lines are an extended set of variations on Virgil's words 'nusquam tuta fides' (4.373). At their height, Dido proclaims: 'Owr tender hearts with pitty which betraying, | Works their advantage, and owr sure decaying' (791–2). Ten stanzas later, Aeneas' moment of decision is again portrayed as a matter of compassion. At first, his 'Pitty withstood what Jove did strictly charge' (2.850). But then he takes his farewell, and Mure exclaims:

> Hard hearted lover to thy loyall love!
> Could not the sunne-set of those lovely eyes,
> (Whil death her senses stopt), to pitty move
> Thy flinty heart?
>
> (2.853–6)

Moreover, in this translation, Mure decided to divide Book 4 of the *Aeneid* into two parts. He chose to end the first of these at the point where 'No pitty can prevale to plead remorce' (2.938). Mure's Book 2 thus leads to the moment when Aeneas' ears are hardened against Dido at the end of the oak simile. He describes this as the point when 'neither pitty, plaints, nor words avail'd' (2.958). In Mure's amatory verse, the 'sweet' pain of unreciprocated love is poised upon a thin edge. His early sonnet sequence 'To Margareit' depicts how his love gradually leads him to his own death because she refuses to pity him.[133] His love sonnets are an account of his 'pleasant dying' and in 'Dido and Æneas' Mure wrote the same tragic love story onto a larger stage.

The 'pleasantness' of dying for love is a theme that Mure found in Virgil's account of Dido. Mure was fond of Petrarchan conceits and in his mind the sweetness of the story was inextricably linked to the pathos of the tragedy. We have seen a similar treatment of the Dido and Aeneas narrative in the anonymous British Library manuscript but Mure takes this connection even further. Mure introduces Virgil as a 'sweit voyce' (1.10), singing 'sweit deliciows ayrs' (29). He writes:

Rap't with delight of thy mellifluous phrase,
Thy divine discant, and harmonious layes,
Whose sugg'red accords, (which thy worth do blaze),
The hearers' senses, at thair ears betrayes.
(1.13–16)

However, Mure does not simply comment on this quality that he finds in Virgil's writing. Instead, much like the anonymous translator, he makes the poem even sweeter and more sensual. As an example, we can take his translation of Virgil's description of Venus:

The heavenly treasure of her golden hair
Was toss'd by sweet-breath'd Zephyr heir and thair;
Her rayment short, her lovely knees wer bair,
With which no snowe in whitnes might compair.
Her eyes shin'd favour, courtessie, and grace,
No mortall ever saw more sweet a face.
(1.343–8)

venatrix dederatque comam diffundere ventis,
nuda genu nodoque sinus collecta fluentis.
(1.319–20)

Mure could compete with any early modern translator of Virgil in expanding upon the sensual aspects of the original.

All of the features of pathos, sweetness, erudition and liberality that mark this translation can be captured in one fascinating, intertextual moment towards the end of Book 1. In modern criticism, the natural-philosophical song that Iopas sings at the Carthaginian banquet is read as an emblem for the cosmic scope of Aeneas' story and how it relates to the nature of the universe.[134] In this passage, Virgil based his description of Iopas in part upon Homeric precedents, including Demodocus in Book 8 of the *Odyssey*. However, unlike the Homeric Demodocus, who 'sang of the love of Ares and fair-crowned Aphrodite', Virgil made his bard into a natural-philosophical poet who sings about the mysteries of the universe.[135] This change was significant, because the song of Demodocus was something of a touchstone in antiquity for the debates about the moral worthiness of Homer. Virgil's change of the bard's subject-matter has been attributed both to ancient allegories of the Homeric Demodocus' song and to the simple fact that 'scandal about the gods had no place in Virgilian epic'.[136]

However, Mure did not share the notion that the lascivious tale of Mars, Venus and Vulcan would be out of place in the story Virgil tells. In this passage, Mure turns back to Homer to supplement the song that Iopas sings and he transforms him into a singer of love poetry.

Mure gives to the Carthaginian bard not only songs about nature, but also the song that Demodocus presented in *Odyssey* 8: Mure's Iopas 'sweetly' tells 'How Mars and Venus Vulcane did ensnare' (1.931). Furthermore, while in Virgil Iopas sings freely until his song is finished, in Mure the bard is interrupted by Cupid disguised as Ascanius: 'Lo! suddenly amids this joyfull throng, | Ascanius, comming, interrupts the song' (1.935–6). Mure makes an allusion to *Amores* 1.1, where Ovid is interrupted by Cupid snatching a foot away from him as he attempts to compose an epic poem. This passage is an extremely fitting reflection upon Mure's project as a whole. This is a translation in which Virgil sings not of cosmic matters, but of love affairs. It is also a translation that takes its cue from amatory poetry, taking away the epic scope of Virgil's narrative and turning it into an erotic epyllion. To do so, Mure, like Cupid, feels free to interrupt the Virgilian narrative at will. After Cupid has interrupted Iopas' song, Mure remarks that the blind boy 'Bears over all the vniverse command' (1.948). The predominance of Cupid is the central feature in this remarkable rewriting of Virgil.

Without this translation by Mure and BL Add. MS 60283, there would not be evidence that a 'suggr'd Virgil' existed during the English Renaissance. This fact alone demonstrates why it is urgent that manuscript translations be incorporated into literary history. Without the three translations in this chapter, we might think that the early English *Aeneid* was always a serious, moral poem. While this is by and large the case, this chapter has shown that there were mischievous and amorous translations of the *Aeneid* in early modern England. Virgil was not always stern and dour. But the more mischievous *Aeneid*s found their audiences through manuscript distribution, while print offered the more obviously useful, or propagandistic, versions of the epic. Furthermore, without these three manuscript translations, we would have believed that there was no translation of the *Aeneid* into stanzaic form before the Civil War. And looking only at the printed texts, we might think that the tradition of Virgil translation had stopped between 1584 and 1620. But manuscript research shows that translations of the *Aeneid* also flourished during this period in a wanton, playful form. Gillespie has argued that paying attention to manuscripts will supplement and modify our current understanding of translation history.[137] In the case of English Renaissance Virgils, this has certainly proven true.

Notes

1. Woudhuysen, *Sidney and the Circulation of Manuscripts*, p. 11.
2. Ibid., pp. 12 and 15.
3. See the edition of Denham's manuscript translation in Sowerby (ed.), *Early Augustan Virgil.*
4. Williams, 'The Castle Ashby Manuscripts', p. 394.
5. London, British Library, Add. MS 60283. I have published a transcription of the translation in: Brammall, '*Aeneid* 4', pp. 81–109. I quote from this translation according to the line numbers in this edition.
6. Williams, 'The Castle Ashby Manuscripts', p. 411.
7. Cauchi, 'Sir John Harington and Virgil's *Aeneid* IV'.
8. Harington, *Sixth Book*; Cauchi, 'Introduction'; Scott-Warren, *Harington and the Book as Gift*, pp. 213–19.
9. Williams, 'The Castle Ashby Manuscripts', pp. 410–11.
10. Christie, *Important Literary and Musical Manuscripts*, pp. 26–7.
11. Beal, *Index*, I, 121, 130.
12. Williams, 'The Castle Ashby Manuscripts', p. 411.
13. Craig, *Sir John Harington*, p. 144, n. 111.
14. Burrow, 'The English Humanist Epic', pp. 178–9.
15. Cauchi, '*Aeneid* IV', p. 245.
16. Ibid., pp. 244–5. See also Woudhuysen, pp. 106–7, 164.
17. Cauchi, '*Aeneid* IV', pp. 244–5.
18. The exclusion of the manuscript from recent works by Gerard Kilroy and Jason Scott-Warren points to their agreement. Kilroy, 'The Pleasant Learned Poet', and Scott-Warren, *Sir John Harington and the Book as Gift*.
19. Lyne, *Words and the Poet*, p. 68.
20. For another example, one could compare the manuscript's rendition of the oak tree simile to the original Latin (*Aen.* 4.441–9; BL Add. MS 60283, ll. 623–30).
21. Douglas, *Virgil's Aeneid*, IV, 189 (ll. 42, 47).
22. Phaer and Twyne, *The .xiii. Bookes of Æneidos*, sig. V1^{v}.
23. Harington, *Sixth Book*, p. 2.
24. Vicars, *Aeneids*, sig. A3^{r}.
25. Fleming, *The Bucolikes*, sig. A2^{r}.
26. Brinsley, *Virgils Eclogues*, sig. A3^{v}.
27. Burrow, 'The English Humanist Epic', p. 182.
28. In some early modern Virgils, such as the 1558 *Universum poema* edition, the Latin here reads 'sinus' rather than 'sinum'. The plural would make the translation less of a leap from the source.
29. Ibid., ll. 129–32.
30. Cauchi, '*Aeneid* IV', p. 247.
31. Scott-Warren, *Sir John Harington and the Book as Gift*, p. 29.
32. Craig, *Sir John Harington*, p. 135; Cauchi, 'Introduction', p. xiv.
33. Burrow, *Epic Romance*, pp. 150, 153.
34. Cauchi, 'Introduction', p. xliv.
35. BL Add. MS 60283, ll. 194, 197, 224, 227.
36. May, *Elizabethan Courtier Poets*, p. 57.

37. Ibid., pp. 57, 68.
38. Gorges, *Poems*, pp. 87–110.
39. For examples from all of these authors see May, *Elizabethan Courtier Poets*, who comments on p. 155: '[Harington] conscientiously limited his use of the popular "sixain" stanza.'
40. About one-third of the Arundel manuscript, for example, was unprinted material, see Hughey, 'The Harington Manuscript at Arundel Castle', p. 388.
41. Beal, *Index*, I, 156.
42. May, *Elizabethan Courtier Poets*, p. 2.
43. Berkshire Record Office, Trumbull Additional MS 23. For a full description and analysis of this manuscript, see Cauchi, 'Introduction', pp. liv–lvii. See also Croft, 'Sir John Harington's Manuscript of Sir Philip Sidney's *Arcadia*', and Miller, 'Sir John Harington's Manuscripts in Italic'.
44. Scott-Warren, *Sir John Harington and the Book as Gift*, p. 215.
45. Harington, *Sixth Book*, p. 2.
46. Scott-Warren, *Sir John Harington and the Book as Gift*, p. 216: 'The vision of Aeneas usually expresses what the new monarch meant to Harington and his contemporaries. In the words of the gratulatory elegy for James, 1603 saw not only an unimpeded succession to the crown, but also "succession stablisht in the crowne".' See also Burrow, Review, p. 249.
47. Scott-Warren, *Sir John Harington and the Book as Gift*, pp. 213–19.
48. Kilroy, 'The Pleasant Learned Poet', p. 17.
49. Skinner, *Foundations of Modern Political Thought*, I, p. 214.
50. King James, *Political Writings*, p. 2
51. Ibid., p. 61.
52. Ibid., p. 2.
53. Harington, *Sixth Book*, p. 59.
54. Harington, *Tract on the Succession*, p. 83.
55. Ibid., p. 83.
56. Harington, *Epigrams*, p. 94.
57. Ibid., p. 209.
58. Harington, *Sixth Book*, p. 19.
59. Ibid., p. 43.
60. Ibid., p. 54.
61. Ibid., p. 55.
62. *Ottava rima* became immensely popular for translations of the *Metamorphoses*, which were considered more similar to the modern *romanze*, but it never became standard for Virgil. See Javitch, *Proclaiming a Classic*, pp. 71–7.
63. Ibid., pp. 76–7.
64. Ibid., p. 77.
65. Cauchi, 'Introduction', p. xix.
66. Cauchi, xix.
67. Harington, *Sixth Book*, pp. 33, 43, 47, 49.
68. Harington, 'Preface', in Ariosto, *Orlando Furioso*, pp. 10–11.

69. Javitch, *Proclaiming a Classic*, pp. 23–6.
70. Ibid., pp. 26–9.
71. Ibid., p. 135.
72. Harington, *Sixth Book*, p. 43.
73. Ibid., p. 47.
74. Craig, *Sir John Harington*, p. 39; Burrow, *Epic Romance*, p. 151.
75. Harington, *Sixth Book*, p. 47.
76. Ibid., p. 1.
77. Craig, *Sir John Harington*, p. 25.
78. Harington, *Sixth Book*, p. 1.
79. Visser, *Reading Augustine*, pp. 22–3.
80. Ibid., p. 5.
81. 'One might say that whereas in the *Confessions*, Vergil sometimes spoke from within Augustine's own sensibilities and emotions, in the *City of God*, the poet spoke to Augustine from the outside. For the Roman society that Vergil represented had espoused values and ideals from which Augustine, once he became a monk, deliberately distanced himself.' MacCormack, *Shadows of Poetry*, p. 227.
82. Harington, *Metamorphosis of Ajax*, p. 90.
83. MacCormack, *Shadows of Poetry*, pp. 194–7.
84. Augustine, *City of God* (5.18), II, pp. 226–7.
85. Smalley, *English Friars and Antiquity*, p. 103.
86. Ibid., p. 106.
87. See Cauchi, 'Introduction', pp. liv–lvii.
88. Harington, *Sixth Book*, p. 17.
89. Ibid., p. 19.
90. Ibid., p. 29.
91. Ibid.
92. Ibid., pp. 21 and 27.
93. Ibid., p. 45.
94. Ibid., p. 51.
95. Ibid., p. 53.
96. Feeney, 'History and Revelation in Vergil's Underworld', p. 120.
97. Galinsky, *Augustan Culture*, p. 364; Hardie, *Epic Successors of Virgil*, pp. 92–3.
98. Harington, *Sixth Book*, p. 59.
99. Ibid., p. 15.
100. Ibid., p. 41.
101. Ibid., p. 20.
102. For example, Craig, *Sir John Harington*, pp. 41–2.
103. Lyne, *Ovid's Changing Worlds*, p. 245.
104. Harington, *Sixth Book*, p. 25.
105. Ibid., p. 61.
106. Ibid., p. 15.
107. Ibid., p. 17.
108. Ibid., p. 33.
109. Ibid., p. 49.
110. Edinburgh University Library, Laing III.453. I am grateful to Stuart Gillespie for having brought this translation to my attention.

111. See Mure, *Works*. I quote Mure's works and translation from Tough's edition.
112. On his debts to Montgomerie and other Jacobean court poets, see Lindsay, *History of Scottish Literature*, p. 137.
113. Mure, *Works*, I, p. 40.
114. Dunnigan, *Eros and Poetry*, pp. 125–48, esp. p. 125.
115. Spiller, 'Poetry after the Union', p. 156. See also Sarah Dunnigan's *ODNB* entry on Sir William Mure.
116. Jack, 'Scottish Sonneteer', p. 247.
117. Mure, *Works*, I, p. 163.
118. Ibid., p. 195.
119. See, for example, Mure, *Works*, I, p. 36: 'Peace! wantone Muse, Leave now thy lovelie layes.' Alternatively, see Mure, *Works*, I, p. 41: 'Forebear to sing thy lovelie layes a space; Leave wanton Venus and his blinded boy.'
120. Lindsay, *History of Scottish Literature*, p. 138; Spiller, 'Poetry after the Union', p. 157; Mure, *Works*, II, p. 269.
121. Douglas, *Virgil's 'Aeneid'*, II, p. 11, l. 299.
122. See Sarah Dunnigan's *ODNB* entry on Sir William Mure.
123. Humphrey, *Interpretatio*, pp. 171–2.
124. Wilson-Okamura, *Virgil in the Renaissance*, pp. 101–42.
125. Ibid., p. 137.
126. Tough, 'Introduction', pp. x–xi.
127. For instance, see Burrow, 'Shakespeare and Humanistic Culture', especially pp. 13–14.
128. I quote the Latin and translation from: Gellius, *Attic Nights*, II, pp. 182–3 (9.10.1–2).
129. I quote the English translation and the Latin from Vida, *De arte poetica*, trans. Williams, pp. 78–9 (2.526–34):

    Postremo, tibi siqua instant dicenda, ruborem
    Quæ tenerum incuterent Musis adaperta, chorisque
    Virgineis, molli vel præterlabere tactu
    Dissimulans, vel verte alio, & rem suffice fictam.
    Si pater omnipotens tonitru cælum omne ciebit,
    Speluncam Dido, dux & Trojanus eamdem
    Deveniant, pudor ulterius nihil addere curet.
    Nam sat erit, tellus si prima, & conscius æther
    Connubii dent signum, ululentque in vertice Nymphæ.

130. Cerda, *Priores Sex Libri Aeneidos*, p. 411: 'SPELUNCAM DIDO, &C.] Vere parthenium, id est, virginalem Virgilium voces, qui tam verecunde amores hos tractaverit. Rem turpem tantum suspicionibus reliquit.'
131. See, for instance, his poems 'Mes Amours et mes Douleurs sont sans comparisoune', 'Ane Reply to I cair not quither I get hir or no', 'Elegie', 'Chausoune', 'Beautie hath myne eyes assailed', and others. Mure, *Works*, I.
132. The pity vs. piety distinction is most helpfully discussed in Burrow, *Epic Romance*, p. 4 *et passim*.
133. Mure, *Works*, I, pp. 47–53.
134. Hardie, *Virgil's 'Aeneid'*, pp. 60–5.

135. I quote the translation from Homer, *Odyssey*, I, pp. 290–1 (8.266–7).
136. Hardie, *Virgil's 'Aeneid'*, pp. 61–2; Austin, *Aeneidos Liber Primus*, p. 223.
137. Gillespie, *English Translation and Classical Reception*, p. 107.

Chapter 4

Virginian Virgil: The Single-Book Translations of Sir Thomas Wroth, Sir Dudley Digges and George Sandys

On 17 November 1619, members of the Virginia Company gathered in London at a private residence to hold one of the Company's 'great' or 'quarter' courts. From 1612 onwards, four times annually, a number of the men involved in the Company would gather on the second last Wednesday of each law term to elect councillors and principal officers, make laws and ordinances, confirm grants and answer trade questions – in other words, to conduct all the Company's important business.[1] At the quarter court held on 17 November 1619, roughly sixty members of the Company were present. The meeting itself was not a particularly eventful one, but from the perspective of a study of English translations of Virgil, it provides a curious prospect. For among those sixty members sitting in that room, there were three translators of single books of the *Aeneid*. Between 1584 and 1632, there were only three new English translations of the *Aeneid* published in print. Remarkably, all three of these were written by prominent members of the Virginia Company who were present on that day in 1619: Sir Thomas Wroth, Sir Dudley Digges and George Sandys.[2] This was probably not the first time these three were sitting together in the same room for Virginia Company business (unfortunately records specifying who attended the meetings prior to 1619 do not exist), and it was certainly not the last.

The use of Virgil's *Aeneid* as a model for colonial practice in the literary publications surrounding the Virginia Company has been demonstrated in several studies.[3] Such uses of Virgil's epic are not surprising. A poem about a *translatio imperii* westward into unknown territory could easily be adapted for thinking about contemporary colonial practice. Susan Ford Wiltshire has shown in a brief essay how Aeneas is the model of William Strachey's 'True Reportory'.[4] Howard Mumford Jones has overviewed a range of examples of early modern colonisers using classical precedents.[5] Jones pointed out in particular that John Smith's account of his activities in Virginia is 'like a prose Aeneid'.[6] Within Smith's 1612 publication, *A Map of Virginia with a Description of the Countrey, the Commodities, People, Government and Religion*, there is a brief history, 'The Proceedings of the English Colonie in Virginia', recounting Smith's adventures in the New World. The narrative is divided into twelve chapters, echoing the twelve books of the *Aeneid*, and in the course of the narrative Smith is portrayed as a hero like Aeneas. For one example, he offers a speech to rally his followers that has echoes of Aeneas' 'O socii' speech.[7] Another recent study by Wilson-Okamura has even argued that Dido's settlement at Carthage offered a model for early colonisation as well.[8] Indeed, there is ample precedent for studies of the *Aeneid* as a literary model for British colonialism in the early seventeenth century. So far, however, there has been no exploration of the circle of Virginia Company translators of Virgil, nor has the connection bringing together this group even been identified before. This chapter conducts an exploration of how these three translators each use a portion of the *Aeneid* as a means to explore British colonialism in the new worlds and its relation to foreign policy closer to home.

It would be nice to imagine that after that meeting of the Virginia Company on 17 November 1619 Wroth, Digges and Sandys found themselves together on some street in London discussing the relevance of the *Aeneid*, and that in this manner they became inspired by mutual discussion to translate Virgil. Unfortunately, however, there is no evidence of these translations being a conscious, united effort. At the same time in France, Marie de Gournay was translating Books 2 and 4 of the *Aeneid* and, in the process, writing herself into a community with Jean Bertaut and Jean Davy du Perron, but no such clear evidence exists in the English context. Rather, with these three English translators, we must look at three men who came separately to the *Aeneid*, all responding to a similar cultural moment. Accordingly, the primary aim of this chapter is to show in what different ways the *Aeneid* could be used to reflect on the colonial activities and foreign policies of England from the years 1615 to 1632. The three translators chose different books of the *Aeneid* and published their translations in very different contexts. By viewing them together, however, we can bring into focus a particularly rich moment for the reception of Virgil in early modern England. Moreover, we can catch a glimpse of how isolating a single book of the *Aeneid* allowed these translators to apply the epic to pointed, political concerns.

The Spectre of Creusa: Prophetic Closure in Sir Thomas Wroth's *Destruction of Troy*

In 1620, Sir Thomas Wroth published a translation of Book 2 of the *Aeneid* under the title *The Destruction of Troy*. This translation has so far received no attention, perhaps because writing about Wroth's translation historically is a challenge. He published very little, and not much is known about his life before the Civil War. For this reason, the connection between *The Destruction of Troy* and the Virginia Company is slightly more elusive than in the cases of Digges and Sandys. As I will show, Wroth was deeply involved in the Company in 1620, and the paratexts of his translation foreground this connection. But I will argue that the most valuable way to approach Wroth's translation is through his rewriting of the role of Creusa. Wroth substantially reconfigures the ending of Book 2 of the *Aeneid* to make his translation into a microcosm of the epic. This new presentation of Creusa, which incorporates material from the commentary tradition into the body of the poem, reinforces the providential closure of Book 2. The self-contained nature of *The Destruction of Troy* reveals parallels between Wroth and other single book translators like Robert Stapylton and it is richly suggestive when read within its Virginian context.

Eyes of Judgment: The Two Dedications in *The Destruction of Troy*

Wroth dedicated his translation 'To the Right Honorable Syr Robert Sidney Knight, Lord Vicount Lisle'. Sidney is a figure of great interest to this translation because it seems that he was not only presented with the work, but that he played a part in its genesis. In a poem accompanying the dedication, Wroth writes to Sidney:

> When first I did thy Patronage implore,
> Promise and Love the chiefe incentives were,
> Which made me bold to set my skill before
> Your eie of judgment.[9]

Wroth evidently sent some of his work to Sidney to seek patronage. Since *The Destruction of Troy* is Wroth's first published work, Sidney must have read some of Wroth's writing in manuscript. As the dedication continues, Wroth introduces his central conceit: his poem is a 'barke' that is about to 'launch into the Maine', and he asks for Sidney's 'Love' to act as a 'Pilot' for his ship. The most revealing part of this conceit, however, comes in the final two lines of the dedication: 'And as thou grac'd her lying in the Docke, | So steere her now aloofe from Envies Rocke.' The implication is that Sidney had some part in this translation before its publication. Would this have been simply as a patron? Robert Sidney, like his brother, was a notable patron of poets: Abraham Fraunce, Thomas Powell, Robert Jones, Robert Dowland, George Chapman and George Wither all dedicated works to him.[10] It is possible he also patronised Wroth's translation in its early stages. But Sir Thomas Wroth was an established wealthy country gentleman: he certainly would not have needed monetary patronage to write. It is more likely that Sidney himself had read this translation before publication and had encouraged it. Perhaps he had even been involved, in a minor way, poetically.[11] We know that Sidney distributed his own manuscripts among literary friends and family and that he read their works as well.[12] Moreover, the two men could have known each other, since Wroth was a cousin of Sidney's son-in-law, Sir Robert Wroth. It thus seems fair to suggest that the two men could have been involved in an early exchange of manuscripts.

In 1620 Sir Robert Sidney was at the height of his success. On 2 August 1618, Sidney received the highest public honour of his life when he became Earl of Leicester.[13] Indeed, the reign of King James on the whole had been favourable to Sidney: he was awarded several important posts, including being Queen Anne's High Chamberlain and Surveyor, as well as a generous pension.[14] Such success, however, did not entail Sidney always being in line with the king. He vigorously opposed the Spanish Match and supported militant Protestant policies.[15] By 1620, the main public engagement in Sidney's life was his involvement in the Virginia Company. In 1619, Sidney's daughter Barbara was married to Thomas Smythe, the nephew of Sir Thomas Smythe, who was Sidney's companion in the Company's administration. This was the first of a series of marriages intertwining the Sidney and Smythe families. Not surprisingly, this marriage allegiance was political as well.[16] When the Virginia Company split into factions at the beginning of the 1620s, Sidney was a prominent figure within Smythe's group, which was soon to join with the Warwick faction of which Sir Thomas Wroth was a leader. Sidney's alliances, both familial and political, were being fundamentally shaped by the Company's disputes at the time when Wroth's Virgil translation appeared in print. Sir Robert Sidney, the translation's dedicatee and patron, is thus one integral part of the Virginian context in which the translation was composed.

In addition to Sir Robert Sidney, *The Destruction of Troy* also points to another major figure of seventeenth-century English colonialism. At the back of the translation of Book 2 of the *Aeneid*, there is another work by Wroth, 'The Abortive of an Idle Houre, or a Centurie of Epigrams'.

This is a collection of one hundred epigrams, which are mostly original, although there is also a direct translation, as well as some adaptations, from Martial. They are generally witty and satirical, often using a classical word or a comedic name derived from Latin to mock a moral fault or an unfortunate physical attribute. For example, epigram 15 is written about 'Magnasus' ('Big-nose').

Among this collection of epigrams, a few are more serious – in particular, epigram 26, which is the only one addressed to a person by name: 'To his worthy friend Captaine Butler, Governour of Bermuda, or the Summer Ilands'. This poem of friendship and political support from Sir Thomas Wroth to Captain Butler is an important piece of evidence for the circle within which Wroth was working:

> I Marveil I, what mischiefes or what evils
> Hath made men call your Iles the Iles of Devils,
> Is't for the perillous Rockes, or for the Swine,
> In whom our Lord the Legion did confine?
> What ere it be, let's heare no more complaints,
> So governe you, they may be Iles of Saints.[17]

Nathaniel Butler was elected governor of Bermuda on 28 April 1619. This friendship between Butler and Wroth also suggests that Wroth was by this time a part of the close circle centring around two of his relatives, the Earl of Warwick and Sir Nathaniel Rich. Butler was close friends with both of Wroth's relatives within the Company, and these relatives would probably have been the means by which Wroth met Butler. The Earl of Warwick was responsible for getting Captain Butler elected as Governor of Bermuda in 1619, and the large number of letters from Captain Butler to Sir Nathaniel Rich (who was Wroth's brother-in-law and who also introduced Wroth into the Virginia Company) witness the close collaboration between them. Certainly by 1623 Wroth was a close member of this circle. One document from the Virginia Company in February 1623 shows the signatures of members of the Warwick/Smith faction. On this list, the Earl of Warwick's signature appears first, with Nathaniel Rich's immediately to the right of his and Sir Thomas Wroth's immediately below. All of these signatures are larger than the others on the page, suggesting something of the close tie between these three men.[18] And yet this close collaboration and friendship, I argue, emerged much earlier than this, as is suggested by this epigram. If the epigrams and the translation were meant to be published together (as they were), it shows us that Wroth would have envisioned Butler reading his Virgil as well. With this poem to Butler and the dedication to Sir Robert Sidney being the only direct references to contemporaries in *The Destruction of*

Troy, the immediate readership we can establish consists of prominent members of the Virginia Company.

'Translated Hence Out of This Mortall Life': Rewriting the Role of Creusa

Sir Thomas Wroth's translation of Virgil is stylistically somewhere between the unreserved domestication of Sir Dudley Digges and the decorous classicism of George Sandys. Wroth completed his translation in fourteeners, which are printed on facing pages across from the Latin. The choice of fourteeners is a testament to the lasting influence of the Phaer-Twyne *Aeneid*: by 1620 the fourteener was past its time, but the Phaer and Twyne translation was reprinted for the last time that very year. Wroth does not echo the Phaer-Twyne very often or very obviously, but his choice of metre shows that the translation begun in Mary's reign still had an audience. Wroth's use of the fourteener, however, is different from Phaer's: he makes no attempt to copy the syntax or line structure of the Latin. Even with the Latin on the facing page, for instance, he does not attempt to copy Virgil's ten unfinished lines in Book 2 into English.[19] This is an unusual choice when Wroth was writing, as is shown by the meticulous rendering of half lines in the translations by Digges and Sandys. Stylistically then, Wroth's principles of translation and imitation are rather free. Yet in spite of this stylistic freedom, only rarely does Wroth veer away from the meaning of the Latin and interpolate something of his own. What I wish to focus on is one instance when he does so, when the ghost of Creusa appears to Aeneas.

The third part of Book 2 of the *Aeneid* tells of Aeneas' return to his house and his escape from the burning city. It is at this point in the narrative that Creusa becomes an important figure. If we recount the end of Book 2 as Virgil tells it, the events are as follows. When Anchises has finally been persuaded by a sign from Jupiter to leave Troy, Aeneas lifts his father onto his shoulders and leads his son in his hand, while he tells his wife to follow at a distance, 'longe' (2.711). In the course of their panicked escape from Troy, however, Anchises believes he sees the Greeks gaining on them and cries out, which prompts Aeneas to run, not realising that he has lost his wife. Only when he is outside the city does Aeneas notice Creusa's absence and, in a fit of grief, he runs headlong back into Troy, where he meets a larger image, a 'nota maior imago' (2.773), of his wife. Although Virgil never specifies what has happened to her, she tells Aeneas, rather mysteriously, that the mother of the gods has detained her on these shores and so she cannot go with him: 'sed me magna deum genetrix his detinet oris' (2.788). She also tells him that he will marry again in Italy and asks him to love and care for their son. Aeneas attempts to embrace her three times, but the image escapes him like a winged dream, 'volucrique simillima somno' (2.794). At last, he returns to his companions and, having taken up his father once again, he sets off.

When Wroth comes to translate these passages about Creusa, he tells the story with certain details not to be found in Virgil. Beginning with the moment when Aeneas describes losing Creusa, Wroth subtly incorporates extraneous material (I will quote also the Latin on the preceding, facing pages in Wroth's translation):

> namq*ue* avia cursus
> Dum sequor, & nota excedo regione viarum;
> Heu misero coniux [sic] fatone erepta Creüsa
> Substitit: erravitne via, seu lassa resedit,
> Incertum.

> for whilst I did advance
> Through wayes most difficult to passe, not minding her behind,
> Whose weale consisted in my care, she by some pow're more kind
> Was ta'ne from her neglecting guide; the Gods, not I, know best,
> Whether she stopt, or lost her way, or wearied, satte to rest.[20]

The Latin tells us Creusa was snatched from Aeneas by 'miserable fate', but in Wroth's translation she is taken away 'by some pow're more kind'. The difference between the Latin and the English is stark: whereas in Virgil the sad fate of Creusa is left unspecified, in Wroth's translation, already at the first point when we learn she is lost, we see traces of a benevolent deity acting behind the scenes. Furthermore, the presence of this benevolent deity is continually reinforced. When Aeneas runs back into Troy, Wroth translates:

> Ipse urbem repeto, & cingor fulgentibus armis.
> Stat casus renovare omneis, omnemq*ue* reverti
> Per Troiam, & rursus caput obiectare periclis.

> backe I return'd againe,
> Thorow the Center of those deaths, which I had past in vaine,
> To find her out who was not lost, and yet no longer mine.[21]

The final line in Wroth's translation here has no source in the Latin. Virgil's Aeneas only declares that he is resolved 'to renew all misfortunes, to retrace his way through all of Troy, and to expose himself again to every peril'. Once more, in Wroth's translation, we find an interpolation reassuring us that Creusa was, indeed, 'not lost'. The benevolent deity moves into the scene once again.

The key moment for Wroth's translation of this passage then comes when Creusa herself addresses Aeneas:

> Quid tantum insano iuvat indulgere labori
> O dulcis coniux [sic]? non hæc sine numine divum
> Eveniunt: nec te hinc comitem asportare Creusam
> Fas: haud ille sinit superi regnator Olympi.
>
> why doest thou toyle in vaine,
> To seeke for her who's neither lost, nor by the Grecians slaine,
> But by the Gods translated hence out of this mortall life;
> Then set thy heart at rest, loe hence thou must not have thy wife,
> For so the King of Heaven commands.[22]

Virgil's text is mysteriously vague. Creusa informs Aeneas that 'not without the will of heaven does this befall; that you should take Creüsa from here in your company cannot be, nor does the mighty lord of high Olympus allow it' (2.777–9). In Wroth's translation, however, we learn much more: Creusa tells us that she has not been slain, that she is not lost, and, moreover, she has been 'translated hence out of this mortall life'. This phrase is actually a fine description of what Wroth does to Creusa in this passage: he translates her clear out of mortal life and moves her speech away from the subdued consolation of the Latin into a sort of apotheosis. By 'translating' her out of earthly life, Wroth invests her with greater authority. The moment when Creusa vanishes is suggestive: the Latin reads, '& multa volentem | Dicere, deserüit, tenuesq*ue* recessit in auras', whereas Wroth translates, 'and ev'n as she was ready to declare | Much more of her prophetick minde, she vanish't into ayre.'[23] Whereas Virgil's Creusa finishes speaking and leaves Aeneas wanting to say more, Wroth's Creusa is now gifted with a 'prophetick minde' and she is the one with more left to say. By giving Creusa this voice, Wroth gives her the key to the narrative of the *Aeneid* and makes her into a woman who understands her position in the story of Roman Empire. Wroth has translated Virgil's elusive and tragic Creusa into a goddess and prophet at the end of Book 2.

These changes to Virgil's Creusa derive from various commentaries. In his 'Request to the Reader', Wroth writes, 'I stray not from the scope and intent of the Author, justified by the best Commentaries',[24] and he is true to his word. We can be certain that he looked at the Servian commentary while working on the Creusa passage, since his marginal gloss on an element of Creusa's speech is an expansion of a note by Servius. Wroth writes 'She gave him this caveat [to love and care for their son], because she knew her sonne was to have a mother in law, who for the most part with-drawes the husbandes affection from the children they had by their former wife, especially if they have any children.'[25] This is largely a translation of Servius' comment on *Aeneid* 2.789: 'NATI SERVA COMMUNIS AMOREM quasi mater sollicita, quod dixerat, eum aliam habiturum uxorem. bene ergo propter futuram novercam commendatur Ascanius.'[26]

In the Renaissance commentaries, interpretations of Creusa tend to invest a great deal in the two words 'maior imago' in 2.773. The commentators attempt to puzzle out just what these words imply. Servius, for example, offers two possibilities: 'MAIOR IMAGO since a ghost is larger than a body. *And by this Virgil wants to show that she is dead, or that she has been made into a goddess.*'[27] There is quite a difference between the two options Servius presents. The second one is especially influential, however, as it is built upon by several Renaissance commentators. Cristoforo Landino, for instance, offers only that one possibility: 'Maior: since she is divine rather than human.'[28] It is likely that Wroth took his interpretation of Creusa from a commentary like Landino's. [29]

But what difference does Creusa's 'prophetick minde' make to a reading of Book 2? Richard Heinze provided a structural analysis of this book, noting that Creusa's prophecy would have been necessary so long as Virgil was composing Book 2 as a separate poem, but might not have been necessary within the *Aeneid* as a whole. According to tradition, Virgil did, after all, read out the books of his poem separately:

> A conclusion of this kind was an artistic necessity as long as Virgil was composing his Sack of Troy as a separate poem, intended to stand alone. As soon as this separate poem was incorporated into the larger context of the epic, there was no longer a need for any prophecy at this point, or at least no more than the prospect of a *regia coniunx* awaiting Aeneas in a distant land.[30]

In his expansion of Creusa's vision, Wroth's translation develops the one key structural feature that allows Book 2 of the *Aeneid* to work as an isolated microcosm of the full epic. The *Destruction of Troy* is thus complete unto itself, with a prophecy at the end almost as authoritative as Anchises' prophecies at the end of Book 6. In recent classical scholarship, critics have explored how some individual books of the epic encapsulate total visions of Aeneas' journey.[31] Wroth's translation shows an early translator's awareness of this possibility in the case of Book 2. In this particular single book translation, we thus have a sense of consolation, completion and closure. And Wroth is not alone among early modern English translators of Virgil to stress the independence and unity of certain single books. As we shall see in the next chapter, Robert Stapylton produced a stand-alone, political reading of Book 4.

If this translation was, as I suggested in the first half of this section, primarily directed at readers connected to the endeavours of the Virginia Company, what would they have made of the *Destruction of Troy*? This question cannot be answered definitively, but I would like to make some suggestions. The themes of a westward colonial expansion, of carrying one's own gods, of immense suffering and of a prophetic mission would have meant a great deal to a man like Captain Butler, who was then attempting to establish his 'Iles of Saints'. Moreover, Wroth's choice of Book 2 reflects the gloomier spirit of Jacobean colonialism. After the failures of Elizabethan colonial efforts, Jacobean colonial writing tended to be much darker. As Andrew Fitzmaurice writes, during the Jacobean period, 'death replaced gold as the glory of Virginia. Courage was the quality required to achieve such glory.'[32] *The Destruction of Troy*, recounting the horrors of war and the narrow escape of a courageous Aeneas, was an appropriate text for such a colonial culture. That said, with Wroth's creative translation of Creusa's prophetic moment, *The Destruction of Troy* also displays confidence that the entire colonial movement would be sustained by its status as a providential mission.

The 'Schoole of Virtue': Sir Dudley Digges's *Didos Death*

In January 1622 an anonymous duodecimo was printed containing a parallel English and Latin version of Book 4 of Virgil's *Aeneid*. The title page of the work presented the book as *Didos Death* and stated that the translation was completed 'by one that hath no name'. That this translation was the work of Sir Dudley Digges, however, can be demonstrated by a letter from John Chamberlain to Dudley Carleton on 22 March of that same year. Two months after the publication of the translation, Chamberlain wrote to Carleton, 'Here is a litle pamflet goes under his [i.e. Digges's] name, (though he will not be named) which doth him no great credit neither, saving that herupon some flouting witts call him Sir Dido Diggs.'[33] Chamberlain does not go so far as to say explicitly what the work by Digges was, but the timing of the letter makes it quite clear. Moreover, the title of the translation, *Didos Death*, with its rhythmic and alliterative echo of Dudley Digges's name, was surely meant to hint at its authorship.

So why did Digges, at this time a senior and heavily employed statesman in Jacobean politics, decide to publish a Virgil translation anonymously? No other English translation of Virgil during the Renaissance was printed without the translator's name. In 1621, Digges was an outspoken member in parliament; he had an established network of connections; he had funds; he was, moreover, simultaneously playing active roles in the Virginia Company, the Muscovy Company and the East India Company. What was the significance of publishing a Virgil translation – Digges's only translation, and his only poetic publication for that matter – at this point in time? The reason is that the translation acts as a political commentary on a particularly sensitive subject.

Antique Discipline: The Martial Virgil of the *Foure Paradoxes*

Digges's engagement with Virgil begins long before he published his translation of Book 4 in 1622. The *Foure Paradoxes, or Politique Discourses* that Digges published in 1604 display an extended reading of Virgil. This is the first place one must turn to understand what Digges would have made of Book 4. Although eighteen years separate the *Foure Paradoxes* and *Didos Death*, the two texts reveal a striking continuity and a sustained set of political beliefs. The way these two texts employ Virgil's *Aeneid* is similar, and the two works thus lend themselves to being understood together. The political moments that generated them share certain traits as well, since both were moments when King James's foreign policy was being actively debated. In 1603, when James ascended the throne, the question about how he would conduct his foreign policy still appeared to be open.[34] Was he to follow the militaristic programme and political ideals of the Essex circle, launching a hostile confrontation with Spain? Or was King James going to pursue a pacific foreign policy, continuing the negotiations for peace that Cecil had initiated under Queen Elizabeth? King James eventually opted to support Cecil and continue the peace negotiations, but in 1604 James's reign was still young and the political situation appeared uncertain. It is in such a politically unpredictable context that Digges published the *Foure Paradoxes* in 1604.

These *Foure Paradoxes* were written in part by Sir Dudley Digges and in part by his father Thomas Digges. The title page proclaims that two of these four paradoxes – the ones 'concerning militarie discipline' – were written 'long since by Thomas Digges Esquire', who had passed away in 1595. To these two paradoxes by his father, Dudley Digges added two more in 1604, concerning 'the worthinesse of warre and warriors'. Thomas Digges was an ardent supporter of foreign intervention and his son wanted to revive this ideal in the early years of the reign of King James I.

The two paradoxes by Thomas Digges present two interrelated arguments. First, he argues that 'no Prince, or State doth gaine, or save by giving too small entertainement unto Souldiers, Officers, or Commaunders Martiall'.[35] And second:

> that the Antique Romane and Graecian discipline Martiall doth farre exceede in Excellency our Modern, notwithstanding all alterations by reason of that late invention of Artillerie, or fire-shott. And that (unless wee reforme such corruptions as are growne into our Moderne Militia, utterly repugnant to the Ancient) wee shall in time loose utterly the renowne and honour of our Nation.[36]

In the battle between the ancients and the moderns, the ancients exemplify true martial valour whereas the modern English are drifting into decrepitude. Thomas Digges therefore holds up the classics as an example the English need to learn from. While he does concede the difference between modern technology and ancient weaponry, the classics still perform the ultimate didactic role: 'the auncient discipline of the Romane and Martial Graecian States, (even for our time) are rare and singuler Praecedents'.[37]

When Dudley Digges adds his own two paradoxes to his father's, this conception of the classics as models of martial valour continues on seamlessly. What was a critique of the military practices of Elizabeth's reign becomes a challenge at the beginning of James's reign for the nation to rise up and reclaim that 'auncient discipline'. The paradoxes Dudley Digges presents, however, are bolder and more idiosyncratic than those of his father. For example, at the beginning of his third paradox, he portrays himself as a courtier in the tradition of Sir Philip Sidney. For Digges, Sidney was first and foremost a great soldier, and he should have written a defence of the military profession as well.[38] Digges's effusive praise of Sidney in 1604, moreover, could not have avoided exposing a distinct political bias. David Norbrook has described it as a time when people were wondering, 'might not [James's] accession usher in a new age in which those who admired Sidney's political ideals and poetic achievement would be patronized by an enlightened king?'[39] Digges speaks fervently on behalf of those dreams, and he presents the alternatives at that moment as a martial, Sidneian model, on the one hand, and the current trend of an English nobility swayed by the effeminate and 'decaied Gentry',[40] on the other.

To recapture this ancient, martial model of behaviour is a matter of retrieving what is most precious to true Englishness. In the third paradox, Digges traces English civility back to the Roman conquests. He argues that what is best of English culture was planted by the Romans themselves. I quote from this section at length, both because it is central to Digges's perception of English history, and also because it introduces the first of several quotations from the *Aeneid*. Digges writes that if the English should actively wage war for their religion then would our warriours like true auncient souldiers strive to be religious, virtuous, full of honesty, and we might justly thinke with the *Thessalian* those of our contrimen most dull and sottish that went not to the warres: or say with the *Aetolian* the warre is better farre than peace for him that hath a minde to prove an honest man. For then our Campe would be a schoole of virtue where (by dutifull obedience) men should be trained up and taught what appertaind to wise commanding: where religion perhaps the cause of the quarrell should be so fervent, that men would thinke it their cheifest joy, in midst of greatest miseries, to have the feare of God their meditation and an unspotted life their comfort. For them the memorie of *Alexander* that the night before the battle with *Darius* cald for *Aristander* to winne the favor of Gods with sacrifice: or of *Æneas*.

Quo iustior alter
Nec pietate fuit, nec bello maior et armis:
Than whom there was none more upright
in goodnesse, nor more great in fight.
that in *Virgil* leaves his companions busied, *et*
Arces quibus altus Apollo
Praesidet horrendaeq; domat Secreta Sibilla
antrum immane petit &c.
To high *Apollos* temple hies
And to those dreaded mysteries,
The horride vault where *Sibil* lies &c.[41]

Aeneas is the model warrior: he is the ancient example of what Sir Philip Sidney represented among the Elizabethans. These two quotations, from *Aeneid* 1 and 6 respectively, focus upon Aeneas' piety (the second quotation is in fact introduced in the *Aeneid* by 'at pius Aeneas', which Digges has left out here).

Most interestingly, however, the movement in these two paragraphs is a movement from warfare towards virtue. It is in this suggestion in particular that Digges is much bolder than his father, for he espouses warfare not to defend virtue, but rather to *create* virtue. There is a certain Machiavellian colouring to Digges's thought, and he even cites 'Machiavel' at one point in the margin.[42] Indeed, Digges illustrates what Pocock refers to as the 'elements of Machiavellianism in Jacobean thought', which see the state as 'held together by arms, statecraft, and moral ambiguity'.[43] There is little evidence, however, that Digges was a sensitive reader of Machiavelli's critique of humanism and conventional virtue.[44] He seems rather to have latched onto Machievelli simply as an advocate of warfare. Digges wants James and the people to believe that they do not only need warfare on occasion to hold back Spain, but that by actively embracing war with Spain the English nation will avert a decline in virtue and become all the more glorious.

That James is the only one who can effect this change Digges states very clearly, while employing yet another quotation from the *Aeneid*:

> I cannot therefore but most seriously wishe that our King a worthy in the worthiest kinde of Learning as he is the flower of two Stemmes of most renowned warlicke auncesters, whom God hath given us, *To goe out before us and fight our battelles*, to whom the King of Kings
> *Et mulcere dedit fluctus et tollere ventos.*
> Gives power as well as to appease
> with calmes, with stormes to stirre the seas.
>
> Would when it shall please his wisedome adde life, meane practise to our *Militia* that oft dyes at least decaies much through secure idlenesse.[45]

With his martial ancestry and immense learning, James is presented as combining the two traits for which Digges so greatly honoured Sidney. The Latin quotation is drawn from the speech by Juno to Aeolus in Book 1 of the *Aeneid* when she entreats the wind god to stir up the waters against Aeneas. For a moment, it is as if Digges is taking on the role of Juno and entreating James to unleash the winds and start a war. The original context is ironically inappropriate to Digges's martial message, but he seems content to isolate this one line and to use it without regard to its larger setting. Military valour is the key theme that runs throughout the *Foure Paradoxes* and this quotation epitomises its use of Virgil. Even the final words of the *Foure Paradoxes* are a quotation from Virgil's *Aeneid*, glorifying warfare: 'Pulchrumq*ue* mori succurrit in armis' ('I think how glorious it is to die in arms!').[46] It is as if for Digges the infernal horrors of Book 2 do not exist – only the sense, in this one line, that warfare is leading onwards to glory.

In the intervening years from 1604 until November 1621, Digges went on to have an illustrious career. He was knighted in 1609 and thereafter travelled widely. Above all, the new knight immersed himself in the formation of English colonies overseas. He was involved in the colonies in India, Muscovy and Virginia, all of which he ardently supported. His publications during these years are all relevant to these companies. In 1611, he published a brief work, *Fata mihi totum mea sunt agitanda per orbem*, in which he argues for a sustained effort to find a Northwest Passage. The search for this passage, which had been one of the original aims of the Virginian adventurers, was of great interest to Digges. In a letter to Dudley Carleton on 4 December 1611, John Chamberlain wrote: 'Dudley Diggs is in consideration, yf this new discoverie of the north-west passage (wherin he is a great undertaker), will geve him leave to thincke of any thing els, for yt possesseth him wholy.'[47] In 1615, Digges published *The Defence of Trade*, a letter to Sir Thomas Smith, the Governor of the East-India Company, in which he describes that Company as having a 'blest indevour, with good service to the State'.[48]

In this text, Digges quotes from the *Aeneid* twice, both times while arguing that for the East India Company to have lost only four ships in fourteen years is a remarkable feat:

> and is four of so many ships, so long at Sea, so great a losse, especially in foureteene years of our yet infant and discovering trade, while in the farthest and unknowne parts of the world
> *Ignari hominumque locorumque*
> *Erramus, vento vastis & fluctibus acti,*
> *Incerti quo fata ferant, ubi sistere detur,*
>
> While we seeke for trafficke with strange Nations?[49]

This quotation from Virgil conflates two passages from the *Aeneid* (the first two lines being from Book 1, the third from Book 3) and portrays English colonialisation as being in its infancy, with prospects opening up along every horizon. Aeneas plays the role of the archetypal explorer, in whose footsteps the English colonial adventurers are travelling. Virgil's epic thus clearly remained in Digges's mind as a text for thinking about the political situations of his time. What is new to this text, however, is that Digges is applying Aeneas to colonial politics as well. This is an important development which plays a significant role in his translation of Book 4.

From November to December 1621: The Genesis of Digges's Translation

In the months of November and December 1621, James found himself uneasily navigating divided loyalties in a European crisis. In late 1620, the wars on the continent were escalating. Emperor Ferdinand II had forced King Frederick and his wife, Elizabeth, the daughter of King James, out of Prague. The European peace had been shattered. Needing to support his daughter and son-in-law, James summoned parliament to attain the necessary funds in 1621. But the parliament was not so willing to part with the funds on James's terms and wanted the king to declare an open war with Spain, which James was not willing to do. Parliament also urged James to marry his son to a Protestant, whereas the king was still considering a Spanish match. The tension between crown and parliament grew until James dissolved parliament in February 1622.[50]

Sir Dudley Digges had been elected to parliament in 1621 and played a significant role in several of the debates that year – usually appearing as a figure in those relating to trade. His most significant moment, however, came towards the end of November 1621, when he presented a dramatic speech urging for a war against Spain. There are eight separate accounts of this speech in the volumes of diaries from the 1621 parliaments. According to the most complete of these accounts, the gist of Digges's speak was as follows:

> The King of Spain aimeth at war, our King at peace. They go upon open ways, we upon secret; they may hold their friends better . . . we must resolve to do something or else we shall be subject to all the world's censure. The King hath done so much for peace that he must now have a war. Then [Digges] laid down three propositions: 1, we must resolve upon a war; 2, that it's good to maintain the army that is already on foot in the Palatinate, This [is] an easy and thrifty way; 3, whether a diverting war be fit.[51]

Just as he had done in the 1604 *Foure Paradoxes*, Digges makes a bold, public utterance urging the crown towards military action. The speech shows Digges once again envisioning the prospect of a war with Spain and once again casting his full weight behind it. It is true that his rationalisation of the war is now different. In the 1620s, Digges was still involved in military matters: in 1620, for instance, when the Virginia Company formed a committee for 'Military Discipline', Digges was elected to the committee as one of the five 'men most judicious in that profession'.[52] But in this speech to parliament, Digges justifies war for the sake of Protestantism. At the end of this same session of parliament, according to the diarists, Digges urged the king to defend Protestantism by using the colonies to British advantage. By attacking the Spanish colonies, the king could turn the crisis in central Europe into a part of the British religious and colonial venture: 'If the King of Spain's navy were intercepted from the West Indies, if he were kept from it two years, he would be bankrupt as he was in the Queen's time.'[53]

Then, on 27 November, showing his deep involvement with the movement for war, Digges proposed a committee that would act to consider what to do about the Palatinate.[54] This committee would not have much of a chance, since roughly a week later, the king issued his letter forbidding the Members of Parliament from speaking about his son's Spanish match or any of the royal prerogatives. James made clear that, if they spoke about these matters, he 'would punishe the Insolency of any parliament man in the parliament tyme or after'.[55] James thus made his final move to shut down the debates only just over a week after Digges had his grand moment.

Digges's translation of Book 4 of the *Aeneid* was entered in the Stationer's Register one week later, on 11 December 1621. And *Didos Death* is, I argue, an eminently political translation. Leslie Proudfoot, who studied this translation briefly in *Dryden's 'Aeneid' and Its Seventeenth*

Century Predecessors, came up with only negative things to say about it. He was not aware, however, that the translation was composed by Digges. (Instead, Proudfoot surmised based on the style that it was the work of a man 'possibly of rustic origin'.[56]) I would certainly not argue for any aesthetic triumph on behalf of the translation; it is a ramshackle piece of work that most probably was composed in haste. But this translation is much more interesting than it seemed to Proudfoot, and its interest lies primarily with its political intent. In the original context at the very end of 1621, Digges's Aeneas would have acted as a monitory ideal for and a commentary on Prince Charles and King James.[57]

Digges's translation lends itself to being read contemporarily since it is heavily domesticated. Anna's name is Englished as 'Nan'; the temples Dido visits ('delubra') are translated as a 'holy Church'; visiting 'maternal Delos' ('Delum maternam') becomes 'to visite Mothers Dele'; Cretans can 'prance' ('instauratque choros'); and there are 'mad, merry Greekes'.[58] Dido's deeming it worthy to join herself with Aeneas ('se pulchra viro dignetur iungere Dido') becomes 'how *Dido* faire matching her selfe is mating', and we learn that the couple are spending 'too long hugging' ('quam longa fovere').[59] Yet more invasive and aggressive than this continuous Englishing are intruding moments of topicality, the most curious instance of which is Digges's rendering of 'nec me meminisse pigebit Elissæ' by 'nor leave remembring Queene Elizabeth'.[60] This line may refer in part to Queen Elizabeth for her foreign policy, but it would primarily refer to the daughter of James, who was then at the centre of the European turmoil and whom Digges would be calling upon his readers to remember. The context here in Book 4 may be somewhat ambiguous; however, as we saw in the *Foure Paradoxes*, Digges does not hesitate from appropriating individual lines from the *Aeneid* when he sees a chance, even if it means, in some cases, ignoring the context. King James, after all, was accused of having forgotten and abandoned his daughter, who at this time 'personified the Protestant cause'.[61] Some parliamentarians said that if James really loved Elizabeth, then he would promptly declare a war with Spain, and others maliciously hinted that she was not really his daughter.[62] At such a heated moment, this line in a translation by an opposing parliamentarian such as Digges would have been incisive and controversial.

Moreover, Digges would have been drawn to Book 4 of the *Aeneid* because it is a work that seemed thematically relevant to the political situation at the end of 1621. Book 4 is the story of a prince who is drawn off course and ceases to follow his proper, imperial project. It is about a prince who, for a moment, seems about to plant his roots in the wrong place and to give in to effeminate leisure rather than pursuing masculine duty and virtue. The parallels with Charles entertaining a Spanish marriage are manifold and striking. We can see the prince who is being lured towards binding himself and his lineage with Catholic Spain rather than with Protestantism; who refuses to acknowledge who his enemies really are; who has been lured in by a sense of peace when fate has imposed wars upon him; and who all the while is gradually letting his court grow less and less disciplined and more dissolute. For Renaissance commentators, Book 4 of the *Aeneid* demonstrated Virgil's moral rectitude. Aeneas' love affair with Dido showed 'what happens when the will is temporarily seduced by the sensual appetite and rebels against the rule of reason'.[63] But by depicting Aeneas' sacrifice of his love to meet the gods' commands, Virgil 'inspired readers to emulate his self-denying commitment to duty'.[64] As Digges translates Jupiter's speech to Mercury, the king of the gods accuses Aeneas of 'forgetting thine owne State affaires'.[65]

With such a monitory moral in mind, the admonitions from the gods gain a particular poignancy. Much as Digges had used Juno's words to Aeolus to appeal to King James in 1604, feigning that the words were from the King of Kings to James, the words of the gods speak to Charles and James at the end of 1621. Thus Jupiter tells Mercury to rebuke Aeneas:

> If glory of so great things move him not,
> Nor his owne praise with paine and labour got,
> Envies the sire his sonne *Ascanius*
> Should rule in *Rome*? what plots, hopes make him thus
> In foes land linger, laying *Italy*,
> And all thoughts of his *Latine* off spring by?
> Get him to sea, that's all, from us this tell,
> Quoth *Iupiter*.[66]

Digges's call for James to forgo peace negotiations and to strike against Spain in the colonies is refracted through this translation of Virgil. Speedily published after James had forbidden parliamentarians from discussing foreign politics, Digges's partial translation of Virgil's epic shows how a single book, as opposed to a full translation, could issue a pointed and timely call to duty.

'What Hercules Would Be': George Sandys's Essay upon the *Aeneid*

> And with it that Essay, which lets us see
> Well by the Foot, what Hercules would be.

All fitly offer'd to his Princely Hands;
By whose Protection Learning chiefly stands:
Whose Vertue moves more Pens, then his Power Swords;
And Theme to these, and Edge to those affords.[67]

The preceding verses are a part of Lord Falkland's prefatory poem to Sandys's 1638 'Paraphrase upon the Psalms of David', the second part of his *Paraphrase upon the Divine Poems*. In this poem he overviews the achievements of Sandys's life and dedicates verses to each of Sandys's publications. Falkland gives only ten lines to the complete translation of Ovid, but the six lines above he dedicates to Sandys's translation of Book 1 of the *Aeneid*. As Falkland's response to this Virgil translation suggests, Sandys's version of Book 1 requires a different approach from the translations by Wroth and Digges. Whereas Wroth and Digges each select one book from the *Aeneid* without giving any sign of intending to translate more, Sandys's translation is incomplete: he presents it as an aborted 'assay' upon the whole of the epic. What we have of Sandys's Virgil should thus be understood as a sort of synecdoche. It is a 'foot' of Hercules that represents the entire hero. As the translation itself gives us only very little material to discuss – a point I will pick up later – the best approach is via the representation of the *Aeneid* in relevant works by Sandys. The *Aeneid* has a continuous and central presence in Sandys's writing. It plays particularly prominent roles in *A Relation of a Journey* and the Ovid commentary, being among the most quoted sources in both texts. Moreover, there is a demonstrable development in Sandys's engagement with the *Aeneid* and this development can provide an idea of what Virgil's epic would have meant to Sandys when he published his translation in 1632.

The exact composition date of Book 1 is difficult to ascertain. From the translations in *A Relation* and the Ovid commentary it is clear that the Virgil translation must have been composed between 1615 and 1632.[68] A translation of one book of the *Aeneid* could be completed within a few weeks: Phaer needed only sixteen days to complete his translation of Book 1, and Sandys could have found sixteen free days at many different points during these years. But there are several hints that the Virgil translation dates from the end of this window. A nineteenth-century study of the stylistic features of Sandys's translations noted that in its use of 'unstopped lines', Sandys's Virgil stylistically matches his translation of Book 15 of Ovid (and not the earlier books), which would suggest a translation date around 1626.[69] It would make sense if he completed it in the order in which it appears in the 1632 folio: after Ovid, an essay upon Virgil. Furthermore, in the poem quoted at the beginning of this section, Lord Falkland, who knew Sandys well, goes over Sandys's writing in chronological order, and he treats the Virgil translation after the Ovid.[70]

Given that the translation was more likely composed in the late 1620s and first published in 1632, in this section I intend to look at the translation in the context of Sandys's developing thoughts on the *Aeneid*. His most sustained interest lies in the historical value of the poem and the elusive shadows of truth he believes are flickering below the surface. But there is also a growing concern in Sandys's later work with the epic as an instance of rhetorical persuasion and as a model for colonial practice.

The Leaves of the Sibyl: Virgilian Credibility in *A Relation of a Journey*

Sandys's engagement with Virgil in *A Relation* is extensive and begins with the title page itself. The 1615 title page presents images of the four different parts of Sandys's journey. First, at the top centre of the page, we see Christ rising in glory. This oval image is enwrapped with the words 'sic redibit' above and 'mons olivarum' below. The location and content of this image represent the Holy Land, displaying its central position in the narrative as the destination to which Sandys is travelling. On the right of the page, the figure of 'Isis, sive Ægyptus' obviously represents Egypt. Sandys explores the fable of Isis within *A Relation* and understands this fable as particularly rich, containing 'sundry allegories'.[71] On the left of the page is Achmet, 'sive tyrannus', who represents Turkey. This image of the tyrant Achmet is the only representative figure on the title page that is wholly negative. Sandys tends towards a wholesale rejection of Turkish culture, which is portrayed throughout the narrative as the antithesis of Christianity.[72] Finally, at the bottom of the page, directly opposite the image of Christ, there is a picture of the Cumaean Sibyl sitting in her cave. This picture, like that of Christ, is enwrapped with words above and below. The words above present her as 'Sibylla Cumæa', and the words below are a quotation from Book 3 of the *Aeneid*: 'foliisque notas et nomina mandat' (444). The Sibyl as portrayed by Virgil is thus chosen as the representative figure for the fourth and final part of Sandys's journey – his time in Italy.

The Latin verse below the image is taken from a passage in Book 3 that describes the Sibyl and encapsulates many themes of *A Relation*:

> huc ubi delatus Cumaeam accesseris urbem
> divinosque lacus et Averna sonantia silvis,
> insanam vatem aspicies, quae rupe sub ima
> fata canit foliisque notas et nomina mandat.
> quaecumque in foliis descripsit carmina virgo,

> digerit in numerum atque antro seclusa relinquit.
> illa manent immota locis neque ab ordine cedunt;
> verum eadem, verso tenuis cum cardine ventus
> impulit et teneras turbavit ianua frondes,
> numquam deinde cavo volitantia prendere saxo
> nec revocare situs aut iungere carmina curat;
> inconsulti abeunt sedemque odere Sibyllae.
> (3.441–52)

> (And when, thither borne, you draw near to the town of Cumae, the haunted lakes, and Avernus with its rustling woods, you will see an inspired prophetess, who deep in a rocky cave sings the Fates and entrusts to leaves signs and symbols. Whatever verses the maid has traced on leaves she arranges in order and stores away in the cave. These remain unmoved in their places and do not quit their rank; but when at the turn of a hinge a light breeze has stirred them, and the open door has scattered the tender foliage, never thereafter does she care to catch them, as they flutter in the rocky cave, nor to recover their places and unite the verses; inquirers depart no wiser than they came, and loathe the Sibyl's seat.)

In *A Relation*, the *Aeneid* features as a text that is in some way divinely inspired but in other ways hopelessly confused. There is for Sandys a truth resting behind part of the *Aeneid*, but this truth is mixed with fiction, like the leaves of the Sibyl having been blown out of order. Attempting to sort out the truth from the fiction is the central impulse behind the sifting of Virgil in *A Relation*. At the top-left corner of the title page we find the word 'veritas', and this word encapsulates what Sandys is searching for behind Virgil. While the *Aeneid* does still hold a moral authority, Sandys does not read the poem as a sustained allegory or as epideictic rhetoric. Rather, he writes a 'topographical commentary',[73] in which the primary concern is Virgil's authority as a historian and as a conveyor of prophecies. Every time in *A Relation* that Sandys quotes Virgil at length, he does so to analyse the truth behind the poem.

The first of these instances regards Virgil's presentation of history. Antony Grafton, in *New Worlds, Ancient Texts*, provides a model for this encounter. Grafton stresses that the 'classics' did not provide the Renaissance with a single scientific viewpoint or a single account of history, but rather that the 'classics' contained an abundance of different voices. This abundance explains part of the adaptability of classical texts and how they could maintain their authority for such a long time, through the many discoveries of the Renaissance. This same abundance, however, also meant that there were fissures within the canon that could challenge its authority: 'Cracks and contradictions within the canon – above all religious ones – brought on the most radical challenges to the authority of books.'[74] Raphael Lyne, in *Ovid's Changing Worlds*, explores this precise challenge to classical authorities in Sandys's Ovid commentary, and his discussion can be extended back into *A Relation* as well.[75] For in *A Relation*, these fissures become focal points. Sandys often notes where one classical source says one thing but another source claims something else, and he then attempts to sort out which one is the better authority. The *Aeneid* is not spared from this treatment, and we find it weighed against many other historical sources. I offer here two examples, one that falls in favour of Virgil, the other against him.

In the first, Sandys is near Constantinople and is reflecting upon traditions that claim Aeneas never fled from Troy but rather stayed with the Greeks:

> They that favour not the inventions of *Virgil*, report that *Æneas* removed not from hence; but succeeded in this kingdome, which for a long time after remained in his posteritie: highly honoured by the *Grecians* themselves for his wisedome, valour, and pietie, (he not consenting to the Rape of *Helena*) who forbare to damnifie both his person & fortunes. Whereupon suspected it was, that he betrayed the Citie. But the prophesie that *Homer* makes of him in the person of *Neptune*, then readie to be done to death by Achilles, in my opinion is a testimonie for *Virgil*.[76]

We see a series of historical sources at play: Dictys and Dares (who are unnamed in this passage but are the main source of the tradition that Aeneas was actually a traitor who joined with the Greeks), Virgil and Homer. Virgil's *Aeneid* stands in between two other authorities. A fissure opens up, but here it is closed in favour of Virgil since Homer serves as a 'testimonie' for Virgil's account. Elsewhere, however, the judgement is often against Virgil, as for example in Sandys's reflections upon the story of Dido and Aeneas. It was common in the Renaissance to note that the historical Dido and the Dido of the *Aeneid* were not the same person. Boccaccio, for instance, made much of this discrepancy and Stapylton will note it in his translation as well.[77] Sandys writes:

> But the coming thither of *Æneas*, and cause of her death, is held by diverse no other then a fiction. For *Appian* (if his credite may ballance with *Virgils*) reports that *Carthage* was built full fiftie yeares before *Troy* was destroied.[78]

Sandys then quotes a poem by Ausonius, which charges Virgil with slander. The 'balancing' of authorities in this passage is particularly telling: sources pile up, and the *Aeneid*, while it does claim a special weightiness, has the scales tip against it. Sandys uses the word 'credite' very effectively here, highlighting the issues of trust and belief. In rhetoric, one of the three kinds of persuasion is 'ethos', which concerns the personal character of the speaker.[79] Sandys weighs the credibility of Virgil and Appian, as if they were in a court and he were judging between them. Moreover, unlike Petrarch and Boccaccio, Sandys does not offer a theoretical defence as to why Virgil would have feigned about Dido. Usually, as John Watkins has shown, the 'two-Dido thesis exonerated Virgil himself from suspicions of slander, since his didactic aims justified his departure from historical fact'.[80] But Sandys leaves the *Aeneid* in this passage as potentially being 'no other then a fiction'.

Were these dubious historical matters all that Sandys found in Virgil, the *Aeneid* would probably not have left such a great mark upon his work. As the fourth part of *A Relation* proceeds, however, the Sibyl becomes a figure of great interest. For if there is a profound truth concealed behind the text of the *Aeneid*, then it is glimpsed in her prophetic pronouncements. Many medieval Christian commentators on the *Aeneid* would distinguish between the prophecies that the Sibyl makes and the poetry of Virgil: they have different levels of authority.[81] Likewise, on the one hand, Sandys can display great contempt for the ancient poets when he believes they have speculated incorrectly on their own about divine matters.[82] On the other hand, the Cumaean Sibyl has a great claim to authority, since Sandys considers her a historically authentic oracle who at times revealed Christian truths. According to Sandys, she 'flourished both before, and after the *Trojan* warres; with whom *Æneas* consulted. The manner of her prophesying thus *Virgil* describeth.'[83] There were, Sandys believed, many Sibyls in the ancient world, and, although most were possessed by devils, it was possible for these Sibyls to prophecy about Christianity. Christ had been 'foretold by heathen Oracles',[84] and the Cumaean Sibyl was such an oracle. For Sandys in *A Relation*, Virgil was thus not an 'anima naturaliter Christiana', and he is certainly no magician or prophet; rather, he is a poet who came across ancient prophecies and mixed them in his poetry, without properly understanding them. The result is that Virgil's poetry can at points have a greater authority than the writings of almost any other pagan poet. But his work is an impossibly complex web of divine truth and pagan fiction. Sandys wants to put Virgil back into order but finds that he cannot. In Haynes's words, for Sandys, whenever the truth lurking behind Virgil 'is seen there are problems with decorum; when it is analyzed it falls apart'.[85]

In a remarkable passage near the end of *A Relation*, Sandys draws together his thoughts about the Sibyls. 'Such turbulent extasies', he writes, 'proceeded without question from a diabolical possession. But surely a peaceable, and better spirit did inspire them with those heavenly divinations of our Saviour.'[86] The problem then becomes, how does one sort out what is true from what is not, where the true prophecy ends and the pagan fiction begins:

> So that the whole being to be misdoubted, in that falsified in part, or the true from the untrue not distinguishable; we are rather to beleeve those that have the testimony of time for their approbation. As that prophesie of our Saviour by this of *Cuma*; borrowed from her by *Virgil* (as he confesseth) though perhaps not applied by him where it was meant, but lest at random to be construed by event, and mixt with his fictions.[87]

In this passage we also return to the problem we found in the quotation from Book 3 of the *Aeneid* on the title page of *A Relation*. It is as if the leaves of the Sibyl had been blown into confusion: Sandys's attempts to move behind Virgil and to determine their proper order are constantly frustrated. This attempt by Sandys to locate a deep historical source behind a text has been described as 'Baconian': Lee Pearcy has argued that Bacon's interpretation of myth was the key to Sandys's 1632 *Ovids Metamorphosis*.[88] But while their approach to the history of sources may be similar, Sandys differs from Bacon in so far as he is also interested in Christian revelation hidden in pagan fables.[89] With regard to the Sibyl, Sandys is concerned with the hermeneutical challenge to distinguish theological truth from its pagan corruption.

The search in *A Relation* for elements of truth behind the *Aeneid* thus results in a complex and multilayered approach towards Virgil. While there are facts Sandys is quite certain about – for instance, that Virgil read traces of a divinely inspired Sibyl – the Virgil in *A Relation* is far from the all-knowing philosopher of the prominent late-classical and medieval commentary traditions.

'The Two Maine Columnes of a Common-wealth': Virgilian Politics in the 1632 *Ovids Metamorphosis*

The seventeen years between the publication of *A Relation* and the 1632 *Ovids Metamorphosis* were eventful years in Sandys's life. In 1621, Sandys was appointed to the new post of 'treasurer' of the Virginia Company. He set off to the New World that year, where his job was to take the collection of all rents and duties and to carry out directions from the council at home.[90] He spent the next four years in Virginia. During this time, the colony suffered the Jamestown massacre, which took place in March 1622, when 300–400 colonists were killed in an uprising by the natives. Six letters home to England show Sandys deeply shaken by this incident, and Ellison describes it as resulting in a 'profound sense of personal crisis'.[91] Nevertheless, Sandys continued to live the life of a colonial officer from 1622 to 1625, and during this time he completed his translation of Ovid. The Virginia Company, however, was dissolved by James in 1624, and although Sandys was reappointed under a royal commission, he decided to return to England in 1625.[92] While Sandys never returned to the New World, the major non-literary interest of these later years was still the Virginia colony and he seems to have expected to return at some point.[93] In this section, we must approach the question of what effect these seventeen years had on Sandys's reading of Virgil.

The translation of Book 1 of the *Aeneid* does not immediately offer many hints. If one approaches Sandys's translation looking for points of deviation – moments where Sandys moves away from the meaning of the Latin or adds something of his own for artistic or ideological reasons – one finds remarkably little of note. Sandys is consistently faithful to his source and his translation is neatly contained. Pearcy uses the word 'compression' to describe Sandys's style, a word which is very apt.[94] Sandys keeps impressively close to a one-to-one line ratio while translating Latin dactylic hexameter into English iambic pentameter. He does not allow himself to expand, but rather keeps his translation under a constant pressure to stay within the boundaries of the Latin. Whereas Wroth and Digges both felt free to interpolate at points, according to their interpretative purposes, Sandys displays a greater deference to the Latin original. Studies that have explored the language of Sandys's Ovid translation have also shown the extent of Sandys's Latinisms. Deborah Rubin has argued that Sandys's Ovid translation is 'generally Latinate in its diction',[95] and Raphael Lyne's close readings have shown different ways in which these Latinisms are manifested and the dynamic that consequently emerges between the original and the target languages.[96] Sandys's style and diction in his Virgil translation is, substantially, the same as his style and diction in his Ovid: it continues Sandys's practice of being highly Latinate and compressed, staying very close to the original throughout, notably rendering all of Virgil's half-lines. This imitative closeness and respect for the Latin is significant as we consider Sandys's reading of the *Aeneid* as conveyed by the texts it was printed with.

Even though the Ovid commentary of 1632 is on the *Metamorphoses*, within it Sandys frequently quotes from Virgil and analyses passages of the *Aeneid*. The commentary is not an exploration of Ovid's representation of a fable, but rather of the fables themselves in their various manifestations. In particular, Books 13 and 14 of the *Metamorphoses*, in which the story of Aeneas is retold, provide an opportunity for Sandys to quote from Virgil extensively and to write about the character of Aeneas. There seems to be a marked change in Sandys's thoughts about Virgil, although we find that many of the concerns from *A Relation* are reiterated. Sandys's interest in the historical aspects of Virgil, for instance, is once again foregrounded. In the preface to the Ovid commentary, Sandys writes, 'I have also endeavored to cleare the Historicall part, by tracing the almost worne-out steps of Antiquitie.'[97] Above, we saw Sandys considering the historical authenticity of the Dido and Aeneas episode. The same material appears in his Ovid commentary:

> But others upon better grounds have determined that this was meerely a fiction of *Virgils*; and that *Æneas* never came thether. Among the rest *Ausonius* on her picture . . . For it is more then probable, that *Dido* arrived in *Africa*, two hundred eighty and nine yeares after the destruction of *Troy*; being supposed to bee the Neece of *Jezabell*.[98]

In fact, Sandys has taken this passage almost directly out of *A Relation*. He even uses the same quotation from Ausonius to prove his case both times and copies his original translation of it word for word.[99] The complete reuse of this passage is a fine example of how there is a clear continuity in Sandys's thought and how he did not start his interpretations anew, but built upon what he had already written. Likewise, Sandys repeats many of his reflections on the Sibyl. In the commentary, her humility is

> resembling that of the Saints and Angels, who refused divine worship, as onely due unto God; perhaps taught her by that Spirit, which by an extraordinary dispensation revealed unto her those excellent Mysteries, whereby shee yet speaketh.[100]

We once again find the divine revelation of the Sibyl embedded within Virgil's fiction.

The Sibyl of the commentary, however, does not point the reader in quite the same direction as the Sibyl of *A Relation*. She provides a good place from which to explore the most significant changes. In the commentary, we encounter the Sibyl's prophecy not only as a source of divine revelation, but also of imperial prophecy:

> *Sibyll* was feigned to bee beloved of *Apollo*, in that a prophetesse: Prophesying of old ascribed unto him, & to proceed from his spirit unto others. And because she prophesied of the warres and Empire of the *Romans*; she was said to reveale what should follow to *Æneas*, as to the originall of that nation.[101]

In contrast, I have not found a single instance of prolonged consideration of the *Aeneid* as a colonial or imperial poem in *A Relation*. The colonial aspect of Sandys's 1632 Virgilianism is something new. Although the commentary does not set out a systematic reading of the *Aeneid*, its many references to Virgil's epic show the themes that would have been foremost in Sandys's mind when he published his translation, and there is a consistent awareness of the *Aeneid* as a fable of empire.

It is not surprising to find that Sandys's years as a colonist in Virginia and his extended involvement in the New World had some impact upon which themes from the *Aeneid* attracted him.

In *Humanism and America*, Andrew Fitzmaurice stresses the central role of rhetoric, and especially oratory, in English Renaissance theories of the founding of commonwealths: 'Oratory, as we shall see, was believed to constitute the central act in the foundation of a commonwealth.'[102] As Fitzmaurice argues, the political language of the Virginia Company was profoundly humanistic, not commercial, and this humanistic and rhetorical language was the source of the colonists' justifications and anxieties: 'Humanism provided the aims and the design for the ambition to establish colonies: the design was the foundation of a new commonwealth through virtuous action undertaken for the ends of honour and glory.'[103] The early English colonists saw their undertakings through the lens of the *studia humanitatis*. Fitzmaurice's insistence on the role of rhetoric as a fundamental part of the formation of commonwealths is eminently relevant for Sandys's treatment of Virgil in his commentary. He associates the *Aeneid* both rhetorically and narratively with the act of founding a new commonwealth. The political relevance of Sandys's *Aeneid* is not to be located in any sort of specific topicality, but rather in the humanistic language he uses while discussing Aeneas as the founder of a nation.

Throughout the commentary Sandys often notes that poets have the ability to feign: poets 'had, and have, the liberty to faine what they listed'.[104] In his introduction 'To the Reader', Sandys remarks upon the power inherent in this liberty. Employing an argument reminiscent of Sir Philip Sidney's *Defence*, he writes:

> For the Poet not onely renders things as they are; but what are not, as if they were, or rather as they should bee; agreeable to the high affections of the *Soule*, and more conducing to magnanimitie: juster then either men or Fortune in the exalting of *Vertue* and suppressing of *Vice*, by shewing the beautie of the one and deformitie of the other, pursued by the divine *Vengeance*, by inbred terrors, and infernall torments.[105]

This passage is a collection of humanist commonplaces: poets are presented as feigners, who through the use of epideictic rhetoric can sway their audience towards 'magnanimitie'. But one should compare this passage with one of the most explicit political moments in the commentary. Sandys portrays the Cyclopses as being a barbarous people, uncivil and lawless:

> and no marvaile; when lawlesse, and subject to no government, the bond of society; which gives to every man his owne, suppressing vice, and advancing

vertue, the two maine columnes of a Common-wealth, without which it can have no supportance.[106]

What Fitzmaurice writes about in *Humanism and America* – rhetoric being a foundational force within a commonwealth – is illustrated by these two passages. Those two abilities the rhetorical poet has, the advancing of virtue and the suppressing of vice, are here viewed as 'the two maine columnes of a Common-wealth'. The responsibility that is given here to 'government' is given above to 'poets', and we can see by the interchangeability of poetry and government how rhetorical literature could be an active force in colonisation. Later in this passage, Sandys compares the Cyclopses to the 'the *West-Indians*', who are also lacking 'the two maine columnes'. Thus there is a real need for rhetorical influence in Virginia. Just as the Romans brought civilisation to Britain ('wherein the conquered were the gainers, having got thereby civility and letters, for a hardly won, nor a long detained dominion'[107]) so the British are in a position to bring civility to the New World.

Raphael Lyne has argued that those who consider Sandys's *Ovid* translation as fused with his colonial politics do 'not pay attention to the elements of confusion that predominate' in the commentary.[108] This confusion, however, should be regarded as part of Sandys's treatment of Ovid and not his treatment of the *Aeneid*. While there is some doubt about the theological value of Virgil's writing, Sandys offers a unified and positive interpretation of the political implications of Aeneas.

If the two foundations of a state are its advancing of virtue and its suppressing of vice, then Rome must have accomplished these two feats exceptionally well to have endured so long. Sandys is particularly interested in Aeneas' role as the 'originall of that nation'.[109] The most important passage on the creation of Rome in Sandys's commentary is a brief exploration of how Aeneas enabled Rome to be as magnificent a nation as it became. The answer lies in arguably the most important word in Virgil's *Aeneid*, the adjective 'pius'. For Aeneas,

> by bearing away his house-hold Gods, and aged father on his shoulders (as his chiefest treasure) purchased the perpetuall attribute of *Pious* . . . This piety of *Æneas* was rewarded in his posterity with the greatest, & longest continuing Empire, that ever virtue or fortune afforded.[110]

Sandys here subsumes the language of commerce within the language of humanism. Aeneas *purchased* his attribute of pious, his father is 'his chiefest *treasure*' and Rome is the greatest empire that 'ever virtue or *fortune afforded*'. In each case, a humanistic principle is controlling the commercial terms. The message is that only humanistic ideals can 'afford' an empire and, in particular, it is Aeneas' 'perpetuall' piety that founds the greatest of states. Piety is thus placed at the summit of the humanistic virtues necessary for founding a successful state. For another example, we can turn to Sandys's description of Aeolus, who is described using a quotation from Book 1 of the *Aeneid*. Sandys finds an image of the wise and benevolent ruler in '*Æolus*, who is said to bee beloved of the Gods, in regard of his piety; and of men for his temperance and hospitality: insomuch as the neighbouring nations, though in contention among themselves, submitted to his Empire.'[111] Here the themes of Virgilian piety and virtue creating a successful state reappear. Were Sandys to have completed his Virgil, I believe this theme – the role of virtue as the basis for founding a proper state – would have been central to the translation. And we can moreover surmise that this theme, which emerges in Sandys's response to the *Aeneid* only after he returns from Virginia, would have been of especial interest to him for its resonances with contemporary British developments in the New World in which he was still deeply involved.

While discussing the significance of Hercules in Book 9 of the *Metamorphoses*, Sandys adds a brief section on the story of Hercules and Cacus, for which he uses *Aeneid* 8 as his source. Sandys expounds the story as follows: 'Now Cacus is by interpretation Evill, which lurkes in Caves, in that never secure: when Hercules, or Virtue, vindicates his owne, by the destruction of the other.'[112] Perhaps now we are also in a position to understand more of the significance of Falkland's brief prefatory poem with which I opened this section on Sandys. Falkland describes the translation as 'that Essay, which lets us see | Well by the Foot, what Hercules would be'.[113] With Sandys's Virgil, we have a synecdoche of the whole image of heroic, Herculean virtue conquering vice. Sandys's translation is indeed just like the foot of Hercules, from which we can perceive an epideictic interpretation of the whole. And it would be from that total vision of Aeneas that Sandys would have been able to offer his readers the 'two maine columnes of a Common-wealth' – the sort of commonwealth he hoped to establish in Virginia.

When viewed together, Wroth, Digges and Sandys constitute an important moment in the history of Virgil in English translation. The aim of this chapter has been, first, to show that between the years 1620 and 1632 the affairs of the Virginia Company dominated the reception of Virgil's epic in English translation; and, second, to show the different ways the *Aeneid* could be translated in response to the colonial activity of England. As we have seen, each translator draws upon Virgil in a unique way. Wroth uses Book 2 as a means of depicting the trials of Jacobean colonialism and the aspiration of founding 'Iles of Saints'; Digges uses the *Aeneid* to make a pointed comment on royal affairs at a particularly sensitive moment; and Sandys provides an image of the virtuous pillars needed to found a new commonwealth. By viewing the three together, I have thus attempted to bring to light a rich moment in the reception of Virgil in early modern England. This moment in the history of *Aeneid* translations has been completely overshadowed, in modern criticism, by the Civil War translations that follow in the middle of the seventeenth century. For their political ramifications, however, these Virginian texts deserve a substantial place in any history of English *Aeneid*s.

Having explored these three texts, I would also like to suggest a further point about the phenomenon of single book translations. In a 1931 essay, 'Virgile en France au XVIe siècle: éditions, traductions, imitations', Alice Hulubei made some general comments on sixteenth-century French partial translations of the *Aeneid*. Hulubei saw French partial translations flourishing from 1540 to 1560 and considered them as a middle phase between the early Virgil translations (e.g. the translation printed by Le Roy in 1483 or Saint-Gelais's *Eneydes* from 1509), which domesticate Virgil's writing to please the reader, and the later humanist translations (e.g. Des Masure's *L'Eneide* from 1560 or Le Blanc's *Églogues* of 1554), which aim to be faithful to the original.[114] In her account, the ability to select and isolate particular episodes allowed the translator freedom to domesticate the poem by focusing on relevant and popular incidents in the epic. As we have seen, the fact that partial translations lend themselves more easily to domestication is one of the reasons why two of the authors chose to render only a small part of the epic. As the translations by Wroth and Digges also show, however, this domesticating potential of partial book translations is not an isolated phenomenon in a middle phase of vernacular translations, nor is it simply a question of domesticating for pleasure. Rather, in the case of early modern Virgilian translators, an explanation needs to be sought in their rhetorical value and their specific, local contexts. By rendering only a portion of Virgil's epic, Wroth and Digges were able to actualise very specific strands of interpretation in their translations in order to apply the text to their immediate needs. The flexibility of partial translations is one of the reasons they flourished well into the seventeenth century.

Notes

1. Kingsbury (ed.), *Records of the Virginia Company*, I, p. 72.
2. Ibid., p. 345.

3. Jones, *O Strange New World*, p. 238; Wiltshire, 'Aeneas in America'; Ziolkowski, *Virgil and the Moderns*, pp. 146–7.
4. Wiltshire, 'Aeneas in America', p. 2.
5. Jones, *O Strange New World*, pp. 227–50.
6. Ibid., p. 238.
7. Smith, 'Proceedings of the English Colonie in Virginia', pp. 31–2. Cf. *Aeneid* 1.198–207.
8. Wilson-Okamura, 'Virgilian Models', p. 713.
9. Wroth, *Destruction of Troy*, sig. A1^{v}.
10. Hay, *Life of Robert Sidney*, p. 207.
11. Another ambiguous dedication suggests that Sidney may have done some translation as well: Kelliher and Duncan-Jones, 'A Manuscript of Poems by Robert Sidney', p. 115.
12. On the circulation and revision of Robert Sidney's poetry, see Croft, 'Introduction', pp. 1–16.
13. Hay, *Life of Robert Sidney*, p. 223.
14. Ibid., p. 210.
15. Ibid., p. 217.
16. Ibid., p. 226.
17. Wroth, *Destruction of Troy*, sig. H1^{v}.
18. For a facsimile image see Rich, *The Rich Papers*, p. 251.
19. Book 2 has ten unfinished lines, which is more than any other. See Austin's comment on 2.66 in *Aeneidos liber secundus*, p. 55.
20. Wroth, *Destruction of Troy*, sigs. F3^{v}–F4^{r} (but note that this page is incorrectly signed as E4^{r}).
21. Ibid., sigs. F3^{v}–F4^{r}.
22. Ibid., sigs. F4^{v}–G1^{r}.
23. Ibid.
24. Ibid., sig. A2^{r}.
25. Ibid., sig. G1^{r}.
26. Servius, *In Vergilii carmina*, I, p. 330.
27. Ibid., p. 328: 'MAIOR IMAGO quia umbra maior est corpore. *et per hoc mortuam vult ostendere, aut ex homine deam factam.*'
28. Landino, *Publii Virgilii*, fol. 158^{v}: 'Maior: quia divina potius q*uam* humana esset.'
29. Not all Renaissance scholars reach the same interpretation: Jodocus Badius Ascensius does not say that Creusa has become divine (*Universum poema*, fol. 180^{r}).
30. Heinze, *Virgil's Epic Technique*, pp. 36–7.
31. See Galinsky, '*Aeneid* V and the *Aeneid*', and Hershkowitz, 'The *Aeneid* in *Aeneid* 3'. See also Fowler, 'Second Thoughts on Closure', pp. 18–19.
32. Fitzmaurice, *Humanism and America*, p. 76.
33. Chamberlain, *Letters*, II, pp. 429–30.
34. Norbrook, *Poetry and Politics*, pp. 172–4.
35. Digges, *Foure Paradoxes*, p. 1.
36. Ibid., p. 40.
37. Ibid., p. 41.
38. Campbell, 'Sidney as "The Learned Soldier"', p. 175.
39. Norbrook, *Poetry and Politics*, p. 172

40. Digges, *Foure Paradoxes*, p. 79.
41. Ibid., pp. 82–3.
42. Ibid., p. 98.
43. Pocock, *Machiavellian Moment*, p. 357.
44. I rely on the discussion in Skinner, *Foundations of Modern Political Thought*, I, pp. 129–38.
45. Digges, *Foure Paradoxes*, p. 93.
46. Ibid., p. 111; *Aeneid* 2.317.
47. Chamberlain, *Letters*, I, pp. 311–12.
48. Digges, *Defence of Trade*, p. 1.
49. Ibid., p. 22.
50. See Redworth, *The Prince and the Infanta*.
51. Notestein (ed.), *Commons Debates*, II, p. 445.
52. Ibid., I, pp. 395–6.
53. Ibid., II, p. 451.
54. Ibid., III, p. 472.
55. Ibid., VI, p. 224.
56. Proudfoot, *Dryden's 'Aeneid'*, p. 107.
57. Erskine-Hill, *Poetry and the Realm of Politics*, p. 205.
58. Digges, *Didos Death*, sigs. A2^{v}, A4^{v}, A7^{v} and A7^{v}. The Latin in the Digges section of this chapter is quoted from the Latin printed on the facing pages of Digges' translation. This is one of the few occasions where we have a Latin text the translator saw, and thus I quote it here.
59. Ibid., sig. A8^{v}.
60. Ibid., sigs. B1^{v} and B2^{r}.
61. Redworth, *The Prince and the Infanta*, p. 19.
62. Ibid., p. 28.
63. Kallendorf, *In Praise of Aeneas*, p. 95.
64. Watkins, *The Specter of Dido*, p. 4.
65. Digges, *Didos Death*, sig. A11^{v}.
66. Ibid., sig. A10^{v}–A11^{v}.
67. Sandys, *Paraphrase*, sig. G6^{v}.
68. The translations from Book 1 of the *Aeneid* in *A Relation* are different from the translation of Book 1, but those in the Ovid commentary are taken directly from the translation. This suggests it must have been composed after 1615.
69. Wood, 'Beginnings', pp. 73–5. Wood's study has been explored more recently in Davis, *George Sandys*, p. 212. Whereas Book 1 of the Ovid translation contains 14 per cent unstopped lines and 1.8 per cent unstopped couplets, there is a gradual progression until Book 15 contains 29 per cent unstopped lines and 10.4 per cent unstopped couplets. Sandys's translation of Virgil contains 32 per cent unstopped lines and 10 per cent unstopped couplets.
70. For a different account of the composition date and of Sandys's translation in general, see Ellison, *George Sandys*, pp. 101–9 and pp. 172–4.
71. Sandys, *A Relation*, p. 103.
72. Haynes, *Humanist as Traveler*, p. 72
73. Ibid., p. 43.
74. Grafton, *New Worlds, Ancient Texts*, p. 157.

75. Lyne, *Ovid's Changing Worlds*, p. 239.
76. Sandys, *A Relation*, p. 20.
77. Kallendorf, *In Praise*, pp. 58–76.
78. Sandys, *A Relation*, p. 207.
79. Vickers, *In Defence of Rhetoric*, pp. 19–20.
80. Watkins, *The Specter of Dido*, p. 51.
81. See Comparetti, *Vergil in the Middle Ages*, pp. 101–2.
82. For example, when Sandys comes to Lake Avernus, he writes: 'This was supposed the entrance into hell by ignorant Antiquity: where they offered infernall sacrifice to *Pluto*, and the *Manes*, here said to give answers. For which purpose *Homer* brought hither his *Ulysses*, and *Virgil* his *Æneas*.' *A Relation*, p. 279.
83. Ibid., p. 283.
84. Ibid., p. 144.
85. Haynes, *Humanist as Traveller*, p. 134.
86. Sandys, *A Relation*, p. 284.
87. Ibid., p. 284.
88. Pearcy, *The Mediated Muse*, p. 63.
89. See Lewis, 'Francis Bacon'; Hartmann, 'Light from Darkness'.
90. Davis, *George Sandys*, p. 111.
91. Ibid., pp. 134–58, and Ellison, *George Sandys*, p. 128.
92. Davis, *George Sandys*, p. 196.
93. Ibid., p. 255.
94. Pearcy, *The Mediated Muse*, p. 82.
95. Rubin, *Sandys as Translator and Mythographer*, p. 99.
96. Lyne, *Ovid's Changing Worlds*, pp. 201–19.
97. Sandys, *Ovids Metamorphosis*, p. [vii]. This is the first page of Sandys's address 'To the Reader'.
98. Sandys, *Ovids Metamorphosis*, p. 476.
99. Sandys, *A Relation*, p. 208 and *Ovids Metamorphosis*, p. 476.
100. Sandys, *Ovids Metamorphosis*, p. 476.
101. Ibid., p. 477.
102. Fitzmaurice, *Humanism and America*, p. 65.
103. Ibid., p. 68.
104. Sandys, *Ovids Metamorphosis*, p. 162.
105. Ibid., p. [vii].
106. Ibid., pp. 477–8.
107. Ibid., p. 526.
108. Lyne, *Ovid's Changing Worlds*, p. 248.
109. Sandys, *Ovids Metamorphosis*, p. 477.
110. Ibid., p. 449.
111. Ibid., p. 478.
112. Ibid., p. 327.
113. Sandys, *Paraphrase upon the Divine Poems*, sig. G6v.
114. Hulubei, 'Virgile en France', p. 53.

Chapter 5

Rome at War: The Military Virgils of John Vicars, Robert Stapylton and Robert Heath

In previous scholarship on mid-seventeenth-century translations of the *Aeneid*, the so-called 'Augustan' Virgil has dominated the attention of critics. Starting with Ben Jonson's *Poetaster*, extending through translations by famous poets such as Sandys, Waller and Denham, and culminating in Dryden's *Complete Works of Virgil* (1697), the Augustan *Aeneid* has often been treated as the English *Aeneid* of the century.[1] The values that constitute the Augustan *Aeneid* are sometimes vague, but they cluster around three main concepts. The first is stylistic: the progressive development and refinement of English versification and the closed couplet. Augustan poetics are characterised by purity, clarity, decorum and ornament – qualities for which Virgil was the touchstone. This narrative has most recently been told by Robin Sowerby in his study *The Augustan Art of Poetry*. Second, Augustan Virgil employs this refined style to express praise and gratitude to a prince. Howard Erskine-Hill's *The Augustan Idea in English Literature* has shown how a panegyric strand of Virgilian reception developed in the seventeenth century through a new emphasis on the *pax Augusta* under the Stuart kings. In this way, Virgil's epic could become a poem primarily prophesying a stable future that was made possible through the peace preserved by the monarch. The third main aspect of the 'Augustan' *Aeneid* gained impetus from James's advice to his son in *Basilikon Doron*: that he should rule with clemency. In this tradition of royal *Aeneids*, Aeneas as the expression of royal sympathy is set in opposition to rebels against a monarchical system, who are portrayed as expressions of wrath.[2] Refined versification, gratitude for a monarchical peace and royal sympathy form the pillars of the best-known narrative in the history of Virgil reception in England. Unfortunately, the prominence of this important strand of reception has led to the erroneous impression that there is no other important line of Virgil reception in this era.

This chapter aims to show that there was another tradition of Virgil interpretation and translation of great consequence in the first half of seventeenth-century England. If George Sandys is sometimes taken as a starting point for the 'Augustan' Virgil, then Dudley Digges could be seen as the founder of this alternative tradition. According to this alternative line of reading, the *Aeneid* is a poem celebrating war and urging the nation to develop more of a military culture, rather than a poem celebrating the harmony and peace that a monarch brings. An admirable, militant Roman Empire becomes a foil to an insufferable Stuart peace, and Virgil translation becomes an activity for the opposition. I shall show that these translations tend not to seek the precision and purity of style that characterises Augustan Virgils. Instead, they offer Virgil in messier, more explorative English, stretching the language past the breaking point of decorum. This chapter will bring to light a new aspect of Virgil in seventeenth-century England by exploring three never before studied translations which appeared from 1632 to 1646: the *XII Aeneids* by John Vicars, the *Dido and Aeneas* by Sir Robert Stapylton and the manuscript 'Æneis' by Robert Heath.

A Horrible Travesty in Earnest? Providence and Parliament in John Vicars' *The XII Aeneids* (1632)

In 1662, two years after the Stuart Restoration, the royalist Samuel Butler published the first part of *Hudibras*. Towards the end, in a satiric address to the parliamentary muse, Butler scoffed at three parliamentary writers who had been active during the Civil War. The passage is worth quoting in full because it is through this address that John Vicars – the first Englishman to produce a complete translation of Virgil's *Aeneid* by himself – is today best known:

> Thou that with Ale, or viler Liquors,
> Didst inspire *Withers*, *Pryn*, and *Vickars*,
> And force them, though it was in spight
> Of nature and their stars, to write;
> Who, as we find in sullen Writs,
> And cross-grain'd Works of modern wits,
> With Vanity, Opinion, Want,
> The wonder of the Ignorant,
> The praises of the Author, penn'd
> By himself, or wit-ensuring friend,
> The Itch of Picture in the Front,
> With Bays, and wicked Rhyme upon't
> All that is left o' th' forked Hill,
> To make men scribble without skill,

Canst make a Poet spight of fate,
And teach all people to translate;
Though out of Languages in which
They understand no part of speech:
Assist me but this once, I 'mplore,
And I shall trouble thee no more.[3]

John Vicars is then singled out by an annotation, in which Butler derides him for having been a particularly irreverent and incompetent translator of Virgil's epic:

> This *Vickars* was a Man of as great Interest and Authority in the late Reformation as *Pryn*, or *Withers*, and as able a Poet; He translated *Virgils Æneids* into as horrible [a] Travesty in earnest, as the French *Scaroon* did in Burlesque, and was only out-done in his way by the Politique Author of *Oceana*.[4]

For Butler, Virgil was a poet of royalty, and Vicars, being a dissident and parliamentarian like William Prynne and George Wither, was unable to do justice to Virgil's writing. Reinforcing the connection between the supposedly inept translation and Vicars' republican politics, Butler links Vicars with the republican theorist James Harrington ('the Politique Author of *Oceana*'), who published translations of Virgil in 1658 and 1659.

This early dismissal of Vicars' *XII Aeneids* as a 'horrible Travesty in earnest' has proved a remarkably influential and enduring response. Few critics have written anything about Vicars' translation of the *Aeneid*, and those who have typically cite Butler's attack and then move on. John Conington, the great nineteenth-century Virgil commentator and translator, passed this laconic and damning judgement upon Vicars:

> The year 1632 saw a complete version of the 'Æneid' by Vicars . . . Vicars, a Parliamentary fanatic, is known to the world as a poet only by the savage lines in 'Hudibras' . . . There seems to be no merit in Vicars.[5]

More recently, in a survey of Virgil in English translation, Colin Burrow makes mention of Vicars' *XII Aeneids*. But he too simply refers to Butler's satiric judgement, commenting that Vicars was 'laughed into oblivion'.[6] It is the contention of this chapter, however, that Vicars' translation merits close attention and should be restored to its polemical place within the history of Virgil reception in seventeenth-century England. And while Butler is right to put Vicars into the context of the Civil War parliamentarians, it is misleading to take this as the primary context for this translation from 1632. As I shall argue, Vicars' *Aeneid* is first and foremost a product of the radical puritanism of the 1630s. Vicars' form of puritanism is the basis for both this translation's reading of Aeneas and its unique parliamentarian perspective on Virgilian politics. While literary histories have taught us that Virgil's *Aeneid* was usually appropriated as a royalist text in seventeenth-century English culture, no critic has so far explored why one English parliamentarian decided to translate the entirety of Virgil's epic.[7] This section will explore how Vicars came to translate the *Aeneid* as a tool of resistance in 1632.

'Virgiliae Vindiciae' in Bodleian MS. Ashmole 38

Although Samuel Butler's lines in *Hudibras* have shaped the reception of Vicars' translation, they are not the only extant seventeenth-century reply. In fact, a much more elaborate response is to be found in a Bodleian manuscript, which contains a poem entitled 'Virgiliae Vindiciae'.[8] This poem is 143 lines long, and at the end the author notes that it was 'wrighten A gainst John Vicars the Author of | the schole of Christ church=hospitall'. The writer's identity is unknown, but the poem is signed by the initials E. C. The 'Virgiliae Vindiciae' is a fascinating testament to the contemporary reception of Vicars' *Aeneids*: it exhibits the sort of ire that his translation could provoke. As it is also a well thought-out response, it offers a fitting place to begin a fresh look at Vicars' translation.

Internal evidence suggests this poem was most likely written sometime between 1637 and the early years of the 1640s. Robert Cummings, who included a small portion of the 'Virgiliae Vindiciae' in *Edmund Spenser: The Critical Heritage*, wrote that the poem 'must immediately postdate [Vicars'] *XII Aeneids of Virgil* (1632)'.[9] In a part of the poem Cummings does not quote, however, E. C. addresses Ben Jonson and implores him to rise from his grave and scourge Vicars: he exclaims to Jonson that this outrageous translation 'would rayse thy troubled dust from grave a gayne' (100). It is thus quite clear that the poem was written after the death of Ben Jonson in 1637. It is more difficult to establish a *terminus ante quem*, but there are at least two substantial pieces of evidence. First, all of the poem's references to people and places seem to be pre-1640: the poem alludes to popular, early seventeenth-century figures such as Tom Coryat, Martin Parker and John Trundle with an easy familiarity. And second, there is not a single reference to the Civil War in which Vicars was polemically involved from the early 1640s onwards. The evidence thus points towards a date of composition sometime between 1637 and 1642. As such, the poem is a more contemporary response to Vicars' translation than Butler's *Hudibras* and affords a glimpse of how Vicars' work was received early on.

At the heart of the 'Virgiliae Vindiciae', there is a contrast between two types of authors. One type is set out in a series of three invocations to Virgil, Spenser and Jonson. Each of these laureate poets is asked to rise up from his grave and seek retribution against Vicars for the harm he has done to their royal art. Virgil is described as the 'Prince of Latin Bardes' (40) and Jonson as the 'prince of English scenicks' (103). Spenser is represented as having received the 'Mantuan gemms' (84) with which he embellished 'th'embroydred robes of thy blest Fayrie Queen' (86). The second group, in contrast, includes the balladeers, popular authors and hack-writers of London. This group features figures such as Martin Parker, the balladeer and tavern keeper, and John Trundle, an infamous dealer in ephemeral literature and a tavern-keeper as well. In this twofold division, Vicars is situated in the second category and is thus made the subject of mockery: he had no business handling Virgil. Towards the end of the poem, for example, E. C. exclaims, 'Parker washe thou his brayne in Trundells ale' (125). E. C. likewise writes that because Vicars dared to assault one of the muses, he 'deserves noe other than the Bridewel pay' (28). In 1629 Martin Parker was brought before the Bridewell governors in London and accused as a balladeer and vagrant; it is likely that E. C. alludes to this episode. In a striking couplet which comes at the end of the poem, E. C. then exclaims: 'Oh . . . that I had some Furyes snakye curle | wch In thy face I might wth Vengeance hurle' (140–1). This couplet is an allusion to the end of the *Aeneid*, when Jupiter hurls a Fury, wreathed with 'serpentum spiris' ('snaky coils') (12.848), into the face of Turnus. E. C. presents himself as Jupiter striking down Vicars so that the proper hereditary line can flourish. Virgil, Spenser and Jonson represent the proper lineage; Vicars represents an illegitimate claimant to the poetic throne.

Like the scathing lines in *Hudibras*, the 'Virgiliae Vindiciae' is a bitter attack upon Vicars' translation. In fact, it is even more brutal than Butler's and shows that Vicars' translation was extremely controversial from the moment it appeared. But whereas Butler tarnishes Vicars by associating him with the Civil War parliamentarians Wither and Prynne, E. C. suggests another disreputable context: the popular hack-writers of London. E. C. tells Vicars, 'th; art a translatour in the vulgar phrase' (34), and the word 'vulgar' is especially resonant. As we shall see, there is much justification for this association, and it dovetails into the later satiric verses by Butler.

Englands Hallelu-jah: The Context of Vicars' *XII Aeneids*, 1617–31

By 1632, Vicars' output was already prolific. But for all the quantity that he produced, there are only a few major themes that dominate his publications from 1617 through to the 1650s. The most prominent of these themes is a virulent strain of anti-Catholicism. Vicars' first major publication was *Mischeefes Mysterie*, a translation of a Latin poem by Francis Herring chronicling the Gun Powder Plot. The tone of this translation is struck on the title page, where it states that the plot was 'invented by hellish malice, prevented by heavenly mercy'. In a preface dedicating the translation to the mayor of London, Vicars warns that 'the deluge of destruction intended by the barbarous butchers of Rome' is universal and thus still relevant to Londoners.[10] In 1619, Vicars then translated selected epigrams of John Owen. He included several of Owen's sharply anti-Catholic pieces such as one he titles 'Against the Romish Catholike'.[11] Continuing with this pattern, in 1624 Vicars published *Babels Balm, or The Honey-Combe of Romes Religion*, a translation of ten satires by George Goodwin against the various ills of the Roman Catholic Church. The first satire mocks 'the Popes Supremacie', the second 'the Authoritie of the Pope of Rome', the third the Catholic 'Interpretation of Scriptures', and so on.[12] This antipathy to Catholicism was to pervade Vicars' writing all the way through the Civil War. At the same time as Vicars was composing histories of the Civil War parliaments, he was publishing short, polemical tracts such as *Behold Romes Monster on his Monstrous Beast!* and *A Looking-Glasse for Malignants, or Gods Hand against God-Haters*. Before 1632, Vicars published only one work that was not stridently anti-Catholic, *A Prospective Glasse to Looke into Heaven* (1618), which was an attempt to describe and map the New Jerusalem.[13] In this poem, Vicars describes such spectacles as the second coming, the walls of the New Jerusalem, the foundations of the city, the twelve gates, the golden streets, the tree of life and the rivers of honey.[14] The poem fits into Vicars' form of apocalyptic puritanism, but it is unusual for its relative lack of polemic.

It is thus not surprising that the main references to Virgil's *Aeneid* in Vicars' writing before 1630 all share in his controversial and anti-Catholic outlook. The most substantial, and significant, reference comes in the 'Epistle Dedicatory' to his first publication, *Mischeefes Mystery*, the translation of *Pietas pontificia* by Francis Herring. Writing about the tragedy of the Gun Powder Plot, Vicars laments:

> Such an endlesse boundlesse extent of greevous aggravations, that I might with the sorrowfull Trojan Prince, *Infandos renovare dolores, & totos vos in lachrymas resolvere*, Tell you such a wofull tale as might with the Prophet Jeremy turne your heads into fountaines of teares: for *Quis talia fando* (*nisi Papista crudelis*) *temperet a lachrymis*, none doubtlesse but the *Pharaonicall* hard-hearted Papist could choose but be exceedingly sorrowfull thereat.[15]

Vicars adapts verses from the opening of Book 2 of the *Aeneid*, when Aeneas begins to tell the tragic story of the fall of Troy to Dido and the Carthaginians. But Vicars changes the second of the Virgilian quotations by interjecting 'nisi Papista crudelis'. The Papists are thus conflated together with the duplicitous Greeks, while the English Protestants are represented by the pious Trojan prince. The poem by Francis Herring contains many Virgilian allusions and frequently makes this connection as well. Guy Fawkes is stirred up by an Allecto sent by the Catholic Church ('Alecto be thy guide'[16]) in an incident that mirrors Juno's stirring up the Latins in Book 7 of the *Aeneid*. Fawkes is then compared to '*Bi-lingued Sinon*' from Book 2 of the *Aeneid*.[17] The poem wonders, 'Oh is it possible such wrath should rest, | In Romes un-erring Popes most sacred brest?',[18] which reworks Virgil's famous question pertaining to Juno: 'tantaene animis caelestibus irae?' The Gun Powder Plot is even compared to the Greek men in the Trojan horse, since the Catholics also operated 'with Grecian craft'.[19] Throughout the poem, however, Virgil himself is regarded as an ethical marvel. At the beginning of the second part of *Mischeefes Mystery*, the poem asks, who could cleanse the current age of sin? The answer is 'Nay non (unlesse we could from death recall, | And cause the Ghost of *Virgil* to appeare)'.[20] What Vicars does in his 'Epistle' is thus to apply the same connections that he found in Francis Herring's reception of the *Aeneid*. In this early work, Vicars develops a polemical message out of the epic, which portrays the piety and righteousness of a whole nation battling a Catholic threat.

This mode of using Virgil to reinforce anti-Catholicism comes up again in Vicars' most original poetic effort, *Englands Hallelu-jah, or Great Brittaines Gratefull Retribution, for Gods Gratious Benediction*. Published in 1631 and thus contemporaneous with his Virgil translation, this poem is especially significant for a reading of the *XII Aeneids* in its original context. *Englands Hallelu-jah* offers a highly partisan view of English history from the time of the Reformation onwards. It relates in 145 stanzas what Vicars thought about Caroline England and its immediate past. Alexandra Walsham, in *Providence in Early Modern England*, has sketched out the religious context within which we must place this text. Walsham has shown that in the late Jacobean period there developed a full industry of works commemorating God's benevolence to England: an 'ever-widening range of publications gave expression to [an] intoxicating mixture of jingoism, xenophobia, and anti-popery welded together by providentialism'.[21] By the time we reach the late 1620s and early 1630s, this edgy providential discourse was becoming ever more factious and ever more polemical.[22] Moreover, by 1629, the shift in religious orthodoxy was 'clearly biting in London',[23] where Vicars was working as a schoolmaster at Christ Church Hospital. He was evidently astonished by the turn of events and the rising status of new Arminian leaders. In *England's Hallelu-jah*, England is portrayed as a nation chosen by God for glory. But, according to Vicars, the times were rapidly changing, because England had been obstinately ungrateful. God's patience had been tested, as England had left God waiting, 'each day, weeke, moneth, yea Yeare by yeare expecting | Thy due *Conversion*'.[24]

In 1631, Vicars was extremely anxious about the course the nation was taking. The years of Elizabeth's reign were England's halcyon days, and Vicars was eager to restore their glory:

> Witnesse, o ever witnesse, may those dayes,
> Those *Halcyon-Dayes* of sweet *Eliza's* Raigne;
> *Eliza*, worth *Englands* endlesse praise,
> That *Friend* to *Faith*, That *Scourge* to *Rome*, & *Spaine*:
> All *present*, *past*, and *future* Ages *Glorie*,
> Worth prime *Place* and *Grace* in datelesse Storie.[25]

During the age of Elizabeth, the English were tested by the Spanish Armada, but God's special providence protected them. Indeed, the defeat of the Armada marked the miraculous high point of Elizabeth's years.[26] In Vicars' narrative, God's favour remained with the English for a time after Elizabeth's death. The Gun Powder Plot was a key moment, when 'our supernall *Isre'ls Shepheard* good . . . Close by us (by his *Providence*) then, stood'.[27] God also protected England during the years of the Spanish Match, when a Catholic threat loomed large once again. Vicars describes this incident using the metaphor of the Trojan horse, the same metaphor that is applied to the Gun Powder Plot in *Mischeefes Mystery*:

> Some *Troian-Horse*, by *Spaines Pelasgan Art*,
> With sacred shew, our Kingdome might have entred;
> A *Spanish Fleet* (at least) t'uphold the part,
> Of urged Reformation had bin ventred:
> A *Fleet* (I saw) full fraught with arm'd protection,
> To bring the *Puritans* to due subjection.[28]

However, Spain's deceptive, Grecian methods were thwarted by God and their plans to prevent England from aiding the King and Queen of Bohemia were foiled. For a short time longer, England remained in God's favour.

But the times were changing, because England continued to prove unfaithful: 'but, how unthankefull, *England*, hast Thou bin, | For *These*, *all these*, *Gods* Mercies unto *Thee*?'[29] While Vicars praises Queen

Elizabeth profusely, he offers no such compliments to either King James or King Charles. England had recently been afflicted by the plague as a punishment, but it had still not converted. Vicars commemorates the public fast (a subject which caused great tension between King Charles and the more zealous puritans[30]) held on 2 August 1626, but since then there had been no more signs of conversion. As a consequence, Vicars prophesies that grave terrors would soon come to England: 'but, oh, o woe, I tremble to relate it!'[31] He rebukes his nation with the strongest rhetoric he can muster: 'O *England*, *England*, call to mind these things, | Recant, repent, thy great *Ingratitude*.'[32] In 1631, Vicars was clearly aggrieved at the course England was taking.

What exactly did Vicars hope to see happen? A glance forward to 1641 suggests an answer. In that year, after the parliament had been reconvened, Vicars published a short poem with the title *Englands Remembrancer, or A Thankfull Acknowledgement of Parliamentary Mercies to Our English-Nation*, which closely echoes the language of *Englands Hallelu-jah*. Vicars asks all Christians to see 'How, though two former Parliaments were broke, | A third is cal'd, hopefull to strike the stroke | Of blessed reformation.'[33] The words which previously Vicars had only applied to the reign of Queen Elizabeth, he applies to their current time: 'O, who cannot these Halcyon-dayes admire, | And with enflamed Zeale be set on fire.'[34] The recalling of the strongly Calvinist parliament and the possibility of eradicating Catholicism from England satisfy the conversion that Vicars was calling for in his providential poem in 1631. And it is thus in this context – with Vicars eagerly waiting for a full, puritan reformation of English hearts – that one must approach his translation of the *Aeneid*.

Providence and Parliament in *The XII Aeneids of Virgil*

In the early 1630s, England produced a few major responses to Virgil's epic. It is revealing to contrast Vicars' *The XII Aeneids of Virgil* (1632) with works such as George Sandys's 'The First Booke of Virgils Æneis' (1632) and Alexander Ross's *Virgilius Evangelisans* (1634). Even just comparing the dedications, Vicars' *Aeneids* stands out. The other two are both dedicated to King Charles, whom they endorse as a glorious English Augustus. Sandys addresses Charles as 'the Poets Theame and Patron; who at will | Canst adde t'Augustus Scepter Maro's Quill'.[35] In a Latin prefatory poem, Sandys also hails Charles as 'Augustissimo Carolo' and 'Cæsar Britannice'.[36] Ross likewise dedicates his cento 'ad Augustissimum Carolum Magnæ Britanniaæ, &c. Monarcham'.[37] In the accompanying poem, adapting verses from the *Georgics*, Ross writes, '*Virgilium* Cæsar *dilexit; dilige nostrum* | Carole, *Virgilium; sic mihi* Cæsar *eris*' ('Caesar loved Virgil: may you love my Virgil, Charles; thus you will be Caesar to me').[38] Ross suggests that poetry flourishes through the support of kings ('Regibus illa virent'[39]) and even places Charles in the position of Jupiter, as father of the Ausonian chorus.[40] In contrast, Vicars does not directly mention Charles but instead dedicates his work to George, John and Bernhard Stewart, three young boys of Katherine Stewart, the Duchess of Lenox. Vicars presents his translation as an educational tool for noble youths rather than as a piece honouring the king.

The place where Vicars' difference from Sandys and Ross comes through most pervasively, however, is in the language and style of the translation. As has been noted, Sandys marks the beginning of a line of translators of Virgil who worked in an austere, compressed and Latinate English.[41] Vicars' style places him outside of this developing tradition. Indeed, Vicars' translation is marked by its lively indecorum. He does not adhere to any single tone or register and Colin Burrow's word 'ramshackle' is a good one to describe his work. Vicars employs a style in which Latinisms and Englishisms, quaint diction and exaggeratedly ornate diction jumble for space on a single page. This exuberance is the source of both the absurdities that have exasperated critics and the occasional gems that can be found throughout. In *Dryden's 'Aeneid' and Its Seventeenth-Century Predecessors*, Leslie Proudfoot remarked that Vicars is very remote from the 'Augustans', but suggested that his writing is 'less simple'.[42] Vicars' verse has 'something quaint, farouche and excessive' about it, since he treats 'language as if it were still plastic'.[43] Vicars will not be bound to the single line or the couplet as a formal element, but rather looks to looser formal principles: alliteration, assonance and often internal rhyme.[44] All things considered, Proudfoot passed a favourable judgement upon Vicars' experiment, which he deemed eccentric but spirited.[45] And it is indeed worth emphasising that Vicars does have some artistic qualities, however unusual they may be. One will not find another translator of Virgil in the seventeenth century producing bees, for instance, that buzz so gleefully: 'like busie-buzing bees in flowery May, | Working most nimbly in a sun-shine day'.[46]

One way of exploring the stylistic range that Vicars exhibits is to consider a few examples of his malleable language. There are several words in Vicars' translation he coined himself.[47] Some of these words are overtly Latinate. He creates the word 'aequiparate'[48] to render 'eruam et aequa solo fumantia culmina ponam' (12.569) ('I will overthrow and lay its smoking roofs level with the ground'). Much like the words 'concomitate', 'obtestate', 'denudate' or 'properate' (all of which Vicars is fond of using[49]), this word is almost a direct borrowing from the Latin. Vicars also seems to have created for himself the word 'ignipotent', which is his rendering of 'ignipotens' (8.414), one of Vulcan's epithets.[50] On the other hand, he also created words that have a much less Latinate air. For 'bacchatur' (4.301), he creates the colourful word 'drunkard-ize',[51] and, for the anchors that hold the Trojan ships, he creates the adjective 'fangy'.[52] Vicars often uses exaggerated 'Englishisms', such as referring to food as 'heps and haws'.[53] There is thus an exceptionally wide range of verbal innovation. Another instance of this lexical creativeness appears in his habit of combining words to create new adjectives or onomatopoeic phrases. In Vicars' *Aeneids*, sailors can be 'sea-tired', a corpse 'lightning-half-burn'd', a man 'mischief-minded', a mouth 'gore-bloud-gushing', a strike 'thunder-smart' or a groan 'heart-string-breaking'.[54] This *Aeneid* contains 'bouncing blows', 'tinkering strokes', 'thumping thwacks', 'tinckling tangs', 'wringling wreathes', 'frisks and skips' and 'ratling roaring'.[55] It is perhaps most indicative of the indecorousness of Vicars' translation that these 'thumping thwacks' and the word 'ignipotent' can appear on the same opening.[56]

This style of translating Virgil becomes more significant in the context of a particular group of seventeenth-century translations of the *Aeneid*. If the austere, classical *Aeneid*s make up one line of seventeenth-century Virgil reception, I would argue that the less decorous Virgils of Dudley Digges and John Vicars are part of another side of the tradition, which generally flourished among militarists in the 1620s and 1630s. Later in the seventeenth century, the republican James Harrington, while he does not rely directly on Vicars, refers to 'the Thunder-thumping way of Grandsire Virgil', a phrase which David Norbrook states would have been 'liable to cause offence'.[57] It seems to me likely, however, that Vicars would have thought the adjective 'thunder-thumping' quite appropriate. Proudfoot described Harrington's translation as 'licentious' and 'promiscuous', and he suggested that it was an eccentricity like Digges's *Didos Death* (1622). I would go a step further and argue that we should see Digges and Vicars not simply as randomly eccentric translators of Virgil but as a group of often provocative, oppositional readers of the *Aeneid*.

The different parliamentarian readings by Digges and Vicars are united by a perspective on the *Aeneid* that sees the epic as a poem of war. They urge their nation to abandon a peace that (for different reasons) threatens England's greatness. The same motivation will lie behind the oppositional reading of Robert Stapylton, although he is not an advocate of parliament. The Stuart supporter Stapylton will tie in with Vicars and Digges in so far as he wishes that King Charles I would return to military action. Finally, I will suggest that this tradition of Virgil translation proved productive even for the staunch royalist Robert Heath whose 'Æneis' can be described as a royalist emulation of Vicars' military reading of the *Aeneid*.

It is evident from Vicars' translation of Book 4 that he had read Digges's *Didos Death* and that he appreciated his predecessor's colourful choices of words. Vicars follows Digges in referring to Dido's sister, Anna, as 'Nan'.[58] Digges, Vicars and Heath, who used *Didos Death* and the *XII Aeneids* as sources, are the only English translators in the sixteenth and seventeenth centuries who domesticated Anna's name in this casual manner. On the very next page, Vicars echoes an idiosyncratic choice of diction that Digges alone had made at this specific point. Digges refers to the temples that Dido visits as a 'holy Church'. Vicars, who nowhere else in his *Aeneids* translates 'templum' with this word, renders these temples as a 'church': 'then to church they go'.[59] For one more example we can turn to another highly idiosyncratic point in Digges's translation. This moment comes when, at the end of Jupiter's command for Aeneas to leave Carthage, Digges translates Jupiter's majestic 'naviget: hic summa est' (4.237) as 'Get him to sea, that's all'. Vicars, in turn, translates these words, 'Let him to sea: here's all'.[60] How different this style is from the early Augustan verse of Sidney Godolphin: 'This message to the Phrygian Prince convay, | And bid him hoise his sayles.'[61] If the Augustan translators of the seventeenth century were keen to make Virgil adhere to linguistic decorum, the parliamentarian translators were more open to translating the *Aeneid* in various tones and registers. In his own words, Vicars does not hesitate to dress Virgil in 'a home-spun english gray-coat plain'.[62]

But what did this London schoolmaster with a fervent belief in providential puritanism find in Virgil in the 1630s? As is clear from our look at *Englands Hallelu-jah* of 1631, John Vicars was inspired by a particularly hot form of providential zeal at the same time that he was translating Virgil. In the dedicatory poem, he claims that his translation is fit to promote 'learning, vertue, grace and godlinesse' in its young readers.[63] The final two of these qualities are especially interesting. Providence, piety and the gods are all prominent themes in the *Aeneid*; not surprisingly, these themes are especially foregrounded in Vicars' translation. Even though he is occasionally perturbed by the poetic licence Virgil takes with the gods, it seems that Vicars saw in Virgil the hazy outlines of puritan belief, with an emphasis on providence and individual duty.

In his translation Vicars is typically content to understand Virgilian 'fatum' as an expression of Christian providence. These two ideas were sometimes conflated in the Renaissance reception of Virgil, such as in the commentary by Sir John Harington who wrote, '*the fates* wear vnderstood by the Pagans [as] the gods decrees not vnlyke to that wch Christians call predestinacion'.[64] Harington's source for this opinion might have been St Augustine's *De civitate Dei*, in which the church father states:

> Without any doubt, it is by divine providence that human kingdoms are set up. If any one ascribes them to 'fate' because he uses that term for the will or power of God, let him maintain his conviction but correct his language.[65]

Another example from the Renaissance can be found in Chapter 13 of Philippe de Mornay's *A Woorke Concerning the Trewnesse of the Christian Religions*, in which de Mornay explains that pagans 'also easely perceived the Providence', although they may have lacked specific terminology or understanding.[66] Even more than in Harington's translation, however, in *The XII Aeneids of Virgil* the distinctions between the poetic gods, fate, predestination and providence are often completely elided. This can be seen in how Vicars frequently translates 'deus' as 'fate' or even as what the gods 'destinate': he frequently will substitute personified, pagan gods for an abstract principle of destiny or providence.[67]

Making such a substitution is of course not always easy in Virgil's epic. And Vicars seems to have discovered this in the act of translating. Sometimes, Virgilian gods behave mischievously and cruelly.[68] As Denis Feeney has eloquently explained, there is no one single trope that can encapsulate them.[69] When Vicars came across Virgilian gods behaving inappropriately (and thus when he could not combine them with a serious conception of destiny), he tends to remove their divine status. When Fama is spreading malicious reports about Dido and Aeneas in Book 4, Vicars translates Virgil's phrase 'dea foeda' (195) as 'godlesse Goddesse'.[70] Caelano, the harpy who curses Aeneas in Book 3, is never referred to as a possible god in Vicars. And the most interesting case is Vicars' treatment of the Furies in the second half of the *Aeneid*. Allecto is frequently referred to in Virgil as a 'dea'. Vicars seems to have felt this was inappropriate. To avoid bestowing upon them any role within the poem's conception of divinity, Vicars systematically translates them as 'hellish hags' (a phrase he picked up from Thomas Phaer, who uses it on occasion).[71] But when the final, fatal Fury appears before Turnus' face, he was posed with a conundrum. Could a hellish hag decide the outcome of this morally edifying epic and be the instrument of providence? Modern critics tend to regard this scene as either a final sign of Virgil's ambivalence towards the Roman Empire, or at very least a sign of his acknowledgement of the paradox that the Roman Empire used violence in the cause of order.[72] Vicars, however, creates moral clarity. And so his translations reads: 'Thus 'twas with *Turnus*, where his power was bent, | Fierce fates made all his facts in vain be spent.'[73] Here, 'fierce fates' is a translation of 'dea dira' (12.914). This is the first and only time Vicars does not translate 'dea' referring to a Fury as 'hag'. Instead, the final appearance of the Fury is as Fate itself. Vicars changes his mode of translation at the very end of the epic in order to sustain his vision of the role destiny plays in the poem – everything takes place under its careful eye.

The providential tone of this translation is set early on with the character of Aeneas. In Book 1, when Aeneas meets his mother in the forests near Carthage, he introduces himself with a word that is rich in Christian overtones: 'I a poore pilgrim range through Libyan woods, | From Europe, Asia forc'd.'[74] These lines translate the Latin, 'ipse ignotus, egens, Libyae deserta peragro, | Europa atque Asia pulsus' (1.384–5). This image of Aeneas as a quasi-Christian pilgrim is then reinforced throughout the first book. When Aeneas is encouraging his followers to endure, he delivers the famous line, 'sunt lacrimae rerum et mentem mortalia tangunt' (1.462). Vicars translates these words as 'These are materiall teares, crosses come neare'.[75] In a moment of overt Christian moralising, Vicars' Aeneas informs his followers that their tears are merely worldly. The Trojans will have to carry their burdens like Christ in order to fulfil the divine will. They are thus engaged in a sort of *imitatio Christi*. As to what they are heading towards, Vicars gives us a hint in Jupiter's prophecy, which announces that, in the end, the world shall be governed by Christian values: 'pure Faith and Pietie, *Remus* and's brother | Shall reigne, give laws, & warres rage smoothly smother'.[76] This translates 'cana Fides et Vesta, Remo cum fratre Quirinus | iura dabunt; dirae ferro et compagibus artis | claudentur Belli portae' (1.292–4). Vicars' first line here reveals a bit of his puritanism, as he veers slightly away from the original. Whereas George Sandys's translation stresses the Latinate names, '*Faith*, *Vesta*, *Romulus* with *Remus*', Vicars' rendition provides a glimpse into the less ceremonial and more spiritual perspective he brings to Virgil's *Aeneid*. Instead of a personified virtue and a Roman goddess, Vicars has Protestant values destined to rule.

In most translations of the *Aeneid* the word 'pius' can serve as an indicator for the translator's views on Virgil's epic.[77] Vicars is aware of the wide semantic range that the Latin word can cover. He is aware, for instance, that both 'piety' and 'pity' derive from and are contained in the same Latin word, as is shown when he renders a single 'pietas' into both of these English nouns: 'pietas nec mitigat ulla' (5.783) becomes 'Nor piety or pity stops or stayes'.[78] Elsewhere, he employs a wide range of terms: 'brave', 'grave', 'great', 'honest', 'pious', 'fillial' and 'Kinde' are all words he will use to render this most distinctive of Aeneas' epithets.[79] The translation he uses most often, however, is the unostentatious English 'good'.[80] What Vicars means by 'good' becomes clearest in one passage in Book 3, which is the only time in the whole poem that he elaborates the word 'pius' into a full phrase: 'Great Gods (sayes he) spare threats, avert these ills, | Appeased, save good men that do your wills.'[81] This phrase, 'good men that do your wills', comes out of the single word, 'pios'. Vicars makes his hero foremost an obedient servant of the gods and an agent of providence. In this role, Aeneas seems to be an unproblematic and wholly admirable character in Vicars' translation. Moreover, 'good' avoids markedly royalist overtones. The simplicity of the word 'good' suggests that Vicars found in the *Aeneid* a quality that could be approached by all men who read the poem, and not only by princes. It shifts the poem to a more approachable level.

This shift is especially important because Vicars did not consider the *Aeneid* a poem glorifying an absolute monarch but rather a poem representing a society of mixed monarchies.[82] And it is in this vision that he seems to have been most provocative. In Book 9 of the *Aeneid*, the Latins convene at King Latinus' palace to discuss what course they should take in light of their heavy losses. Turnus wants to keep fighting; Drances and King Latinus are pleading for a truce. At the moment when this meeting is about to take place, Vicars introduces a particularly suggestive word into his translation:

> The Gods great wrath, and graves fresh 'fore their eyes,
> Made them conclude, *Æneas* enterprise
> Fatall to be, and with heavens cleare consent;
> Therefore in haste they call a parliament.
> Straight all the empires Peeres are call'd to court,
> And thither with huge confluence resort.[83]

The word 'concilium' (11.234) becomes 'parliament' in Vicars' English. This word then comes up again in the same book, when Turnus says bitterly to Drances, 'Thou wilt be foremost at a parliament',[84] where 'parliament' this time is a translation of 'patribusque vocatis' (11.379). Vicars took his clue for reading the *Aeneid* in this manner from the translation by Thomas Phaer and Thomas Twyne. In their work, the word 'parliament' is occasionally used to render the senates and courts of Troy, Carthage and Latium,[85] and Vicars even reproduces the word 'parliament' in an 'argument' exactly where Twyne did.[86] But whereas the word 'parliament' was not a loaded word for Phaer or Twyne and was incorporated as a matter of metrical convenience, in Vicars the word is used much more systematically and takes on a new ideological relevance in the context of the 1630s. King Latinus' court (and his court alone) turns out to be a functioning parliament over which Latinus presides. What Latinus rules over is certainly a monarchy, but the elders are a respected, parliamentary body, even if the haughty Turnus should seek to override their voices. The significance of this should not be underestimated: in the *Aeneid* the Trojans bring their gods to Italy, but they are fated to accept the name, language and *laws* of the Latin people. 'I'le guide you to the Gods and sacred rites', says Aeneas in Vicars' English, but the Latins shall still have their 'soveraigntie'.[87] Vicars thus finds in Virgil's vision of early Rome an example of a functioning parliament – albeit a parliament dangerously close to falling apart because of internal tensions.

A corresponding and corroborating episode is the council of the gods at the beginning of Book 10. For here Vicars uses the same word to describe the gathering of the gods themselves. 'The Gods convoke a parliament',[88] the argument to Book 10 proclaims. At the close of the council, 'hic finis fandi' (10.116) becomes 'here ceast the parle of all the Gods assembled'.[89] It is thus not only the destined mortal sphere that operates within the model of a mixed monarchy. Jupiter in Virgil is presented as 'the one who has the first power of things' ('rerum cui prima potestas', 10.100). Vicars interprets these words as referring to Jupiter's specific position within the parliamentary gathering: '*Jupiter* then, who had prime power to speak'.[90] As the 'aeterna potestas' (10.16), Jupiter fills the role of 'the mightie moderatour, wise, eternall'.[91] The politics of Vicars' *XII Aeneids* thus stand out sharply from the politics of the other major translations of the *Aeneid* in the early 1630s. Vicars' translation, like the others, likens the power and structure of the gods to the power and structure of the Roman state. [92] But the political imagery that envelops this equivalence between the divine cosmos and the human *imperium* is different from the absolute royalist imagery of the Augustan tradition of translating Virgil. Vicars' *Aeneids* present a picture of mixed monarchies and active parliaments operating at both human and divine levels of the cosmos.

In the letter to his readers, Vicars had described his concern in translating the *Aeneid* as 'especially the common good and publick utility, which I hoped might accrew to young schollars and grammaticall *Tyroes*'.[93] His dedication to three young men who were not princes further emphasises the point of 'common good' which Vicars claims here as his purpose. Instead of glorifying and encouraging an absolute prince, as one typically finds in the Augustan translations of this period, Vicars provocatively uses the *Aeneid* to provide a model for active members of a godly society. And as such, Vicars' translation deserves recognition as a major translation of Virgil's *Aeneid* which appeared on the eve of the Civil War. His work shows that the middle of the seventeenth century was not a period solely of royalist *Aeneids* and that one of the major English translations of Virgil from this period is the work of a committed puritan and parliamentarian. Above, we witnessed E. C. attacking Vicars' translation primarily because it was too common; for Vicars, however, the 'publick utility' of his poem was precisely its purpose. He creates an English Aeneas who is simply 'good' and who can offer a model for all young Englishmen in pursuit of godliness. For such young scholars, Vicars' Aeneas was to represent an impeccable, active member of a parliamentary nation destined by God for great things. He is an agent of providence, at a time when Vicars felt the English nation was not fulfilling its divine course.

Arms and the Man, or Merchandise and the Woman? Robert Stapylton's *Dido and Aeneas*

Much like John Vicars' complete *Aeneid*, Robert Stapylton's translation of Book 4 has been the object of more derision than study. The critics who have opened Stapylton's *Dido and Aeneas* have remarked on the exceptional literalness of the work, which manages to match Virgil's Latin line by line in English.[94] The condensed result, however, has generally not been admired. Proudfoot described the translation as 'straining after literal compactness', which gives the impression of crudity, congestion and rapidity.[95] Robin Sowerby has remarked that 'the best that can be said about Stapylton's version is that it is easier to read and understand than that of Vicars',[96] and he describes Stapylton's rendition as 'another lame version'.[97] In the history of early Augustan Virgils, Stapylton's translation is not afforded a place, unless perhaps as a foil against which the balanced and harmonious closed-couplets can stand out advantageously. In an account of oppositional translations of Virgil in the early seventeenth century, however, *Dido and Aeneas* occupies an important position and can be fruitfully considered alongside the translations by Sir Dudley Digges and John Vicars.

One of the mistakes in previous approaches to Stapylton's translation is that it has often been regarded as a private work written by a nobleman to amuse or console other nobles.[98] For example, in the *ODNB* article on Stapylton, L. G. Kelly has suggested that that translation was undertaken to console Lady Catherine Twisleton of Barley, whose husband died in 1635. The dates, however, do not line up with this scenario, as the translation was entered in the Stationers' Register in 1634. Moreover, since Book 4 tells the story of an abandoned lady who commits suicide out of despair, it seems an inappropriate choice to send to a grieving woman. Instead, I argue that the Stapylton translation of Book 4 is a predominantly political work. Book 4 of the *Aeneid* may have gained its exceptional popularity for its portrayal of a love affair, but its political implications were often just as important for early modern readers. As Wilson-Okamura has noted, Book 4 offered a description of one of the two colonial states in the *Aeneid* to which Renaissance authors responded.[99] Most commentators also regarded this book as the most *useful* piece of work by Virgil. The influential Pontanus edition of the *Aeneid* cites Maioragius, noting 'although all the books by this author are extremely useful, Book 4 is the most useful of all'.[100] The book was especially valuable because it portrayed the greatest challenges to virtue and to the state. The love story was not admired in private terms in most Renaissance commentaries, but rather because it weighed the competing demands of personal desire and public duty. It also treated the very foundations of a commonwealth, since Dido is just setting out to establish Carthage. Donatus makes this explicit when he writes that Dido loved Aeneas in large part because he was 'necessary to her, as she was building a new state and desiring to strengthen the new foundations of an empire'.[101] In *Didos Death*, we have already witnessed how a translation of Book 4 could appeal to a topical political moment. In this section, we will consider another way that a translation of Book 4 was brought to comment upon contemporary English politics.

Stapylton is unique among the early modern English translators of the *Aeneid* because he offers his own allegorising interpretation in the 'Preface'. In Stapylton's account, Book 4 becomes a self-contained entity, not as a love story, but as a political allegory.[102]

> If any should question him for the *truth* of *History*, the verse is transparent, they may onely intend their sight, and looke quite through the *Fained worke*: and in the Founders of the *Carthaginian* and *Roman* Empires *Dido* and *Aeneas*, they shall read the mysteries of their *Foundations*, the *Fœminine* and *Masculine* governements of those two great Citties, by *Merchandise*, and *Armes*; And if it be a fiction that *Aeneas* ever saw *Dido*, it is true that *Rome* fell into the power of *Carthage*, till by a Faction growing in the bosome of this State, it was perswaded, like a love-sicke Lady, to trust it self in the armes and imbrace of *Rome*, that would seeme commanded by *Fate* to breake all mutuall tyes; till cursing the *Roman* false-hood, the reputation and spirit of poore *Carthage* glided into winde.[103]

Dido and Aeneas are treated as allegories of their respective cities and their opposing value systems. Much like modern critics such as David

Quint, who find contrasting sets of values throughout the *Aeneid*, Stapylton found two discrepant approaches to commonwealths in Book 4.[104] Aeneas, representing Rome, portrayed a masculine state built upon military prowess; on the other hand, Dido, representing Carthage, portrayed a feminine state that was built upon merchandise. As Carthage eventually fell to Rome, the allegory stresses how Rome's military power was ultimately superior to the commercial enterprises of Carthage. Stapylton's reading of Book 4 thus fits into the militarist reception of the *Aeneid* that I have explored in the oppositional translations by Digges and Vicars. Reading the *Aeneid* as a poem in defence of military affairs was a central strand of the epic's reception among translators in the early seventeenth century.

The ultimate sources of Stapylton's allegory are Polybius and Cicero, who both contrasted the values of Carthage and Rome. In these accounts Carthage is portrayed as a precarious state which relied upon its commercial and maritime strengths. Instead of building on its own people's valour, as the Romans did, the Carthaginians used mercenary and foreign armies. Polybius offered the following account:

> They indeed devote their whole energies to [military service on land], whereas the Carthaginians entirely neglect their infantry, though they do pay some slight attention to their cavalry. The reason of this is that the troops they employ are foreign and mercenary, whereas those of the Romans are natives of the soil and citizens. So that in this respect also we must pronounce the political system of Rome to be superior to that of Carthage, the Carthaginians continuing to depend for the maintenance of their freedom on the courage of a mercenary force but the Romans on their own valour and on the aid of their allies.[105]

Cicero agreed with this analysis, noting how the distractions of commerce undermined Carthage's military pursuits and promoted luxury instead:

> In fact, no other influence did more to bring about the final overthrow of Carthage and Corinth, though they had long been tottering, than this scattering and dispersion of their citizens, due to the fact that the lust for trafficking and sailing the seas had caused them to abandon agriculture and the pursuit of arms. Many things too that cause ruin to states as being incitements to luxury are supplied by the sea, entering either by capture or import; and even the mere delightfulness of such a site brings in its train many an allurement to pleasure through either extravagance or indolence.[106]

For Polybius and Cicero, the political system of Rome was better than that of Carthage. They both stressed that military affairs and virtues must be cultivated and cannot simply be bought. In Renaissance Italy, these comments came to stand behind Machiavelli's and Guicciardini's advocacy of citizen militias as opposed to mercenary troops.[107] Although Stapylton does not specify a link to mercenary armies, his idealisation of Roman military culture in contrast to Carthaginian rule by money makes him fall into line with Cicero and Polybius, as well as, closer to home, Sir Dudley Digges.

Stapylton seems to have developed the details of his political allegory of Virgil on his own as there is no precise parallel in the Renaissance. However, he was well read in Greek and Roman historians, as the commentaries to his later translations demonstrate. In 1644, Stapylton published *The First Six Satyrs of Juvenal*, which also contains 'Annotations clearing the obscurer places out of the History, Lawes, and Ceremonies of the *Romans*'. The annotations, which make up almost half of this work, range widely over Greek and Roman antiquarian interests, although Stapylton rarely acknowledges his direct sources. Similar information is provided in his translations of a speech by Pliny and of Musaeus' *Hero and Leander*.[108] It is therefore highly probable that he was familiar with the standard texts by Polybius and Cicero. And there are some possible links to contemporary Virgil commentaries. The commentators on Book 4 often stress the femininity of Dido and the masculinity of Aeneas. When glossing the phrase 'quam tu urbem, soror' (47), as Anna seeks to persuade Dido that a match with Aeneas will bring glory to Carthage, Pontanus notes that Anna speaks

> from a hope of the highest advantages and of the highest dignity. If you will join in marriage with Aeneas, a man so strong and vigorous, you will place your state in the greatest safety. Then you will have a kingdom most flourishing with arms and riches, so that you will be able to help a friend or destroy an enemy, with the greatest glory.[109]

Here, Aeneas will presumably bring the 'arms' to the kingdom which under Dido's command is already flourishing with riches. In the commentary tradition, Dido often represents Carthaginian wealth, luxury and femininity while Aeneas is the warrior, dutiful and masculine. Stapylton could have found support for his allegory in these texts.[110]

The topical significance of this allegory becomes apparent when it is considered in the context of Charles I's personal reign. Charles had signed peace treaties with France on 14 April 1629 and with Spain on 5 November 1630. As Pauline Gregg describes in her book *King Charles*, in the ensuing period of peace, English trade with the continent flourished, to the point that the king's sister spoke of the 'incredible profit' that was flowing into English ports.[111] The English became leading traders in the wool industry, and as Spain and France grew more hostile to each other, England picked up more of their trade. English ships were even starting to be used to transport goods around Europe for other nations. The resulting situation was sketched as follows by Gregg:

> Charles had only to look down from his wife's palace at Greenwich onto the veritable forest of masts in the river below, or take one of his frequent journeys by barge down river past the bustling wharves that lined the Thames, to feel the beat of a commercial nation. Increased trade induced merchants, including the Merchant Adventurers, to put profit before principle and concede tonnage and poundage.[112]

The changing international role of England under the Personal Rule was greeted by some with great consternation, as we have seen with John Vicars. Others, such as Thomas Carew, praised Charles as an Augustus who was spreading English influence through a new *pax Augusta*. In his 1631 poem 'New-yeares gift. To the King', Carew celebrated Charles for having closed the doors of the Temple of Janus, which were only closed in Rome during times of peace: 'But *Byfront*, open thou no more, | In his blest raigne the Temple dore.'[113] Stapylton's contrast of military and mercantile culture should be read in this context. Based on the dichotomy Stapylton makes between Roman and Carthaginian modes of government, one could say that, in the early years of the Personal Rule, Charles was following the mercantile, seafaring, Carthaginian model, rather than the self-sufficient, military, Roman model. In other words, he was behaving like Dido rather than Aeneas.

Stapylton's stress on the contrast between these two different types of government is not only apparent in the allegory in the preface. He makes the contrast apparent throughout his translation. As modern scholars have noted, Virgil himself emphasises the importance of wealth in Dido's story and Carthaginian history. In *The Commerce of War*, for example, Neil Coffee has argued that 'the mercantile nature of Dido and her Carthaginians contributes to the picture of the Punic city as the antitype of Rome.'[114] Coffee has documented how money plays a crucial role in the story of Dido's exile and her foundation of Carthage, whereas it plays no role in the account of Aeneas' exile and his state-founding in Italy.[115] Stapylton's literal translation carefully recreates and stresses this contrast. Dido's wealth is portrayed in the gifts she gives to Aeneas: 'he glowd | In Tyrian dyes: a Robe from's shoulder flow'd, | A gift rich *Dido* wrought' ('Tyrioque ardebat murice laena | demissa ex umeris, dives quae munera Dido | fecerat').[116] In this translation, Dido shares her 'estates' with Aeneas, while he contributes arms to her rising kingdom. In one of the less literal moments of translation, Stapylton has Dido proclaim: 'I tooke him up, did with him share estates' ('excepi et regni demens in parte locavi').[117] On the other side, when Anna remarks upon what the match between Dido and Aeneas could bring to Carthage, she exclaims, with 'Troians accompanying | In Armes, how high will Punicke glory spring?' ('Teucrum comitantibus armis, | Punica se quantis attollet gloria rebus!')[118] We have already seen how Pontanus views this as foreseeing Roman arms combining with the Carthaginian wealth. Or to take one more example, we can consider Stapylton's slightly misleading translation of the prophecy that Aeneas would be 'qui gravidam imperiis belloque frementem | Italiam regeret' as 'to rule *Italy*, with *Empire* great, | And lowd in War'.[119] In Stapylton, the great empire and prowess in war seem to fit with the Trojans instead of the Italians. Through many such small touches, Stapylton's translation portrays the allegorical contrast between mercantile Carthage and martial Rome. The allegory is thus not external to the translation but pervades the project.

Stapylton may not have taken such a strong oppositional stance as Digges and Vicars, but his allegorical translation is part of the same line of Virgil reception. Proudfoot has shown that Stapylton had read and relied on Digges's *Didos Death*, much as Vicars did.[120] But the important similarities go beyond the verbal echoes noted by Proudfoot. As a young Catholic and royalist, Stapylton's ideal of a military English state would not have been anything like that of Digges's or Vicars' militant Protestantism. But his translation also pleads for a renewed attention to the military side of politics, and it should be read as a critique of Caroline policies rather than as a panegyric. Kevin Sharpe has emphasised that the Caroline cavalier and court poets could remain royalists while speaking 'ambivalently, and sometimes critically' of the political culture.[121] *Dido and Aeneas*, which includes harsh satirical remarks on the contemporary court culture in its prefatory poems, is an example of such a piece of criticism from a royalist. While the translation's dedicatee, Lady Twisleton, and Stapylton's biographical details place him firmly in royalist circles, the translation itself summons Virgil in support of a form of government that opposed Charles I's policies during the early 1630s. Stapylton's opening frontispiece asks the question, 'What mov'd these *Princes* to their *fates*? behold | A Cypresse-garland and a Crowne of gold.' According to his allegory, this crown of gold is won in battle, not bought with money.

Stapylton's allegorical Book 4 must thus be added to a fascinating collection of oppositional *Aeneid*s in the early seventeenth century. His translation interprets and applies the epic politically without falling into the pattern of the early Augustans. If George Sandys's translation of Book 1 was at the beginning of the Augustan tradition, then Digges's translation of Book 4 could be seen as the beginning of a new oppositional strand of translation to which Vicars and Stapylton also belong.

Perhaps most importantly, Stapylton also offers further proof that in the decade leading up to the Civil War, the *Aeneid* was still an unpredictable text. He shows another way that Book 4 could be isolated from the whole epic and made to stand on its own. Far from being stable in its political meaning, its applications varied widely and the translators found new ways to recreate the epic in the ever-changing political climate.

'Drad Wars, and that Brave Hero's Fame': Robert Heath's Manuscript 'Æneis' (1645–6)

Placing the complete translation of the *Aeneid* by Robert Heath into the same tradition of English Virgils as those of Digges and Vicars may at first seem surprising. Robert Heath was the son of Sir Robert Heath, one of the leading politicians of early Stuart England, serving as Chief Justice and as the king's lawyer on multiple occasions. When the translation was composed between 1645 and 1646, the younger Robert Heath was living with his father and siblings in Oxford, where the senior Robert Heath found important positions in the royal camp for his children.[122] The younger Heath seems to have inherited most of his beliefs and allegiances from his father and he himself is counted as one of the cavalier poets.

Further reason not to suspect a connection between these translations is given by the fact that Vicars and Digges were not on the best terms with the Heath family. Vicars attacked the Heaths on several occasions. In one of his parliamentary chronicles, recounting the fall of Denham's Farnham Castle in Sussex, Vicars wrote:

> The taking of this castle so terrified the Cavaleers in *Sussex* that those of them of the long-robe (Master *Lukener*, the Corporation *Proctour*) Master *Aderson*, Master *Heath* (Son to that dry and barren *Heath* the Judge, like Father like Son) and others of the same stamp began now to traverse the commands of their Cavaleers.[123]

The son in question could very well have been Robert Heath, the poet and translator. In 1626, the senior Sir Robert Heath was also a part of the Court's persecution of Sir Dudley Digges.[124] Thus uniting Digges, Vicars and Heath in a history of Virgil reception might not have met with the translators' own approval, but there are good grounds for doing so. As I shall argue in this section, Heath's complete translation of the *Aeneid* is an important example of the non-Augustan Virgil, both for its representation of military affairs and for its highly idiosyncratic poetic style. Furthermore, it demonstrates how the oppositional, military reception of the *Aeneid* in early Stuart England carried on into the early part of the Civil War and could even be transformed to support royalism. I show that Heath's translation relies on John Vicars' *XII Aeneids*, but it rewrites Vicars' oppositional poem for the royalist cause during one of its darker moments.

'Girt a la mode with Skins': The Attribution to Robert Heath

The Heath translation has never been studied before, so there are still general uncertainties surrounding the manuscript. What can be easily determined are the date of the translation and the name of its author. Each book, except the first, is followed by a date, in much the same way as in the Phaer-Twyne *Aeneid*. These dates show that Book 2 was completed on 11 March 164[5] and Book 3 on 13 August 1645, and that the remaining nine books were completed from 26 May 1646 to 9 September 1646. These dates make the Heath translation the first major *Aeneid* of the Civil War period.

The manuscript also contains four signatures, from which we know that the author's name was 'Robert Heath'. George N. Crosland, who was the first to publicise the manuscript in a short column in *Notes and Queries*, asserted that this was Robert Heath (*c.*1620–*c.*1685), the son of the prominent politician Sir Robert Heath (1575–1649).[125] Crosland, however, provided no evidence for attributing the translation to this specific Robert Heath, and fifteen years later, in an Appendix to *Works of John Dryden*, William Frost questioned the basis for this claim.[126] Since then nobody has studied the translation and the question has remained open. Based on my research, I believe that Crosland's attribution is accurate. The elder Heath was still alive and would have been a possible author, especially given his formidable classical education.[127] But the father never wrote poetry and the signatures in the manuscript do not match his. The signatures in the manuscript are in a more upright hand than Heath's and Sir Robert Heath's 'R' has a flat top while those in the manuscript have tall stems and flourishes. Moreover, in the several dozen manuscripts I have seen by the senior Heath, he never uses his initials alone. This combination of facts would make the senior Heath extremely unlikely.

His son, however, fits perfectly. He was an active poet in the 1640s and it seems that he kept all of his writing in manuscript. Only one collection of his poetry was published, which appeared as *Clarastella* in 1650 and includes love poems, elegies, epigrams and satires. However, the printer, Humphrey Moseley, stated that it was 'ventured to the Press without [Heath's] knowledge'.[128] Robert's brother John also produced a lengthy manuscript translation of Martial, and it is plausible to see the two brothers writing and circulating classical translations during their time together in Oxford in the 1640s.[129] The case for Robert Heath is also strengthened because certain characteristics of the translation match his other writings. I will explore many of these later in this section, but one example is the translator's tendency to insert words in French. Thus, for a few examples, Memnon has an 'equipage', Potitius is 'girt a la mode with skins', and Turnus is 'armd cap a pe'.[130] Similarly, in *Clarastella*, Linus wears a 'peruque', another person has a 'leiger demein' and other people are 'best pleas'd with quelquechoses vain'.[131] Robert Heath had a great affection for French culture. He honoured his private French teacher Gabriel Dugres with a prefatory Latin poem in the *Grammaticae Gallicae compendium* (1636) and he cites Du Bartas admiringly in *Clarastella*.[132]

The one major difference between Heath's work in *Clarastella* and the poetry of the *Aeneid* translation is that the printed work is a much more refined and accomplished product, but this can be explained by the unpolished state of the translation. Even though the Clarke Library manuscript is a fair copy, it is still possible to see how the rough copy was unfinished in several places. Heath progressed line by line while translating, and it appears that he sometimes composed multiple versions of a single line and only later chose one and crossed out the others. This technique of translation can be seen in a rawer state in another, later seventeenth-century *Aeneid* translation in the British Library, where up to four versions of a single line are composed.[133] From the manuscript in the Clark Library it is apparent that the version from which the fair copy was made still contained places where no decision had been made between the multiple renditions of a single line. In these instances, the wrong line was occasionally copied. Thus, for example, one finds moments such as this:

> Summon up Hells pale Ghosts, cause th'Earth to quake
> ~~Stop swiftest Riuers streams ba make stars, start back~~
> Under her Feet, stop swiftest Currents, make
> The stars retreate.[134]

Or the following:

> Hyrtacide warlike Nisus kept a gate
> (Whom huntresse Ida, as Aeneas mate
> Had sent) expert with's Bow, and darts: at th'place
> [His deare Euryalus was whose comely face
> The rest surpast; - - - - - - -]

His dear Euryalus was: a lovelier face
No Trojan, no brave Dardan souldier had.[135]

There is even an instance where a couple of possible rhyme words in parentheses have been mistakenly copied.[136] This manuscript translation therefore was not polished to the level of the translations studied in Chapter 3. Rather, it is a nearly finished text produced during the years Heath spent with his family and the royal court in Oxford.

A Song Sung in a Siege: Robert Heath's 'Æneis'

The first reason for reading Heath alongside Vicars is that Heath clearly had the other man's translation in front of him as he worked. A few examples can display the range of his borrowing and reworking. On the level of specific wordings, there are many echoes. We could compare their translations of a single phrase, such as 'Enceladi semustum fulmine corpus' (3.578). Vicars translated this as 'Encelads lightning-half-burn'd corps', which Heath recreated almost precisely as 'Enceladus Lightning-half-scorcht Corps'.[137] Sometimes, these imitations place Heath into a line with both Digges and Vicars. Earlier in this chapter, I showed how Vicars followed Digges in having Dido refer to her sister as 'Nan'. Heath copies this name, probably from Vicars, and uses it throughout Book 4.[138] In Heath, as in Vicars, the winds are referred to as 'puffs'.[139] Most of the furies are also 'Hells-hags' in Heath, except for in the last instance in Book 12, where Heath follows Vicars by referring to the Fury as a 'Fate'.[140] And perhaps the most striking examples are places where Heath takes over Vicars' love of hyphenations, alliterations and coinages. Heath, alongside Vicars and Stanyhurst, is the only other English translator of Virgil to create phrases such as 'dire-death-dying Dido', 'barb'rous butcheries' and 'fury-flashes his fierce Eyes flush fire'.[141] Like Vicars, Heath would fit James Harrington's description of 'the Thunder-thumping way of Grandsire Virgil'. In fact, he even translates 'fulmine deiecti' (6.581) as 'thunder-thumpt downe'.[142] The imitation of Vicars' style in this translation runs deep.

Moreover, as I have shown, Vicars' use of language had a type of promiscuity that could make his translation appear to critical contemporary readers as almost a parody. Its exuberance breaks free from the normal bounds of 'chaste' Virgilian translation. Heath displays a similar exuberance, but he can be even freer than Vicars. In Chapter 3, I showed how manuscript translation seems to have liberated translators to take less reverential attitudes towards Virgil's epic. Heath's manuscript once again displays that there could be a lighter side to Virgilian translation in this period. Indeed, I would suggest that humour is something to search for in greater detail in manuscript reception of the classics. In Heath's translation, unlucky Aeneas and his companions are chased by Fortune like 'Tennis-balls'.[143] Both a great tree and Atlas turn out to be wearing fashionable 'periwigs',[144] but they may not be as fashionable as Potitius, who is 'girt a la mode with skins'.[145] Even in the midst of battle, Heath sometimes adds in a light touch: in order to kill off the giant Pandarus, Turnus 'rose on th'Tip-toe-stand'.[146] These moments display a playfulness that is courtlier than Vicars', but they also show a willingness to break the severity of Virgil's high style. In this regard, Heath is a follower both of Vicars and of one of the major trends in early modern English manuscript translations of the *Aeneid*.

However, there are two key differences. First, Heath's translation is a line-by-line translation whereas Vicars' is not. Much like Phaer, Heath tries to live inside the poetic metre of the original, and his translation is almost precise. Heath uses 9,868 lines in his translation, while the Latin has 9,897. Considering that he uses rhyming couplets of iambic pentameter, this is a remarkable compression. It also seems that Heath's affection for hyphenations and combining words has more than just stylistic grounds. For Heath, these hyphenations were important because they allowed for an unprecedented compression of the content. Sometimes the results are absurd as poetry, but they always keep the verse curt. Thus the phrase 'hic Cacum in tenebris incendia vana vomentem' (8.259) becomes 'vaine-flame-spewing Cacus', and 'nigranti picea trabibusque obscurus acernis' (9.87) becomes 'a maple-pitch-tree-shady Grove'.[147] Heath rarely worries about what theorists such as Humphrey would have called the *proprietas* or *puritas* of his target language. He insists on working line for line, even when the English word order is barely comprehensible. The two lines 'Hic manus ob patriam pugnando vulnera passi, | quique sacerdotes casti, dum vita manebat' (6.660–1) become a mess in the English: 'Here Troops of for their Country Fighters slaine | And Priests that all their lives did chast remaine'.[148] This pursuit of brevity leads to the impression that everything is done in staccato and it even affected Heath's choice of ornamentation. When the poetry rises to a high pitch, one technique he often uses is to repeat monosyllabic words, as this is a very concise way of adding stress: 'tollite cuncta' (8.439) becomes 'Leave, Leave these works', and 'neve armate manus' (9.115) becomes 'Leave, leave those arms'.[149] The condensed English results in an *Aeneid* that is decidedly different from the more expansive version of Vicars, even if they share their disregard for *proprietas*.

The second key difference between Heath and Vicars is that Heath rewrites the politics of the *XII Aeneids*. With respect to their royalist politics, Vicars seems to have been correct in calling the Heaths 'like Father like Son'. The senior Robert Heath was extremely loyal to Charles, and he believed that a king's political powers were practically unlimited.[150] Unity was essential in a nation and the king provided the focal point for such a bond.[151] Nevertheless, Sir Robert Heath certainly felt that parliament had a crucial role to play as advisor to the king: they should not twist the king's arm, but they always should be asked for advice on the important matters. At times, Sir Robert Heath even took parliament's side (to his own detriment with the royalists), even if he remained committed to the king's cause.[152] This careful balance can also be witnessed in the translation by Robert Heath, the son. Politically, his *Aeneid* is markedly different from Vicars' from the outset, as any monarchical suggestion is stressed. This can be effected through small wordings, such as 'gentem' (1.33) becoming 'Romes Monarchy' and 'rerum dominos' (1.282) becoming 'the worlds triumphant Monarchs'.[153] More extended emphasis on monarchy comes in Jupiter's early prophecy: Heath translates 'populosque feroces | contundet moresque viris et moenia ponet, | tertia dum Latio regnantem viderit aestas' (1.263–5) as 'subdue feirce Nations | New Lawes impose, and ore them sov'raigntize | Thus shall three sumers see him Monarchize'.[154] Turning 'sovereignty' and 'monarchy' into verbs may not be eloquent, but it stresses the monarchical framework unmistakably.

On the other hand, Heath also recreates one of the parliaments that Vicars has in his translation – the 'parliament' that Jupiter calls in heaven in Book 10. And at the beginning of this book, Heath adds some wonderful domestications of his own. The passage that in Vicars introduced the celestial parliament – 'Panditur interea domus omnipotentis Olympi | conciliumque vocat divum pater atque hominum rex | sideream in sedem' (10.1–3) – becomes in English: 'Meanwhile Heav'ns glorious Father, King of mortalls | Opens all-spreading heav'ns eternall Portalls | To Heav'ns Star-chamber calls a Parliament'.[155] Heath's father had worked on several cases in the Star Chamber. Robert raises its importance here onto the celestial sphere and follows Vicars in making Jupiter listen to his advisors. However, Heath is never quite as ready as Vicars to yield rule to the parliament in these books. As noted above, Vicars transforms 'o pater, o hominum rerumque aeterna potestas' (10.18) into 'the mightie moderatour, wise, eternall'. But Heath renders these words as 'great Father, heav'n and earths eternall King'.[156] His version pulls Vicars' back towards a safely royal sphere. And when he comes to the court of Latinus, Heath makes no mention of a parliament whatsoever. There are only the 'Peers of State' and a strong royal precedent.[157] Politically, Heath's translation is a royalist reigning in of its model Vicars.

But along with Stapylton's *Dido and Aeneas*, Heath's 'Æneis' is a good example of why a translation of the *Aeneid* by a royalist is not necessarily 'Augustan', at least in the stereotypical sense. Augustan *Aeneid*s are generally portrayed as including the theme of gratitude and elements of panegyric.[158] In spite of its monarchical bias, there is no hint of this ideal within the Heath translation. Furthermore, Augustan readers of the *Aeneid* placed great store in contrasting Aeneas as a royal and pitiful prince with the angry and vengeful rebels.[159] In contrast, Heath carefully avoids this distinction. Instead, his translation focuses on the virtues that are needed by all parties in a time when the world is in a state of chaos. In *Clarastella*, Heath frequently writes about the national discord he was experiencing. He laments 'the new world's sins | Are so deep di'd no floud can rinse. | Nothing but lightning and Heav'ns fire | Can purge our pestilential aire.'[160] In a world where 'kingdomes thus turn'd, and overturned are', Heath looks to the *Aeneid* as a poem that relates the experience of war and the values that can redeem a nation.[161] Based upon the elegies Heath wrote for his fallen friends in *Clarastella*, it appears that Heath himself had some experience on the battlefield in 1645.[162] From the dates in the manuscript, we also know that the translation was being composed during the 'Siege of Oxford' by the parliamentary forces. Most of the poem was written from late May 1646 to early September 1646, a time during which the treaty for Oxford's surrender was being arranged. In *Clarastella*, Heath wrote a 'Song in a siege', a comedic poem promoting drink as a way to keep up one's courage.[163] The Virgil translation was also a sort of 'song in a siege', even if it takes a much more serious approach to the times.

The translation's key themes are loyalty and bravery. These values are not isolated to any one group or figure in the poem. Instead, Heath admired loyalty and bravery in principle and hated those who turned on their allies, whatever side they supported. These values come through in *Clarastella*. Much like Dante attacks neutrals in the third Canto of the *Inferno*, Heath mocks 'John Newter' who 'was nor for King or Parliament':

> What side his soule hath taken now
> God or Div'l? we hardly know:
> But this is certain, since he dy'd,
> Hee hath been mist of neither side.[164]

Just as his father was a loyal royalist who never lost sympathy for parliament, Heath saw valour on both sides of the war. In his translation, neither Aeneas nor Turnus is consistently privileged. Aeneas is subject to moments of violent rage, just as fiercely as Turnus is. Heath has Aeneas proclaim, 'yea my Minds revengefull spleene | T'will satisfy, and please the Ghosts of mine | Thus fuming I was going with furious mind'.[165] Similarly, all of the major heroes are capable of moments of valour. Heath's exploration of warfare is not as dichotomous as those of Digges and Vicars.

The people who are ridiculed in this translation are thus not those of a single side, but rather those who lack bravery: the braggarts and the opportunists. When dealing with these characters, Heath introduces elements of satire into his epic. In the 'Discourse Concerning the Original and Progress of Satire', John Dryden argues that Virgil 'cou'd have written sharper Satires, than either *Horace* or *Juvenal*, if he wou'd have employ'd his Talent, that way'.[166] Early modern readers were used to spotting moments of satire in Virgil's epic and, on occasion, Heath's Aeneas himself speaks in 'satyre-straines'.[167] Heath's interpretation of Book 5 makes the games in Sicily into little satires of vices. When Entellus takes offence at the overly boastful Dares, he exclaims, 'were I now as young as ere I was, | Or as this daring Bragadochio here | Ide match him straight', before humiliating the younger boaster.[168] In *Clarastella*, Heath also satirises a 'braggadochio' who relies upon his legs rather than arms.[169] If there is one character that is most subjected to mockery in Heath's *Aeneid*, however, it is Drances, who is freely mocked in Book 11 as 'th'mischiefe Master'.[170] Drances too is portrayed as a braggadochio. Heath's irate Turnus exclaims, 'but th'Court must not be fild with words which fall | From thee secure, Big Brags while the strong wall | Keeps of the foe'.[171] Drances is then mocked, 'why dost stay? shall valour still | Ly in thy toad-like tongue and hart-like heele?'[172] This is a liberal adaptation of the Latin, 'an tibi Mavors | ventosa in lingua pedibusque fugacibus istis | semper erit?' (11.389–91). Heath introduces the toad because the creature was associated with illusion and deception in the early modern period. In Book 4 of *Paradise Lost*, the final and lowest stage of Satan's transformations is into a toad who squats beside Eve's ear:

> Squat like a toad, close at the ear of Eve;
> Assaying by his devilish art to reach
> The organs of her fancy, and with them forge
> Illusions as his list, phantasms and dreams.[173]

As both a braggart and a master of deception, Drances occupies the negative end of the scale of values in Heath's *Aeneid*.

At the other end of this scale are the characters who exhibit bravery. 'Brave' is one of the most repeated words in Heath's 'Æneis' and its importance is similar to the word 'good' in Vicars. The opening words of the *Aeneid*, 'Arma virumque', are translated by Heath as 'drad Wars, and that brave Hero's Fame'.[174] This opening line sets out the principle virtue in this translation succinctly: courage in the face of fierce war. If there is a discernible purpose behind this translation, it is the portrayal in English of admirable examples of martial courage. While 'brave' had a wider range of meanings in early modern English than it does today, the most common usage of the word in the translation is in contexts that praise heroic actions in battle. One could draw on a host of examples as there are, for instance, twenty-one uses of the word in Book 12 alone, but a few can serve to illustrate the point. When Aeneas tells Evander, 'sunt nobis fortia bello | pectora, sunt animi et rebus spectata iuventus' (8.150–1), Heath translates, 'we have stout martiall breasts | Brave spirits and war-tride youth'.[175] The word is used often in phrases associated with glory in battle, so that 'inclute Mavors' (12.179) becomes 'brave Mars' or 'insignis gloria facti' (12.322) becomes 'the brave acts fame'.[176] Most often, however, it refers to specific admirable actions that a character has carried out and that others should emulate. And it is remarkable to see how the word honours acts carried out by figures of all different allegiances in this translation. Turnus' 'claris . . . factis' (7.474) becomes his 'brave exploits, high merits'.[177] Lausus' deeds defending his father are praised in grand terms: 'tuaque optima facta' (10.791) becomes 'this brave Act' and his 'laudibus istis' (10.825) become 'such brave acts'.[178] In Aeneas' final speech to his son (12.435–40), Heath makes the parting words of fatherly advice, 'calst thy Allies | Brave Acts, to mind'.[179] Even the figures in the opposing camp could have moments of bravery. Messapus, a friend of Turnus who nevertheless fights honourably, is described by Heath as 'brave Cavalier Messapus', which translates 'Messapus equum domitor' (12.550).[180] Camilla, 'o decus Italiae virgo' (11.508), is likewise a 'brave Maid | Ausonias glory'.[181] Even the atheistic Mezentius, when he finally meets Aeneas in battle, is praised by Heath for meeting him without deceit: he 'meets him face to face and Arms to Arms | Braver by force, not fraud'.[182] And of course Aeneas himself is described as brave time and again. It is by far his most common epithet in the translation.[183]

The final reward for 'bravery' is renown and, in exceptional cases, sainthood, as it is in the elegies that Heath wrote for his friends who had fallen in the Civil War. In a typical elegy, honouring 'Gent. Ed. Sackvil', Heath writes, 'For now he lives fam'd to posteritie, | Both for his Virtues and his Loyaltie.'[184] In Heath's *Aeneid*, Nisus and Euryalus are two characters who achieve the highest rewards for their courage. The 'aliquid . . . magnum' (9.186) that they set out to perform is a 'brave Enterprise', and Aletes praises them for their 'brave hearts and fearles spirits'.[185] In the same speech, Aletes promises them that their bravery will not be unrewarded, stating in the Latin: 'quae vobis, quae digna, viri, pro laudibus istis | praemia posse rear solvi? pulcherrima primum | di moresque dabunt vestri' (9.252–4). At this moment, Heath makes the English rather more explicit: 'brave youths: first heav'n, and your renowne | Gallant rewards will be.'[186] For their bravery in war, Nisus and Euryalus will gain an acceptance into heaven, as well as the honours that Aeneas will bestow upon them.

This praise from Aeneas is of great value in Heath's translation because Aeneas is the greatest exemplar for the sainthood and renown that a character can gain. At the beginning of this book, we have seen how Aeneas winning glory for virtuous acts was the underpinning of the Phaer-Twyne's epideictic reading of the *Aeneid*. In Heath, the context of Aeneas' virtue is much more specifically martial than it is in the Phaer-Twyne, and the reward may seem less consoling, given the reality of dreaded war that surrounded the translation. Nevertheless, the passage when Jupiter assigns Aeneas a place among the immortals is equally climactic. I will quote the passage at length, both to give a longer sample from this translation, which is not readily accessible, and to show how Heath describes the rewards for the bravery that his translation advocated. Here Heath translates *Aeneid* 12.791–806:

> Heav'ns potent Prince to Juno speaks meanwhile
> That viewd from the bright cloud this fight ith plains
> What end, Wife shall we have? what more remains
> Thou know'st (yea dost confesse) that fates decree
> Aeneas shall heav'ns Saint, and star shall be.
> What plotst thou? what hopes thee ith'clouds retaine
> Wa'st fit that mortall wound a ~~sh~~ saint should staine
> Or th'sword (for th'Nymph could nere alone pursue't.)
> To Turnus give and Conqu'reds force recrute?
> Cease now at last, and yield t'our prayers: nor let
> Such grief thee silent gnaw, nor sad cares fret
> Which from thee flow so oft to me: the last
> Cast now is throwne: ore sea and land thou hast
> Had power to th'Trojans tosse, move dreadfull war
> Deforme the house: with griefe the marriage mar
> I farther plots forbid: thus Jove first spake.[187]

Almost a century after the Phaer-Twyne, at the heart of the Civil War, the prospect of the glory and bravery of Aeneas was still providing solace.

The martial values of the Heath *Aeneid* and its extensive debts to the style and content of Digges and Vicars make it a late instance of the military line of Virgil in early modern England. However, whereas Digges,

Vicars and Stapylton used this military reception of the epic to oppose peaceful Stuart policies, Heath's translation is different because it is not written as a gesture of opposition but rather strikes a tone of consolation in the midst of conflict. His translation is an emulation of Vicars' puritan and parliamentarian *Aeneid* and he transforms Vicars' military Virgil from puritan polemic into royalist encouragement. His translation could thus be said to look towards the preponderance of royalist Virgils in the second half of the seventeenth century. But it shares none of the essential qualities of the early Augustan Virgil. Its origins and context are rather the tradition of oppositional *Aeneids* from early Stuart England.

Notes

1. It should be noted that several scholars have disputed this label, especially in application to Dryden. See Hammond, *Dryden*, p. 40.
2. Burrow, *Epic Romance*, p. 148.
3. Butler, *Hudibras*, I, 639–58.
4. Butler, *Hudibras*, I, Butler's note to lines 639–40.
5. Conington, *Miscellaneous Writings*, I, p. 140.
6. Burrow, 'Virgil in English Translation', p. 25.
7. Ibid., p. 25; Venuti, *The Translator's Invisibility*, pp. 35–53; Norbrook, *Writing the English Republic*, p. 36 and *passim*; Quint, *Epic and Empire*, p. 8 and *passim*.
8. Bodleian Library, MS Ashmole 38, fols 129^{r}–131^{r}. The 'Virgiliae Vindicae' has so far not been fully printed. I quote from the manuscript by referring to the line numbers as they would be in a modern edition.
9. Cummings, *Edmund Spenser*, p. 165.
10. Herring, *Mischeefes Mysterie*, sig. ¶2^{r}.
11. For example, see Owen, *Epigrams*, sig. D4^{v}.
12. Goodwin, *Babels Balm*, sig. B4^{r}.
13. Vicars, *A Prospective Glasse*, sig. ¶^{r}.
14. Ibid., sigs. B3^{v}, B6^{r}, C2^{v}, C5^{v}, C6^{r}, C8^{v} and D6^{r}.
15. Herring, *Mischeefes*, sig. ¶3^{v}.
16. Ibid., sig. F3^{r}.
17. Ibid., sig. F4^{r}.
18. Ibid., sig. D3^{v}.
19. Ibid., sig. K2^{v}.
20. Ibid., sig. I3^{r}.
21. Walsham, *Providence*, p. 246.
22. Ibid., pp. 8 and 249.
23. Tyacke, *Anti-Calvinists*, p. 182.
24. Vicars, *Englands Hallelu-jah*, sig. B8^{r}.
25. Ibid., sig. B2^{r}.
26. Ibid., sig. B3^{v}.
27. Ibid., sig. B4^{r}.
28. Ibid., sig. B6^{r}.

29. Ibid., sig. B7^{v}.
30. Walsham, *Providence*, p. 146.
31. Vicars, *Englands Hallelu-jah*, sig. C5^{r}.
32. Ibid., sig. C5^{v}.
33. Vicars, *Englands Remembrancer*, sig. A2^{r}.
34. Ibid., sig. A3^{r}.
35. Sandys, *Ovids Metamorphosis Englished*, p. [iii]. This is the first page of 'A Panegyricke to the King'.
36. Ibid., sig. ¶4^{v}.
37. Ross, *Virgilius evangelisans*, sig. A2^{r}.
38. Ibid., sig. A2^{r}
39. Ibid., sig. A2^{v}.
40. Ibid.
41. Sowerby, *Early Augustan Virgil*, p. 13.
42. Proudfoot, *Dryden's 'Aeneid'*, p. 111.
43. Ibid., p. 115.
44. Ibid.
45. Ibid., p. 117.
46. Vicars, *Aeneids*, p. 16.
47. For the following examples, Vicars' *Aeneids* is either the first instance of the word cited in the *OED* or prior to the first cited instance by the *OED*. No prior instances of these words appear in a full-text EEBO search either.
48. Vicars, *Aeneids*, p. 401.
49. For examples of these words in the *Aeneids*, see: 'concomitate' (p. 112), 'obtestate' (p. 108), 'denudate' (p. 351) and 'properate' (p. 173).
50. Ibid., p. 239.
51. Ibid., p. 99.
52. Ibid., p. 7.
53. Ibid., p. 235.
54. See Vicars, *Aeneids*: 'sea-tired' (p. 7), 'lightning-half-burn'd' (p. 81), 'mischief-minded' (p. 114), 'gore-bloud-gushing' (p. 314), 'thunder-smart' (p. 219), 'heart-string-breaking' (p. 272).
55. See Vicars, *Aeneids*: 'bouncing blows' (p. 240), 'tinkering strokes' (p. 240), 'thumping thwacks' (p. 240), 'tinckling tangs' (p. 291), 'wringling wreathes' (p. 367), 'frisks and skips' (p. 140), 'ratling roaring' (p. 144). The onomatopoetic element in Vicars' translation may have been inspired by Stanyhurst's efforts. Vicars occasionally echoes Stanyhurst and he seems to borrow a couple of the eccentric (but significant) phrasings which had previously appeared only in Stanyhurst's translation. For one instance, see their translations of *Aeneid* 1.384 ('ipse ignotus, egens, Libyae deserta peragro'): Vicars, 'I a poore pilgrim' (p. 14) and Stanyhurst, 'I lyke a poore pilgrim'. Stanyhurst, *The First Foure Bookes*, p. 11.
56. Ibid., pp. 239–40.
57. Norbrook, *Writing the English Republic*, p. 376.
58. Vicars, *Aeneids*, p. 88; and, Digges, *Didos Death*, sig. A2^{v}.
59. Digges, *Didos Death*, sig. A4^{v}.
60. Ibid., sig. A10^{v}.
61. Godolphin, *Passion of Dido for Æneas*, sigs. C4^{r}–C4^{v}.
62. Vicars, *Aeneids*, sig. A2^{r}.

63. Ibid., sig. A2^{v}.
64. Harington, *The Sixth Book of Virgil's 'Aeneid'*, p. 29.
65. St Augustine, *City of God*, II, pp. 134–5 [v. 1]: 'prorsus diuina providentia regna constituuntur humana. Quae si propterea quisquam fato tribuit, quia ipsam Dei voluntatem vel potestatem fati nomine appellat, sententiam teneat, linguam corrigat.'
66. Mornay, *The Trewnesse of the Christian Religions*, p. 212.
67. For examples from the full range of the epic, see Vicars, *Aeneids*, pp. 51, 57, 119, 142, 339, 390 and 406.
68. One of the ironies in the *Aeneid* is that men are consistently held to a much higher standard of morality than the gods are. See Lyne, *Further Voices*, p. 84.
69. Feeney, *The Gods in Epic*, pp. 141–2.
70. Vicars, *Aeneids*, p. 95.
71. Ibid., pp. 201, 202, 204, 208, 209, 211, 251 and 413.
72. Feeney, *Gods in Epic*, pp. 153 and 159; Hardie, *Epic Successors of Virgil*, p. 73.
73. Vicars, *Aeneids*, p. 416.
74. Ibid., p. 14.
75. Ibid., p. 17.
76. Ibid., p. 11.
77. Different translations of the word *pietas* are a recurring theme in Colin Burrow's study of epic romance. See, for example, his discussion of Ariosto, Caxton, Douglas and the *Roman d'Eneas* in light of their differing translations of Virgil's *pietas*: *Epic Romance*, pp. 59–62.
78. Vicars, *Aeneids*, p. 146.
79. See Vicars, *Aeneids*: 'brave' (p. 327), 'grave' (p. 383), 'great' (p. 389), 'honest' (p. 389), 'pious' (p. 19),'fillial' (p. 329), 'Kinde' (p. 329).
80. Examples can be found throughout the translation. For three early instances, see Vicars, *Aeneids*, pp. 12, 103 and 161.
81. Ibid., p. 69.
82. The late 1620s and 1630s were not a highpoint for theories of mixed monarchies but, as Markku Peltonen has shown, they did not disappear altogether. Peltonen, *Classical Humanism*, p. 289.
83. Vicars, *Aeneids*, p. 344.
84. Ibid., p. 351.
85. For one example, 'sanctumque senatum' (1.426) becomes 'parliament' in Phaer, *Seven*, sig. B2^{r}. Likewise, 'patribusque vocatis' (11.379) becomes 'to parlament when Senatours resort' in Phaer and Twyne, *Whole*, sigs. Dd1^{v} and Hh4^{r}.
86. Phaer and Twyne, *Whole*, sig. Dd1^{v}.
87. Vicars, *Aeneids*, p. 384.
88. Ibid., p. 292.
89. Ibid., p. 298.
90. Ibid., p. 297.
91. Ibid., p. 293.
92. Such an interconnection is integral to the *Aeneid* itself. See Hardie, *Virgil's 'Aeneid'*, p. 298.
93. Vicars, *Aeneids*, sig. A3^{r}.

94. Sowerby, *Augustan Art of Poetry*, p. 171; Proudfoot, *Dryden's 'Aeneid'*, p. 122.
95. Proudfoot, *Dryden's 'Aeneid'*, p. 118.
96. Sowerby, *Early Augustan Virgil*, p. 181
97. Sowerby, *Augustan Art of Poetry*, p. 89.
98. Venuti, *The Translator's Invisibility*, p. 39.
99. Wilson-Okamura, 'Virgilian Models of Colonization', p. 718.
100. Pontanus, *Symbolarum libri XVII*, p. 1108: 'cum omnes huius auctoris libri sint utiles maxime, hic profecto quartus . . . omnium utilissimus est.'
101. Donatus, *In libros duodecim Aeneidos,* fol. 78[r]: 'necessarium condenti civitate*m* nova*m* & nova imp*er*ii fundame*n*ta roborare cupie*n*ti'.
102. 'And so intire a worke I doe esteeme this Booke, as while it remaines solitary, I presume to give it the Title of Dido and Aeneas.' Stapylton, *Dido and Aeneas*, sig. A3[v].
103. Stapylton, *Dido and Aeneas*, sigs. A4[r]–A4[v].
104. Quint, *Epic and Empire*, p. 25.
105. Polybius, *Histories*, 6.52, pp. 427–9.
106. Cicero, *De re publica* 2.4.7–8, pp. 116–17: 'nec vero ulla res magis labefactatam diu et Carthaginem et Corinthum pervertit aliquando quam hic error ac dissipatio civium, quod mercandi cupiditate et navigandi et agrorum et armorum cultum reliquerant. multa etiam ad luxuriam invitamenta perniciosa civitatibus subpeditantur mari, quae vel capiuntur vel inportantur; atque habet etiam amoenitas ipsa vel sumptuosas vel desidiosas inlecebras multas cupiditatum.'
107. Machiavelli, *Discourses on Livy*, p. 199. Guicciardini, 'Popular Government', p. 204.
108. Stapylton, *Pliny's Panegyricke*; Stapylton, *Musæus*.
109. Pontanus, *Symbolarum libri XVII*, p. 1120: 'a spe amplissimorum commodorum, & summæ dignitatis. Si cum Ænea tam forti, ac strenuo viro matrimonio copulaberis, tuas res primo collocabis in tutissimis. Deinde habebis regnum armis, & opibus florentissimum, ut vel amico prodesse possis, vel inimicum perdere, cum summa gloria.'
110. Stapylton certainly read Servius. For example, his translation of *Aeneid* 4.515–16 on sig. D1[v] show a reliance on Servius' gloss *ad loc.* As Servius' commentary was usually printed alongside other important commentaries, it is likely that Stapylton would have known others.
111. Gregg, *King Charles I*, p. 201.
112. Ibid..
113. Carew, *The Poems,* p. 90.
114. Coffee, *The Commerce of War*, p. 82.
115. Ibid., p. 76.
116. Stapylton, *Dido and Aeneas*, sigs. C1[r]–C1[v]. *Aeneid* 4.262–4.
117. Stapylton, *Dido and Aeneas*, sig. C5[r]. *Aeneid* 4.374.
118. Ibid., sig. B2[v]. *Aeneid* 4.48–9.
119. Ibid., sig. B8[r]. *Aeneid* 4. 229–30.
120. Proudfoot, *Dryden's 'Aeneid'*, pp. 105–7.
121. Sharpe, *Criticism and Compliment*, p. 29.
122. Kopperman, *Sir Robert Heath*, pp. 287–8.
123. Vicars, *God on the Mount*, p. 223. This comment seems to be Vicars'

colourful expansion of the account in Blunden, *Special Passages*, p. 141.
124. Kopperman, *Sir Robert Heath*, p. 157.
125. Crosland, 'Note', p. 19–20
126. Dryden, *Works*, VI, p. 1193.
127. Kopperman, *Sir Robert Heath*, pp. 7–9.
128. Heath, *Clarastella*, sig. *2[r]. Furthermore W. H. Kelliher has suggested that the poems in a manuscript at the Rosenbach Library under the initials 'R. H.' are by Robert Heath. These poems have been reproduced in Herrick, *Poetical Works*, pp. 423–39. See Kelliher's *ODNB* entry for Robert Heath. If this attribution is correct, there is even more evidence that Heath circulated poetry in manuscript.
129. This connection of the translations by John and Robert has been suggested by W. H. Kelliher and Stuart Gillespie. See Kelliher's *ODNB* entry for Robert Heath and Stuart Gillespie, 'Sir John Heath's Translation', p. 357.
130. Los Angeles, William Clarke Memorial Library MS.1946.007. This manuscript is titled 'Virgil's Æneis Translated into English Heroick Verse'. As the manuscript contains accurate pagination, I will quote from page number throughout this section. Here, pp. 18, 143 and 163.
131. Heath, *Clarastella*, sigs. F8[r], G8[v] and H3[v].
132. Ibid., sig. H4[v].
133. Anon., BL MS Add. 28644.
134. Heath, 'Virgil's Æneis', p. 68.
135. Ibid., p. 157.
136. Ibid., p. 209.
137. Ibid., p. 52; Vicars, *Aeneids*, p. 81.
138. Six examples can be found at Heath, 'Virgil's Æneis', pp. 56, 66 and 67.
139. See, for example, Heath, 'Virgil's Æneis', p. 64, which translates *Aeneid* 3.310.
140. For example, Heath, 'Virgil's Æneis', p. 129. Unlike Vicars, however, Heath is not systematic. See, for instance, on p. 130 the translation of 7.511 ('Fury'). For his translation of the final Dira into Fate itself, see p. 228.
141. Heath, 'Virgil's Æneis', pp. 64 (translating *Aeneid* 4.308), 147 (*Aeneid* 8.483) and 212 (*Aeneid* 12.101–2).
142. Heath, 'Virgil's Æneis', p. 110.
143. Ibid., p. 7; cf. *Aeneid* 1.240–1.
144. Heath, 'Virgil's Æneis', pp. 33 and 62.
145. Ibid., p. 143; cf. *Aeneid* 8.282.
146. Heath, 'Virgil's Æneis', p. 169; cf. *Aeneid* 10.749.
147. Heath, 'Virgil's Æneis', pp. 143 and 155.
148. Ibid., p. 112.
149. Ibid., pp. 146 and 155.
150. Kopperman, *Sir Robert Heath*, p. 49.
151. Ibid., p. 189.
152. Ibid., pp. 210–12.
153. Heath, 'Virgil's Æneis', pp. 2 and 8.
154. Ibid., p. 8.

155. Ibid., p. 171.
156. Ibid. Some Renaissance editions, such as the 1599 Pontanus, read 'divumque' instead of 'rerumque' and Heath's translation probably reflects the reading.
157. Ibid., p. 195.
158. Erskine-Hill, *The Augustan Idea*, p. 17.
159. Burrow, *Epic Romance*, p. 149.
160. Heath, *Clarastella*, sig. D2^r.
161. Ibid., sig. C8^v.
162. Kelliher has also made this suggestion in his *ODNB* entry on Robert Heath.
163. Heath, *Clarastella*, sig. D8^v.
164. Ibid., sig. F11^v.
165. Heath, 'Virgil's Æneis', p. 32. Cf. *Aeneid* 2.586–8.
166. Dryden, *Works*, IV, p. 64.
167. Heath, 'Virgil's Æneis', p.183. Cf. *Aeneid* 10.591.
168. Heath, 'Virgil's Æneis', p. 84. Cf. *Aeneid* 5.397–8: 'si mihi, quae quondam fuerat quaque improbus iste | exsultat fidens, si nunc foret illa iuventas.'
169. Heath, *Clarastella*, sig. F6^v.
170. Heath, 'Virgil's Æneis', p. 199.
171. Ibid., p. 198. Cf. *Aeneid* 11.380–2: 'sed non replenda est curia verbis, | quae tuto tibi magna volant, dum distinet hostem | agger murorum.'
172. Heath, 'Virgil's Æneis', p. 198.
173. *Paradise Lost* 4.800–3. On the significance of the toad imagery, see especially Danielson, 'On Toads and the Justice of God', pp. 12–14.
174. Heath, 'Virgil's Æneis', p. 1.
175. Ibid., p. 140.
176. Ibid., pp. 214 and 216.
177. Ibid., p. 129.
178. Ibid., pp. 187 and 188.
179. Ibid., p. 219.
180. Ibid., p. 221.
181. Ibid., p. 201.
182. Ibid., p. 186. Cf. *Aeneid* 10.734–5.
183. In Book 12 alone, see, for example, pp. 213, 219, 223 and 224.
184. Heath, *Clarastella*, sig. E3^r.
185. Heath, 'Virgil's Æneis', pp. 157 and 158.
186. Ibid., p. 158.
187. Ibid., p. 226.

Conclusion

The oppositional readings of the *Aeneid* that used the epic to challenge the ideals of the Stuart peace came to an end during the Civil War. The translators of the epic were by no means unified in the second half of the century. In the 1650s, for instance, there were translations of the *Aeneid* according to the Stuart Augustanism of Denham, the Cromwellian Augustanism of Waller and the irreverent republicanism of Harrington.[1] But the grand confidence that was placed in Virgil by all types of translators during the period from Phaer until Stapylton seems to have been shaken. James Harrington's publications from the late 1650s are indicative of a change in how oppositional translators treated Virgil. To the extent that Harrington approaches Virgil seriously, it is because he views the *Aeneid* as a part of the historical moment when the Roman Republic became the Roman Empire. Harrington feels that the new Roman peace was unstable and he thus reflects upon the delicacy of Virgil's hopes for the future. However, Harrington's translation is not only a historical reflection; it is also part travesty.[2] Unlike Digges, Vicars and Stapylton, Harrington did not find a positive example in Virgil's poem. Instead, he saw it as a work that needed taking down a notch. By the late 1650s, the sort of language that Vicars had used seriously in his translation had become the sort of language one found in travesties of Virgil's epic. Such an attitude towards Virgil is foreshadowed in Sir John Harington's translation, but it is not a primary part of the English tradition until the middle of the seventeenth century. At that time, there was no longer a division in *Aeneid* translations between military, parliamentarian readings of the epic and panegyric readings that encouraged gratitude. Rather, the natural division in the translations must be drawn between the Augustan Virgils on the one hand and less decorous travesties on the other. This is the reason Butler associates Vicars with the travesties rather than with his proper context. This contrast reflects the changing position of the *Aeneid* within English culture. The serious side of the poem's history in the later seventeenth century becomes subsumed under the complex history of the Augustan *Aeneid* which was already taking shape. This history has been already been well written by scholars such as Sowerby, Proudfoot and Norbrook.[3]

In the course of this book I have brought to light an earlier history of English Renaissance *Aeneids* that has been lost from view. I have demonstrated that the history of the English translations of Virgil can teach us a great deal about his reception in early modern England. The translations offer invaluable insights into the role that Virgil's epic played in Renaissance literary and political cultures. Given their large number, the translations chart, with considerable precision, Virgil's changing reception during the English Renaissance. This study has followed the English *Aeneid* from the beginning of Elizabeth's reign – when the first complete translation of the epic into early modern English enters the literary tradition – up to the start of the Civil War. In the process, I have offered a new picture of the way that Renaissance readers and writers made use of one of their favourite books. The translators of this highly political Latin epic engaged with early modern English politics in a much more unpredictable and sharp-edged manner than has been previously recognised.

It has recently become fashionable in studies of classical reception to ask what translations of a text can teach us about the original itself. Although the focus of this book has primarily been on Virgil in the Renaissance, this is nonetheless an intriguing question to pose at this point. In the context of English reception, Charles Martindale has been the most prominent critic to make the case that translations 'ought to assume a greater importance within the pedagogic procedures of Classicists'.[4] Likewise, Stuart Gillespie has argued that it can be extremely rewarding to use translations to shed light on ancient texts.[5] In the course of this book, there have been a variety of ways in which the translations offer rewarding insights into Virgil. Sometimes, comparing the translations with the original Latin highlights unexpected contrasts. In Phaer's translation, we found Aeneas sailing through the gap between Scylla and Charybdis, whereas Virgil's hero gives the pass a wide berth. Such a small deviation encapsulates *in nuce* the difference between Renaissance expectations of a hero and Virgil's ambiguous portrayal of Aeneas. A different sort of insight is provided by Marlowe's dramatic translation which engages with the 'openness' of Virgil's epic.[6] By filling in some of Virgil's silences – for instance, by staging Aeneas committing himself to Dido – Marlowe creatively exploits one of the most central features of Virgil's art. The later, single-book translations provide instances of how individual books can stand alone. Recent classical scholars have explored how individual books of Virgil's epic contain microcosms of the whole.[7] As I have argued, Renaissance single-book translations can act as historical test cases of this thesis. And much as C. S. Lewis felt that Gavin Douglas's translation could present the *Aeneid* in full colours, like a picture cleaned of accumulated (neoclassical) dust, the translation by John Vicars sometimes brings to light unexpectedly vibrant moments in Virgil's descriptions.[8] Indeed, the study of these Renaissance translations brings to our attention details in Virgil's Latin that might escape a traditional classicist's approach.

But the main benefit of this book lies, of course, in its reconsideration of the role that Virgil's epic played in the English Renaissance. In the first instance, there has been recent debate regarding the applicability of Virgilian 'pessimism' to this period.[9] The many translations of the *Aeneid* provided a perfect set of texts to illuminate this debate. Based on the substantial responses by English translators to the epic, I have argued that pessimistic readings were, at best, extremely rare. It is seldom that one comes across even hints of such a response. However, they were not non-existent. Marlowe's dramatic translation offers a reading that could reasonably be called 'pessimistic'. In his play, individual suffering is explicitly made to confront, and undermine, the 'Augustan' political claims of the text. Not to find more signs of 'pessimistic' readings of Virgil in this period, however, is certainly not to suggest that there was a uniform reading. The greatest problem of the recent pessimistic/optimistic debate has been that it tends to create a blunt duality where none existed. Instead of focusing on traces of pessimistic readings, the conflicting responses to the *Aeneid* during the Renaissance are best explored through the range of political applications for which the epic was used. By exploring these applications, I discovered that Virgil's *Aeneid* was an extremely capacious poem. The many English translations illustrate the sheer variety of early modern uses and forms of the epic.

Flexibility is a predominant characteristic of the style of these translations as well as their political content. After the 1630s, every major translator of the *Aeneid* in the seventeenth century uses rhyming couplets, with the one exception of Fanshawe. From 1558 to 1646, however, six different forms of verse are used: Virgil speaks English in fourteeners, dactylic hexameters, blank verse, sestets, *ottava rima* and iambic pentameter couplets. For Phaer, the English ballad and the length of the Latin line both play a key role. For Stanyhurst, the Latin hexameter and Chaucerian diction are formative elements. In the manuscript translations, the customs of lovers' complaints and the Ariostean verse form were the basis for new versions of the *Aeneid*. The abundance of forms used by translators in this period stands in stark contrast with the following age when a more uniform style gradually sets in.[10] Stylistic flexibility and exploration is a major part of what makes the earlier period of Virgil translation its own recognisable phase.

Another special characteristic of this period is that these translators were capable of responding to the *Aeneid* both in part and in its whole. This is a point that is almost universally missed in studies of the translations from the Renaissance. At the end of Chapter 4, I considered how isolating a single book of the *Aeneid* enabled early modern translators to actualise specific strands of interpretation. The complete translations of the *Aeneid* that frame the period covered by this book show another side of the early modern reception of Virgil. David Scott Wilson-Okamura has argued that the greatest change between the Virgil of the Middle Ages and the Virgil of the Renaissance is that Renaissance authors read the whole of the epic whereas medieval authors focus upon Books 1–6. The change thus concerns 'not what the poem means, but how much of it people read'.[11] This point should be taken further and made more emphatically. Not only were Renaissance translators Englishing the entirety of Virgil's poem; they were also interpreting it creatively *in its entirety*.[12] In the *Interpretatio*, Lawrence Humphrey states that a translator must read the whole book that is to be translated before starting to work on it: if you have not comprehended the full character of both the text and author your translation will be lacking.[13] Phaer, Twyne, Vicars and Heath do not translate the full epic simply for reasons of *copia* or abundance. Rather, their translations display readings of the *Aeneid* that take in a total vision of Virgil's poem. In Phaer and Twyne, this vision is an account of the *vir virtutis*, and the epic reaches its ultimate conclusion only in the Book 13 by Vegio, where Aeneas is rewarded with divinity and everlasting fame. For Vicars, on the other hand, the political underpinnings of the *Aeneid* reach fulfilment in Books 10 and 11, when we encounter the parliamentary structures of the Latin state and the gods themselves. Heath's exploration of the realities of war spreads out over the course of the whole epic. Any successful exploration of these translations needs to consider each of them in its entirety. This is something that has been greatly lacking from previous studies, which have tended to excerpt passages and focus on isolated instances of prosody or diction. The total visions of the *Aeneid* indicate the range and complexity of the reception of Virgil's epic in the English Renaissance.

By studying in depth for the first time the English translations from 1558 to 1646, this book has delineated how Virgil's reception changes throughout this period. To some extent, the political reception of Virgil's *Aeneid* has already been sketched by scholars. However, the main guides have not been very precise. They tend to go from equating

Dido with Elizabeth to equating Aeneas (particularly in his role in Book 6) with James.[14] Many studies also stress the increasing connection of the *Aeneid* with royalism in the seventeenth century.[15] The diachronic map this study has outlined is more nuanced. We find that the portrayal of Aeneas as a *vir virtutis* flourished in English translations, from all around the British Isles, during the period from 1555 to 1584. It is in this form that Virgil's epic enters the mainstream of the English literary tradition through the translation by Thomas Phaer and Thomas Twyne, which remains in print until the 1620s. In the 1580s, other, more varied approaches to Virgil begin to supplement this view. Oppositional and less serious approaches appear alongside the Phaer-Twyne *Aeneid*. Perhaps it is a sign of a new literary confidence in the later years of Elizabeth's reign. The new current of translations demonstrates that by the time Spenser and Shakespeare were writing their major works, there was already a wide range of views of Virgil – pessimistic, amatory, idolatrous – in circulation in English. This trend holds until the second decade of the seventeenth century. At that point, a new political moment decisively shapes the English reception of Virgil's epic: the colonial ventures in Virginia lend a new significance to the *Aeneid* in English culture. By the early 1630s, we find the English *Aeneid* becoming involved in the polemics just before the Civil War. But unexpectedly, there are translations that use the *Aeneid* to praise the Stuart peace and others which use it to call for a greater military culture.[16] I have shown that the first extended translation of Virgil that could be viewed in the context of the Civil War was in fact the work of the 'parliamentary fanatic' John Vicars. This book has thus been able to provide a sketch of the course that Virgil's epic took over the span of the English Renaissance while bringing to light various sides of its reception that have been previously overlooked.

What turns out to be the most common trait among the translators is not a specific political allegiance; rather, it is a conviction that their act of translating the *Aeneid* will be useful to the English (or British) state. These translators tend to wield Virgil's immense authority with great confidence. An instructive contrast can be made with the translators of Ovid during the same period. For the translators of the *Metamorphoses*, as Raphael Lyne has written, 'Ovid proves an awkward model, not fitting into comfortable positions, not providing easy material for a nationalistic transformation.'[17] In contrast, the translators of the *Aeneid* tend to brandish Virgilian authority much more assuredly. The question to be asked in each case is, how does the translator believe Virgil's text can be beneficial to his country? In some cases, translation provides a medium for commentary on sensitive political subjects. For instance, in the letters between James and Elizabeth with which this book began, the use of the *Aeneid* was topical, aligning characters in the epic with contemporary political figures. This mode of reading the *Aeneid* is prominent in the translations by Sir John Harington, Sir Dudley Digges and Robert Stapylton: in each case, the translators make a pointed comment on national affairs refracted through Virgil's epic. In most cases, however, the translators explore what sort of model Virgil was providing for a general audience. Thomas Phaer, Thomas Twyne, George Sandys and John Vicars present Aeneas as a man to follow. But their versions of the hero provide very different models for their country: in different translations, Aeneas can be a model for an ideal humanity, for imperial kings or for citizens of a mixed monarchy. Virgil's *Aeneid* was thus able to enter the political culture of Renaissance England in a wide variety of ways.

In the introduction, I showed that Lawrence Humphrey presents two central images for the act of translation: translation was like bringing a treasure into circulation or like drawing a sword from its scabbard. At the end of this book, we are now in a position to see how these two metaphors apply to the contemporary translations of the *Aeneid*. Under the metaphor of bringing out a treasure, we could place many of the most influential translations of this age: those of Thomas Phaer, Thomas Twyne, Richard Stanyhurst and George Sandys. These translators operated under the conviction that their work was providing something of immense value to their nation. Under the metaphor of the sword, we can place the translations by Sir Thomas Wroth, Sir Dudley Digges, John Vicars, Robert Stapylton and Robert Heath. For these translators, the *Aeneid* was a call to violent action for the English state. These two metaphors can suggest just how dynamic the politics – the *utilitas* – of translating Virgil's epic was during the English Renaissance.

Notes

1. Norbrook, *Writing the English Republic*, pp. 310–11 and 374–8.
2. Norbrook aptly describes Harrington's translations as 'an uneasy compromise between parody and tribute'. See Norbrook, *Writing the English Republic*, p. 378.
3. See, for example, Proudfoot, *Dryden's 'Aeneid'*; Norbrook, *Writing the English Republic*; Sowerby, *The Augustan Art of Poetry*.
4. Martindale, *Redeeming the Text*, p. 93.
5. Gillespie, *English Translation and Classical Reception*, p. 72.
6. The 'openness' of the *Aeneid* was a concern for many translators: see Reynolds, *The Poetry of Translation*, pp. 101–18.

7. For one example, Galinsky has considered how Book 5 might be an '*Aeneid in parvo*'. See Galinsky, '*Aeneid* V and the *Aeneid*', p. 185. Another such approach can be found in Hershkowitz, 'The *Aeneid* in *Aeneid* 3'.
8. Lewis, *English Literature*, p. 84.
9. Thomas, *Virgil and the Augustan Reception*; Kallendorf, *The Other Virgil.*
10. Proudfoot, *Dryden's 'Aeneid'*; Sowerby (ed.), *Early Augustan Virgil.*
11. Wilson-Okamura, *Virgil in the Renaissance*, p. 222.
12. A similar case of the ability of Renaissance readers to respond to the entirety of a classical epic has been made by Raphael Lyne regarding Ovid's *Metamorphoses*: Lyne, *Ovid's Changing Worlds*, p. 20.
13. Humphrey, *Interpretatio*, p. 419.
14. For examples on Queen Elizabeth, see Williams, 'Dido, Queen of England'; Weber, 'Intimations of Dido and Cleopatra'. For King James, see James, *Shakespeare's Troy*, pp. 19–21
15. See especially Burrow, 'Virgil in English Translation', p. 25; Venuti, *The Translator's Invisibility*, pp. 35–53.
16. Norbrook, *Writing the English Republic*, pp. 310–11.
17. Lyne, *Ovid's Changing Worlds*, p. 259.

Bibliography

Primary Sources

Manuscripts

Edinburgh, University of Edinburgh Library, Laing III. 453.
London, British Library, Add. MS 28644.
London, British Library, Add. MS 60283.
Los Angeles, William Clarke Memorial Library, MS.1946.007.
Oxford, Bodleian Library, MS Ashmole 38.

Printed

Anon., *A Mervaylous Straunge Deformed Swyne* (London, 1570).

Ariosto, Ludovico, *Orlando Furioso: Translated into English Heroical Verse by Sir John Harington, 1591*, ed. Robert McNulty, trans. Sir John Harington (Oxford: Oxford University Press, 1971).

St Augustine, *The City of God Against the Pagans*, ed. and trans. William M. Green and others, 7 vols (Cambridge, MA: Harvard University Press, 1957–72).

Badius Ascensius, Jodocus, and others, *P. Vergilii Maronis, poetæ Mantuani, Universum poema* (Venice, 1558).

Blunden, Humphrey, *Special Passages and Certain Informations from Severall Places* (London, 1642).

Brinsley, John, *Virgils Eclogues with his Booke De Apibus* (London, 1633).

Butler, Samuel, *Hudibras*, ed. John Wilders (Oxford: Clarendon Press, 1967).

Carew, Thomas, *The Poems of Thomas Carew with his Masque Coelum Britannicum*, ed. Rhodes Dunlap (Oxford: Clarendon Press, 1949).

Cerda, Johannes Ludovicus de la, *P. Virgilii Maronis Priores Sex Libri Aeneidos Argumentis, explicationibus notis illustrati* (Lyons, 1612).

Chamberlain, John, *The Letters*, ed. Norman McClure, 2 vols (Lancaster, 1939).

Chapman, George, *The Iliads of Homer* (London, 1611).

Cicero, *De Re Publica; De Legibus*, trans. Clinton Walker Keyes (Cambridge, MA: Harvard University Press, 1988).

Digges, Sir Dudley, *The Defence of Trade* (London, 1615).

Digges, Sir Dudley, *Didos Death* (London, 1622).

Digges, Sir Dudley, *Fata mihi totum mea sunt agitanda per orbem* (London, 1611).

Digges, Sir Dudley and Thomas Digges, *Four Paradoxes, or Politique Discourses* (London, 1604).

Dolce, Lodovico, *Didone: Tragedia*, ed. Stefano Tomassini (Parma: Edizione Zara, 1996).

Donatus, Tiberius Claudius, *Donati in libros duodecim Aeneidos quæ antea desiderabatur absoluta interpretatio* (Naples, 1535).

Douglas, Gavin, *Virgil's 'Aeneid', Translated into Scottish Verse by Gavin Douglas*, ed. David F. C. Coldwell, 4 vols (Edinburgh: Scottish Text Society, 1957–64).

Dryden, John, *The Works of John Dryden*, 20 vols (Berkeley: University of California Press, 1956–2002), IV: *Poems 1693–1696*, ed. A. B. Chambers and William Frost (1974).

Dryden, John, *The Works of John Dryden*, 20 vols (Berkeley: University of California Press, 1956–2002), VI: *The Works of Virgil in English, 1697*, ed. William Frost and Vincent A. Dearing (1987).

Elizabeth I, *Collected Works*, ed. Leah S. Marcus, Janel Mueller, and Mary Beth Rose (Chicago: Chicago University Press, 2000).

Fleming, Abraham, *The Bucolikes of Publius Virgilius Maro* (London, 1575).

Gager, William, *Complete Works*, ed. and trans. Dana F. Sutton (New York: Garland, 1994).

Gellius, Aulus, *Attic Nights*, ed. and trans. John C. Rolfe, 3 vols, rev. edn (Cambridge, MA: Harvard University Press, 1946–52).

Geoffrey of Monmouth, *The History of the Kings of Britain*, ed. Michael D. Reeve, trans. Neil Wright (Woodbridge: Boydell Press, 2007).

Giraldi, Giovambattista, *Discorsi intorno al comporre de i romanzi, delle comedie e delle tragedie* (Venice, 1554).

Godolphin, Sidney, *The Passion of Dido for Æneas: As It Is Incomparably Exprest in the Fourth Book of Virgil* (London, 1658).

Goodwin, George, *Babels Balm; or The Honey-Combe of Romes Religion*, trans. John Vicars (London, 1624).

Googe, Barnabe, *Eglogs, Epytaphes, and Sonnettes* (London, 1563).

Gorges, Arthur, *The Poems*, ed. Helen Estabrook Sandison (Oxford: Clarendon Press, 1953).

Guicciardini, Francesco, 'How the Popular Government Should Be Reformed', in *Cambridge Translations of Renaissance Philosophical Texts*, ed. Jill Kraye, 2 vols (Cambridge: Cambridge University Press, 1997), II, pp. 201–31.

Hall, Arthur, *Ten Books of Homers Iliades, Translated out of French* (London, 1581).

Hall, Joseph, *The Works*, 12 vols (Oxford: D. A. Talboys, 1839).

Harington, Sir John, *The Epigrams*, ed. Gerard Kilroy (Aldershot: Ashgate, 2009).

Harington, Sir John, *A New Discourse of a Stale Subject, Called the Metamorphosis of Ajax*, ed. Elizabeth Story Donno (London: Routledge & Kegan Paul, 1962).

Harington, Sir John, *The Sixth Book of Virgil's 'Aeneid': Translated and Commented on by Sir John Harington (1604)*, ed. Simon Cauchi (Oxford: Clarendon Press, 1991).

Harington, Sir John, *A Tract on the Succession to the Crown*, ed. Clements R. Markham (London: J. B. Nichols & Sons, 1880).
Heath, Robert, *Clarastella, Together with Poems Occasional, Elegies, Epigrams, Satyrs* (London, 1650).
Herrick, Robert, *The Poetical Works of Robert Herrick*, ed. L. C. Martin (Oxford: Clarendon Press, 1956).
Herring, Francis, *Mischeefes Mysterie, or Treasons Master-Peece, the Powder-Plot*, trans. John Vicars (London, 1617).
Holinshed, Raphael, *Chronicles of England, Scotland, and Ireland*, 6 vols (London, 1808).
Homer, *Odyssey*, ed. and trans. A. T. Murray, rev. George E. Dimock, 2 vols (Cambridge, MA: Harvard University Press, 1998).
Humphrey, Lawrence, *Interpretatio linguarum: seu de ratione convertendi & explicandi autores tam sacros quam prophanos, libri tres* (Basel, 1559).
Humphrey, Lawrence, *The Nobles, or Of Nobility* (London, 1563).
James VI and I, *Political Writings*, ed. Johann P. Sommerville (Cambridge: Cambridge University Press, 1994).
Jonson, Ben, *Ben Jonson*, ed. C. H. Herford, Percy Simpson and Evelyn Mary Spearing, 11 vols (Oxford: Clarendon Press, 1925–52).
Juvenal and Persius, *Juvenal and Persius*, ed. and trans. Susanna Morton Braund (Cambridge, MA: Harvard University Press, 2004).
Kingsbury, Susan Myra (ed.), *The Records of the Virginia Company of London*, 4 vols (Washington, DC: Government Printing Office, 1906–35).
Landino, Cristoforo, and others, *Publii Virgilii Maronis opera cum commentariis Servi Mauri Honorati Grammatici, Aelii Donati, Christophori Landini* (Venice, 1499).
Llwyd, Humphrey, *The Breviary of Britayne*, trans. Thomas Twyne (London, 1573).
Machiavelli, Niccolò, *Discourses on Livy*, trans. Harvey C. Mansfield and Nathan Tarcov (Chicago: University of Chicago Press, 1996).
Marlowe, Christopher, *The Complete Works*, ed. Roma Gill et al., 5 vols (Oxford: Clarendon Press, 1986–98).
Marlowe, Christopher, *The Tragedie of Dido Queene of Carthage* (London, 1594).
Maule, Jeremy and Adrian Poole (eds), *The Oxford Book of Classical Verse in Translation* (Oxford: Oxford University Press, 1995).
Milton, John, *Paradise Lost*, ed. Alastair Fowler, 2nd edn (London: Longman, 1998).
Mornay, Philippe de, *A Woorke Concerning the Trewnesse of the Christian Religions*, trans. Sir Philip Sidney and Arthur Golding (London, 1587).
Mure, Sir William, *The Works of Sir William Mure of Rowallan*, ed. William Tough, 2 vols (Edinburgh: Scottish Text Society, 1898).
Nashe, Thomas, *The Works*, ed. Ronald B. McKerrow, 5 vols (Oxford: Basil Blackwell, 1904–10; repr. 1958).
Notestein, Wallace et al. (eds), *Commons Debates, 1621*, 7 vols (New Haven, CT: Yale University Press, 1935).
Owen, John, *Epigrams of That Most Wittie and Worthie Epigrammatist Mr. Iohn Owen*, trans. John Vicars (London, 1619).
Phaer, Thomas, *The Kegiment [sic] of Life, Whereunto Is Added a Treatyse of the Pestilence, with the Booke of Children Newly Corrected and Enlarged by T. Phayer* (London, 1545).

Phaer, Thomas, *The Nyne Fyrst Bookes of the Eneidos of Virgil* (London, 1562).
Phaer, Thomas, *The Seven First Bookes of the Eneidos of Virgill* (London, 1558).
Phaer, Thomas, *Thomas Phaer and 'The Boke of Chyldren' (1544)* (Tempe, AZ: Arizona Center for Medieval and Renaissance Studies, 1999).
Phaer, Thomas and Thomas Twyne, *The .xiii. Bookes of Æneidos* (London, 1584).
Phaer, Thomas and Thomas Twyne, *The Whole .xii. Bookes of Æneidos of Virgill* (London, 1573).
Phaer, Thomas and Thomas Twyne, *The 'Aeneid' of Thomas Phaer and Thomas Twyne: A Critical Edition Introducing Renaissance Metrical Typography*, ed. Steven Lally (New York: Garland, 1987).
Peletier, Jacques, *L'Art poetique* (Lyon, 1555).
Pigna, Giovanni Battista, *I romanzi, divisi in tre libri* (Venice, 1554).
Polybius, *The Histories, Books 5–8*, trans. W. R. Paton, rev. Frank W. Walbank and Christian Habicht (Cambridge, MA: Harvard University Press, 2011).
Pontanus (Jacob Spanmüller), *Symbolarum libri XVII* (Augsburg, 1599).
Putnam, Michael C. J. and Jan Ziolkowski (eds), *The Virgilian Tradition: The First Fifteen Hundred Years* (New Haven, CT: Yale University Press, 2008).
Puttenham, George, *The Art of English Poesy: A Critical Edition*, ed. Frank Whigham and Wayne A. Rebhorn (Ithaca, NY: Cornell University Press, 2007).
Rhodes, Neil (ed.), *English Renaissance Translation Theory* (London: Modern Humanities Research Association, 2013).
Rich, Nathaniel Sir, *The Rich Papers: Letters from Bermuda: 1615–1646*, ed. Vernon A. Ives (Toronto: University of Toronto Press, 1984).
Ross, Alexander, *Virgilius Evangelisans* (London, 1634).
Sandys, George, *Ovids Metamorphosis Englished, Mythologiz'd and Represented in Figures* (London, 1632).
Sandys, George, *A Paraphrase upon the Divine Poems* (London, 1638).
Sandys, George, *A Relation of a Journey Begun An: Dom: 1610* (London, 1615).
Scaliger, Iulius Caesar, *Poetices libri septem*, ed. Luc Deitz and Gregor Vogt-Spira, 6 vols (Stuttgart: Bad Cannstatt, 1994–2011).
Servius, *Servii grammatici qui feruntur in Vergilii carmina commentarii*, ed. Georg Thilo and Hermann Hagen, 3 vols (Leipzig: Teubner, 1923).
Sidney, Sir Philip, *A Defence of Poetry*, ed. Jan van Dorsten (Oxford: Oxford University Press, 1966).
Smith, John, 'Proceedings of the English Colonie in Virginia', in *A Map of Virginia with a Description of the Countrey, the Commodities, People, Government and Religion* (Oxford, 1612), pp. 1–109.
Southey, Robert, *The Poetical Works of Robert Southey: Complete in One Volume* (Paris: A. & W. Galignani, 1829).
Spenser, Edmund, *The Faerie Queene*, ed. A. C. Hamilton, rev. edn (Harlow: Longman, 2007).
Stanyhurst, Richard, *The First Foure Bookes of Virgils Æneis, Translated in English Heroicall Verse* (London, 1583).
Stanyhurst, Richard, *Harmonia, seu catena dialectica in Porphyrianas institutiones* (London, 1572).
Stanyhurst, Richard, *De rebus in Hibernia gestis* (Antwerp, 1584).

Stanyhurst, Richard, *De Vita S. Patricii, Hiberniae apostoli libri duo* (Antwerp, 1587).
Stapylton, Robert, *Dido and Aeneas: The Fourth Booke of Virgils Aeneis Now Englished* (London, 1634).
Stapylton, Robert, *The First Six Satyrs of Juvenal* (London, 1644).
Stapylton, Robert, *Musæus, on the Loves of Hero and Leander* (London, 1647).
Stapylton, Robert, *Pliny's Panegyricke: A Speech in Senate: Wherein Publike Thankes Are Presented to the Emperour Trajan by C. Plinius Caecilius Secundus* (Oxford, 1644).
Stellato, Marcello, *Le Zodiaque de la vie (Zodiacus vitae) XII livres*, ed. and trans. Jacques Chomarat (Genève: Librairie Droz, 1996).
Surrey, Henry Howard, Earl of, *The 'Aeneid' of Henry Howard, Earl of Surrey*, ed. Florence H. Ridley (Berkeley: University of California Press, 1963).
Twyne, John, *De rebus Albionicis, Britannicis atque Anglicis, commentariorum libri duo* (London, 1590).
Twyne, Thomas, *Of Certain Wonderful Effects of Late Dayes Come to Passe* (London, 1578).
Valvassori, Clemente, *Orlando furioso di M. Lodovico Ariosto, ornato di nuove figure ed allegorie in ciascun canto* (Venice, 1553).
Vegio, Maffeo, *Short Epics*, ed. Michael C. J. Putnam with James Hankins (Cambridge, MA: Havard University Press, 2004).
Vicars, John, *The XII Aeneids of Virgil* (London, 1632).
Vicars, John, *Englands Hallelu-jah, or Great Brittaines Gratefull Retribution, for Gods Gratious Benediction* (London, 1631).
Vicars, John, *Englands Remembrancer, or A Thankfull Acknowledgement of Parliamentary Mercies to our English-Nation* (London, 1641).
Vicars, John, *God on the Mount, or A Continuation of Englands Parliamentary Chronicle* (London, 1643).
Vicars, John, *A Prospective Glasse to Looke into Heaven* (London, 1618).
Vida, Marco Girolamo, *The 'De Arte Poetica'*, ed. and trans. Ralph G. Williams (New York: Columbia University Press, 1976).
Virgil, *Virgil*, trans. H. Rushton Fairclough, rev. G. P. Goold, 2 vols (Cambridge, MA: Harvard University Press, 1999–2000).
Webbe, William, *A Discourse of English Poetrie* (London, 1586).
Wordsworth, William, *Translations of Chaucer and Virgil*, ed. Bruce E. Graver (Ithaca, NY: Cornell University Press, 1998).
Wroth, Sir Thomas, *The Destruction of Troy, or The Acts of Aeneas* (London, 1620).

Secondary Sources

Allen, Don Cameron, 'Marlowe's *Dido* and the Tradition', in *Essays on Shakespeare and Elizabethan Drama: In Honour of Hardin Craig*, ed. Richard Hosley (London: Routledge & Kegan Paul, 1963), pp. 55–68.
Attridge, Derek, *Well-Weighed Syllables: Elizabethan Verse in Classical Meters* (Cambridge: Cambridge University Press, 1974).
Austin, R. G. (ed.), *Aeneidos Liber Primus* (Oxford: Oxford University Press, 1971).
Austin, R. G. (ed.), *Aeneidos Liber Secundus* (Oxford: Clarendon Press, 1964).

Bartels, Emily C., *Spectacles of Strangeness: Imperialism, Alienation, and Marlowe* (Philadelphia: University of Pennsylvania Press, 1993).
Baswell, Christopher, *Virgil in Medieval England* (Cambridge: Cambridge University Press, 1995).
Bawcutt, Priscilla, *Gavin Douglas: A Critical Study* (Edinburgh: Edinburgh University Press, 1976).
Beal, Peter, *Index of English Literary Manuscripts*, 2 vols (London: Mansell, 1980).
Binns, J. W., *Intellectual Culture in Elizabethan and Jacobean England: The Latin Writings of the Age* (Leeds: Francis Cairns, 1990).
Bloom, Harold, *The Anxiety of Influence: A Theory of Poetics* (New York: Oxford University Press, 1973).
Boas, Frederick S., *University Drama in the Tudor Age* (Oxford: Clarendon Press, 1914).
Bono, Barbara J., *Literary Transvaluation: From Vergilian Epic to Shakespearean Tragicomedy* (Berkeley: University of California Press, 1984).
Botley, Paul, *Latin Translation in the Renaissance: The Theory and Practice of Leonardo Bruni, Giannozzi Manetti and Desiderius Erasmus* (Cambridge: Cambridge University Press, 2004).
Bowers, Rick, 'Thomas Phaer and the Assertion of Tudor English', *Renaissance and Reformation*, 33 (1997), 25–40.
Braden, Gordon, 'Epic Kinds', in *The Oxford History of Literary Translation in English*, 5 vols (Oxford: Oxford University Press, 2005–), II: *1550–1660*, ed. Gordon Braden, Robert Cummings, and Stuart Gillespie (2010), pp. 167–93.
Braden, Gordon, Review of *The Oxford Book of Classical Verse*, ed. Adrian Poole and Jeremy Maule, *Translation and Literature*, 6 (1997), 111–17.
Braden, Gordon, 'Translating Procedures in Theory and Practice', in *The Oxford History of Literary Translation in English*, 5 vols (Oxford: Oxford University Press, 2005–), II: *1550–1660*, ed. Gordon Braden, Robert Cummings, and Stuart Gillespie (2010), pp. 89–100.
Broecke, Steven Vanden, *The Limits of Influence: Pico, Louvain, and the Crisis of Renaissance Astrology* (Leiden: Brill, 2003).
Brooks, R. A., '*Discolor Aura*: Reflections on the Golden Bough', *American Journal of Philology,* 74 (1953), 260–80.
Buckley, Emma, '"Live False Aeneas!" Marlowe's *Dido, Queen of Carthage* and the Limits of Translation', *Classical Receptions Journal*, 3 (2011), 129–47.
Burrow, Colin, *Epic Romance: Homer to Milton* (Oxford: Clarendon Press, 1993).
Burrow, Colin, 'The English Humanist Epic, 1580–1614' (unpublished DPhil thesis, University of Oxford, 1989).
Burrow, Colin, Review of *The Sixth Book of Virgil's 'Aeneid'*, ed. Simon Cauchi, *Journal of Roman Studies*, 81 (1991), 248–9.
Burrow, Colin, 'Shakespeare and Humanistic Culture', in *Shakespeare and the Classics*, ed. Charles Martindale and A. B. Taylor (Cambridge: Cambridge University Press, 2004), pp. 9–27.
Burrow, Colin, 'Virgil in English Translation', in *The Cambridge Companion to Virgil*, ed. Charles Martindale (Cambridge: Cambridge University Press, 1997), pp. 21–37.
Cairns, Francis, *Virgil's Augustan Epic* (Cambridge: Cambridge University Press, 1989).

Campbell, Lily B., 'Sidney as "The Learned Soldier"', *Huntington Library Quarterly*, 7 (1944), 175–8.
Cauchi, Simon, 'Introduction', in Sir John Harington, *The Sixth Book of Virgil's 'Aeneid': Translated and Commented on by Sir John Harington (1604)*, ed. Simon Cauchi (Oxford: Clarendon Press, 1991), pp. xi–lxvi.
Cauchi, Simon, 'Sir John Harington and Virgil's *Aeneid* IV', *English Manuscript Studies*, 1 (1989), 242–50.
Cheney, Patrick, *Marlowe's Counterfeit Profession: Ovid, Spenser, Counter-Nationhood* (Toronto: University of Toronto Press, 1997).
Cheney, Patrick, *Marlowe's Republican Authorship: Lucan, Liberty, and the Sublime* (Basingstoke: Palgrave Macmillan, 2009).
Christianson, J. R., 'Tycho Brahe's German Treatise on the Comet of 1577: A Study in Science and Politics', *Isis*, 79 (1979), 110–40.
Christie, Manson & Woods, *Important Literary and Musical Manuscripts and Autograph Letters, Wednesday 5 July, 1978* (London, 1978).
Clausen, Wendell, 'An Interpretation of the *Aeneid*', *Harvard Studies in Classical Philology*, 68 (1964), 139–47.
Coffee, Neil, *The Commerce of War: Exchange and Social Order in Latin Epic* (Chicago: Chicago University Press, 2009).
Comparetti, Domenico, *Vergil in the Middle Ages*, trans. E. F. M. Benecke (Princeton: Princeton University Press, 1997).
Conington, John, 'The English Translators of Virgil', in *Miscellaneous Writings of John Conington, Late Corpus Professor of Latin in the University of Oxford*, ed. J. A. Symonds, 2 vols (London: Longmans, Green, 1872), I, pp. 137–97.
Conley, C. H., *The First English Translators of the Classics* (New Haven, CT: Yale University Press, 1927).
Conte, Gian Biagio, *The Poetry of Pathos: Studies in Virgilian Epic*, ed. S. J. Harrison (Oxford: Oxford University Press, 2007).
Conte, Gian Biagio, 'The Virgilian Paradox: An Epic of Drama and Pathos', trans. Elaine Fantham, in *The Poetry of Pathos: Studies in Virgilian Epic*, ed. S. J. Harrison (Oxford: Oxford University Press, 2007), pp. 23–57.
Cope, Jackson I., 'Marlowe's *Dido* and the Titillating Children', *English Literary Renaissance*, 4 (1974), 315–25.
Craig, D. H., *Sir John Harington* (Boston: Twayne, 1985).
Croft, P. J., 'Introduction', in *The Poems of Robert Sidney*, ed. P. J. Croft (Oxford: Clarendon Press, 1984), pp. 1–114.
Croft, P. J., 'Sir John Harington's Manuscript of Sir Philip Sidney's *Arcadia*', in Stephen Parks and P. J. Croft, *Literary Autographs* (Los Angeles: William Andrews Clark Memorial Library, 1983), pp. 39–75.
Crosland, George N., 'Note on an Unpublished Manuscript by Robert Heath (Fl. 1650),' *Notes and Queries*, 217 (1972), 19–20.
Cummings, Robert (ed.), *Edmund Spenser: The Critical Heritage* (London: Routledge, 1971).
Cummings, Robert and Charles Martindale, 'Jonson's Virgil: Surrey and Phaer', *Translation and Literature*, 16 (2007), 66–75.
Danielson, Dennis, 'On Toads and the Justice of God', *Milton Quarterly*, 13 (1979), 12–14.
Davis, Paul, *Translation and the Poet's Life: The Ethics of Translating in English Culture, 1646–1726* (Oxford: Oxford University Press, 2008).

Davis, Richard Beale, *George Sandys, Poet Adventurer* (London: Bodley Head, 1955).

Dunnigan, Sarah M., *Eros and Poetry at the Courts of Mary Queen of Scots and James VI* (Basingstoke: Palgrave Macmillan, 2002).

Ellison, James, *George Sandys: Travel, Colonialism and Tolerance in the Seventeenth Century* (Cambridge: D. S. Brewer, 2002).

Erskine-Hill, Howard, *The Augustan Idea in English Literature* (London: Edward Arnold, 1983).

Erskine-Hill, Howard, *Poetry and the Realm of Politics: Shakespeare to Dryden* (Oxford: Oxford University Press, 1996).

Feeney, Denis, *The Gods in Epic: Poets and Critics of the Classical Tradition* (Oxford: Clarendon Press, 1991).

Feeney, Denis, 'History and Revelation in Vergil's Underworld', in *Why Vergil? A Collection of Interpretations*, ed. S. Quinn (Wauconda, IL: Bolchazy-Carducci, 2000), pp. 108–22.

Feeney, Denis, 'The Taciturnity of Aeneas', *Classical Quarterly*, 33 (1983), 204–19.

Fichter, Andrew, *Poets Historical: Dynastic Epic in the Renaissance* (New Haven, CT: Yale University Press, 1982).

Fitzmaurice, Andrew, *Humanism and America: An Intellectual History of English Colonization, 1500–1625* (Cambridge: Cambridge University Press, 2003).

Fowler, Don, 'Second Thoughts on Closure', in *Classical Closure: Reading the End in Greek and Latin Literature*, ed. Deborah H. Roberts, Francis M. Dunn and Don Fowler (Princeton: Princeton University Press, 1997), pp. 4–22.

Frost, William, 'Translating Virgil, Douglas to Dryden: Some General Considerations', in *Poetic Traditions of the English Renaissance*, ed. George de Forest Lord and Maynard Mack (New Haven, CT: Yale University Press, 1982), pp. 271–86.

Galinsky, Karl, '*Aeneid* V and the *Aeneid*', *American Journal of Philology*, 89 (1968), 157–85.

Galinsky, Karl, *Augustan Culture: An Interpretive Introduction* (Princeton: Princeton University Press, 1996).

Galinsky, Karl, 'Clothes for the Emperor', *Arion*, 10 (2003), 143–69.

Geneva, Ann, *Astrology and the Seventeenth Century Mind: William Lilly and the Language of the Stars* (Manchester: Manchester University Press, 1995).

Gill, Roma, 'General Introduction to *Dido Queene of Carthage*', in Christopher Marlowe, *The Complete Works of Christopher Marlowe*, ed. Roma Gill, 5 vols (Oxford: Clarendon Press, 1986–98), I (1986), pp. 115–20.

Gill, Roma, 'Marlowe and the Art of Translation', in *'A Poet and a Filthy Play-maker': New Essays on Christopher Marlowe*, ed. Kenneth Friedenreich, Roma Gill and Constance B. Kuriyama (New York: AMS Press, 1988), pp. 327–42.

Gill, Roma, 'Marlowe's Virgil: *Dido Queene of Carthage*', *Review of English Studies*, 28 (1977), 141–55.

Gillespie, Stuart, *English Translation and Classical Reception: Towards a New Literary History* (Oxford: Wiley-Blackwell, 2011).

Gillespie, Stuart, 'Sir John Heath's Translation of Martial', *Notes and Queries*, 61 (2014), 355–7.

Gillespie, Stuart, 'Translations from Greek and Latin Classics, Part 2: 1701–

1800: A Revised Bibliography', *Translation and Literature*, 18 (2009), 181–224.

Grafton, Antony, with April Shelford and Nancy Siraisi, *New Worlds, Ancient Texts: The Power of Tradition and the Shock of Discovery* (Cambridge, MA: Belknap Press, 1992).

Graver, Bruce E., 'Wordsworth and the Language of Epic: The Translation of the *Aeneid*', *Studies in Philology*, 83 (1986), 261–85.

Greenblatt, Stephen, *Renaissance Self-Fashioning* (Chicago: University of Chicago Press, 1980).

Greene, Thomas, *The Light in Troy: Imitation and Discovery in Renaissance Poetry* (New Haven, CT: Yale University Press, 1982).

Gregg, Pauline, *King Charles I* (Berkeley: University of California Press, 1984).

Hadfield, Andrew, 'Briton and Scythian: Tudor Representations of Irish Origins', *Irish Historical Studies*, 28 (1993), 390–408.

Hamilton, Donna B., *Virgil and 'The Tempest': The Politics of Imitation* (Columbus, OH: Ohio State University Press, 1990).

Hammond, Paul, *Dryden and the Traces of Classical Rome* (Oxford: Oxford University Press, 1999).

Hardie, Philip, *The Epic Successors of Virgil: A Study in the Dynamics of a Tradition* (Cambridge: Cambridge University Press, 1993).

Hardie, Philip, *Virgil's 'Aeneid': Cosmos and Imperium* (Oxford: Clarendon Press, 1986).

Hardie, Philip, 'Virgil and Tragedy', in *The Cambridge Companion to Virgil*, ed. Charles Martindale (Cambridge: Cambridge University Press, 1997), pp. 312–26.

Hartmann, Anna-Maria, 'Light from Darkness: The Relationship between Francis Bacon's *Prima Philosophia* and his Concept of the Greek Fable', *Seventeenth Century*, 26 (2011), 203–20

Hay, Milllicent V., *The Life of Robert Sidney: Earl of Leicester (1563–1626)* (Washington, DC: Folger Shakespeare Library, 1984).

Haynes, Jonathan, *The Humanist as Traveler* (London: Associated University Presses, 1986).

Heinze, Richard, *Virgil's Epic Technique*, trans. Hazel Harvey, David Harvey and Fred Robertson (Berkeley: University of California Press, 1993).

Hershkowitz, Debra, 'The *Aeneid* in *Aeneid* 3', *Vergilius*, 37 (1991), 69–76.

Hill, Christopher, *Intellectual Origins of the English Revolution*, rev. edn (Oxford: Clarendon Press, 1997).

Hughey, Ruth, 'The Harington Manuscript at Arundel Castle and Related Documents', *Library*, 15 (1934–5), 388–444.

Hulubei, Alice, 'Virgile en France au XVIe siècle: éditions, traductions, imitations', *Revue du seizième siècle*, 18 (1931), 1–77.

Jack, Ronald D. S., 'Scottish Sonneteer and Welsh Metaphysician: A Study of the Religious Poetry of Sir William Mure and Henry Vaughan', *Studies in Scottish Literature*, 3 (1966), 240–7.

James, Heather, *Shakespeare's Troy: Drama, Politics, and the Translation of Empire* (Cambridge: Cambridge University Press, 1997).

Javitch, Daniel, *Proclaiming a Classic: The Canonization of the 'Orlando Furioso'* (Princeton: Princeton University Press, 1991).

Jones, Howard Mumford, *O Strange New World: American Culture, the Formative Years* (New York: Viking Press, 1964).

Kallendorf, Craig, *In Praise of Aeneas: Virgil and Epideictic Rhetoric in the*

Early Italian Renaissance (Hanover, NH: University Press of New England, 1989).

Kallendorf, Craig, *The Other Virgil: 'Pessimistic' Readings of the 'Aeneid' in Early Modern Culture* (Oxford: Oxford University Press, 2007).

Kallendorf, Craig, *Virgil and the Myth of Venice: Books and Readers in the Italian Renaissance* (Oxford: Clarendon Press, 1999).

Kelliher, Hilton and Katherine Duncan-Jones, 'A Manuscript of Poems by Robert Sidney: Some Early Impressions', *British Library Journal*, 1 (1975), 107–44.

Kelsall, Malcolm, *Christopher Marlowe* (Leiden: E. J. Brill, 1981).

Kemp, Janet Karen, 'Laurence Humphrey, Elizabethan Puritan: His Life and Political Theories' (unpublished PhD Thesis, West Virginia University, 1978).

Kerrigan, John, *Archipelagic English: Literature, History, and Politics* (Oxford: Oxford University Press, 2008).

Kilroy, Gerard, 'The Pleasant Learned Poet', in Sir John Harington, *The Epigrams of Sir John Harington*, ed. Gerard Kilroy (Aldershot: Ashgate, 2009), pp. 1–90.

Kinney, Clare R., 'Epic Transgression and the Framing of Agency in *Dido Queen of Carthage*', *Studies in English Literature, 1500–1900*, 40 (2000), 261–76.

Kläger, Florian, *Forgone Nations: Constructions of National Identity in Elizabethan Historiogarphy: Stanihurst, Spenser, Shakespeare* (Trier: Wissenschaftlicher Verlag Trier, 2006).

Kopperman, Paul E., *Sir Robert Heath 1575–1649: Window on an Age* (Woodbridge: Boydell Press, 1989).

Lake, Peter, 'Anti-Popery: The Structure of a Prejudice', in *Conflict in Early Stuart England: Studies in Religion and Politics, 1603–1642*, ed. Richard Cust and Ann Hughes (London: Longman, 1989), pp. 72–106.

Lally, Steven, 'Introduction', in Thomas Phaer and Thomas Twyne, *The 'Aeneid' of Thomas Phaer and Thomas Twyne: A Critical Edition Introducing Renaissance Metrical Typography*, ed. Steven Lally (New York: Garland, 1987), pp. xi–lxii.

Lathrop, Henry Burrowes, *Translations from the Classics into English from Caxton to Chapman, 1477–1620* (Madison: University of Wisconsin Press, 1933).

Lennon, Colm, *Richard Stanihurst: The Dubliner* (Dublin: Irish Academic Press, 1981).

Levin, Harry, *Christopher Marlowe: The Overreacher* (London: Faber & Faber, 1961).

Lewis, C. S., *English Literature in the Sixteenth Century, Excluding Drama* (Oxford: Clarendon Press, 1954).

Lewis, Rhodri, 'Francis Bacon, Allegory and the Uses of Myth', *Review of English Studies*, 61 (2010), 360–89.

Light, Alfred, *Bunhill Fields, Written in Honour and to the Memory of the Many Saints of God Whose Bodies Rest in this Old London Cemetery* (London: C. J. Farncombe & Sons, 1915).

Lindsay, Maurice, *History of Scottish Literature*, rev. edn (London: Robert Hale, 1992).

Lucas, Corinne, 'Didon: Trois réécritures tragiques du livre de l'Eneide dans le théâtre italien du XVIe siècle', in *Scritture di scritture: Testi, generi, modelli nel Rinascimento*, ed. Giancarlo Mazzacurati and Michel Plaisance (Rome: Bulzoni, 1987), pp. 593–604.

Lyne, Raphael, *Ovid's Changing Worlds: English Metamorphoses, 1567–1632* (Oxford: Oxford University Press, 2001).

Lyne, R. O. A. M., *Further Voices in Vergil's 'Aeneid'* (Oxford: Clarendon Press, 1987).

Lyne, R. O. A. M., *Words and the Poet: Characteristic Techniques of Style in Vergil's 'Aeneid'* (Oxford: Clarendon Press, 1989).

McCabe, Richard, *Spenser's Monstrous Regiment: Elizabethan Ireland and the Poetics of Difference* (Oxford: Oxford University Press, 2002).

MacCormack, Sabine, *The Shadows of Poetry: Virgil in the Mind of Augustine* (Berkeley: University of California Press, 1998).

Martindale, Charles, *Redeeming the Text: Latin Poetry and the Hermeneutics of Reception* (Cambridge: Cambridge University Press, 1993).

Matthiessen, F. O., *Translation: An Elizabethan Art* (Cambridge, MA: Harvard University Press, 1931).

May, Steve W., *The Elizabethan Courtier Poets: The Poems and their Contexts* (Columbia, MO: University of Missouri Press, 1991).

May, Steve W., 'Tudor Aristocrats and the Mythical "Stigma of Print"', *Renaissance Papers*, 10 (1980), 11–18.

Miller, R. H., 'Sir John Harington's Manuscripts in Italic', *Studies in Bibliography*, 40 (1987), 101–6.

Morini, Massimiliano, *Tudor Translation in Theory and Practice* (Aldershot: Ashgate, 2006).

Moul, Victoria, *Jonson, Horace, and the Classical Tradition* (Cambridge: Cambridge University Press, 2010).

Nisbet, R. G., '*Aeneas Imperator*: Roman Generalship in an Epic Context', *Proceedings of the Virgil Society*, 18 (1978–80), 50–61.

Norbrook, David, *Poetry and Politics in the English Renaissance*, rev. edn (Oxford: Oxford University Press, 2002).

Norbrook, David, *Writing the English Republic: Poetry, Rhetoric and Politics* (Cambridge: Cambridge University Press, 1999).

Norton, Glyn P., *The Ideology and Language of Translation in Renaissance France and their Humanist Antecedents* (Genève: Librairie Droz, 1984).

Otis, Brooks, *Virgil: A Study in Civilized Poetry* (Oxford: Clarendon Press, 1963).

Panoussi, Vassiliki, *Greek Tragedy in Vergil's 'Aeneid': Ritual, Empire, and Intertext* (Cambridge: Cambridge University Press, 2009).

Parry, Adam, 'The Two Voices of Virgil's *Aeneid*', *Arion*, 2 (1963), 66–80.

Pearcy, Lee T., *The Mediated Muse: English Translations of Ovid 1560–1700* (Hamden, CT: Archon Books, 1984).

Peltonen, Markku, *Classical Humanism and Republicanism in English Political Thought, 1570–1640* (Cambridge: Cambridge University Press, 1995).

Pigman III, G. W., 'Versions of Imitation in the Renaissance', *Renaissance Quarterly*, 33 (1980), 1–32.

Pocock, J. G. A., *The Machiavellian Moment: Florentine Political Thought and the Atlantic Republican Tradition* (Princeton: Princeton University Press, 1975).

Potter, Lucy, 'Marlowe's *Dido*: Virgilian or Ovidian?', *Notes and Queries*, 56 (2009), 540–4.

Proudfoot, Leslie, *Dryden's 'Aeneid' and its Seventeenth-Century Predecessors* (Manchester: Manchester University Press, 1960).
Putnam, Michael C. J., 'Introduction', in Maffeo Vegio, *Short Epics*, ed. Michael C. J. Putnam with James Hankins (Cambridge, MA: Harvard University Press, 2004), pp. vii–lviii.
Putnam, Michael C. J., *The Poetry of the 'Aeneid': Four Studies in Imaginative Unity and Design* (Cambridge, MA: Harvard University Press, 1965).
Quint, David, *Epic and Empire: Politics and Generic Form from Virgil to Milton* (Princeton: Princeton University Press, 1993).
Redworth, Glyn, *The Prince and the Infanta: The Cultural Politics of the Spanish Match* (New Haven, CT: Yale University Press, 2003).
Rener, Frederick M., *Interpretatio: Language and Translation from Cicero to Tytler* (Amsterdam: Rodopi, 1989).
Reynolds, Matthew, *The Poetry of Translation: From Chaucer & Petrarch to Homer & Logue* (Oxford: Oxford University Press, 2011).
Rosier, James L., 'Richard Stanyhurst and Sixteenth-Century Lexical Usage', *Studia Neophilologica,* 33 (1961), 115–27.
Rubin, Deborah, *Ovid's 'Metamorphoses' Englished: George Sandys as Translator and Mythographer* (New York: Garland, 1985).
Saintsbury, George, *A History of Prosody: From the Twelfth Century to the Present Day*, 2nd edn (London: Macmillan, 1923).
Saunders, J. W., 'The Stigma of Print: A Note on the Social Bases of Tudor Poetry', *Essays in Criticism*, 1 (1951), 139–64.
Schwyzer, Philip, *Literature, Nationalism, and Memory in Early Modern England and Wales* (Cambridge: Cambridge University Press, 2004).
Scott-Warren, Jason, *Sir John Harington and the Book as Gift* (Oxford: Oxford University Press, 2001).
Sessions, W. A., *Henry Howard, the Poet Earl of Surrey: A Life* (Oxford: Oxford University Press, 1999).
Sgarbi, Marco, *The Aristotelian Tradition and the Rise of British Empiricism: Logic and Epistemology in the British Isles (1570–1689)* (Dordrecht: Springer, 2013).
Sharpe, Kevin, *Criticism and Compliment: The Politics of Literature in the England of Charles I* (Cambridge: Cambridge University Press, 1987).
Skinner, Quentin, *The Foundations of Modern Political Thought*, 2 vols (Cambridge: Cambridge University Press, 1978).
Smalley, Beryl, *English Friars and Antiquity in the Early Fourteenth Century* (Oxford: Basil Blackwell, 1960).
Smith, Mary E., *'Love Kindling Fire': A Study of Christopher Marlowe's 'The Tragedy of Dido Queen of Carthage'* (Salzburg: Institut für Englische Sprache und Literatur, 1977).
Sowerby, Robin, 'Introduction', in *Early Augustan Virgil: Translations by Denham, Godolphin, and Waller*, ed. Robin Sowerby (Lewisburg: Bucknell University Press, 2010), pp. 11–22.
Sowerby, Robin, *The Augustan Art of Poetry: Augustan Translation of the Classics* (Oxford: Oxford University Press, 2006).
Spiller, Michael, 'Poetry after the Union 1603–1660', in *The History of Scottish Literature*, 4 vols (Aberdeen: Aberdeen University Press, 1987–9), I: *Origins to 1660*, ed. R. D. S. Jack (1988), pp. 141–62.
Steane, J. B., *Marlowe: A Critical Study* (Cambridge: Cambridge University Press, 1965).

Steiner, George, *After Babel: Aspects of Language and Translation*, 3rd edn (Oxford: Oxford University Press, 1998).
Sutton, Dana Ferrin, 'Introduction to *Pareus*', in Richard Eedes and George Peele, *Oxford Poetry by Richard Eedes and George Peele* (London: Garland, 1995), pp. 153–75.
Terpening, Ronnie H., *Lodovico Dolce: Renaissance Man of Letters* (Toronto: University of Toronto Press, 1997).
Thomas, Richard F., *Virgil and the Augustan Reception* (Cambridge: Cambridge University Press, 2001).
Tough, William, 'Introduction', in William Mure, *The Works of Sir William Mure of Rowallan*, ed. William Tough, 2 vols (Edinburgh: Scottish Text Society, 1898), I, pp. vii–xxvii.
Tudeau-Clayton, Margaret, *Jonson, Shakespeare and Early Modern Virgil* (Cambridge: Cambridge University Press, 1998).
Tudeau-Clayton, Margaret, 'Richard Carew, William Shakespeare and the Politics of Translating Virgil in Early Modern England and Scotland', *International Journal of the Classical Tradition*, 5 (1999), 507–27.
Tyacke, Nicholas, *Anti-Calvinists: The Rise of English Arminianism c.1590–1640* (Oxford: Clarendon Press, 1987).
Underdown, David, *Somerset in the Civil War and Interregnum* (Newton Abbot: David & Charles, 1973).
Venuti, Lawrence, *The Translator's Invisibility*, 2nd edn (London: Routledge, 2008).
Vickers, Brian, *In Defence of Rhetoric* (Oxford: Clarendon Press, 1989).
Vickers, Brian, *Shakespeare, Co-Author: A Historical Study of Five Plays* (Oxford: Oxford University Press, 2002).
Visser, Arnoud S. Q., *Reading Augustine in the Reformation: The Flexibility of Intellectual Authority in Europe, 1500–1620* (Oxford: Oxford University Press, 2011).
Wallace, Andrew, *Virgil's Schoolboys: The Poetics of Pedagogy in Renaissance England* (Oxford: Oxford University Press, 2010).
Walsham, Alexandra, *Providence in Early Modern England* (Oxford: Oxford University Press, 1999).
Watkins, John, *The Specter of Dido: Spenser and Virgilian Epic* (New Haven, CT: Yale University Press, 1995).
Weber, Clifford, 'Intimations of Dido and Cleopatra in Some Contemporary Portrayals of Elizabeth I', *Studies in Philology*, 96 (1999), 127–43.
Weil, Judith, *Christopher Marlowe: Merlin's Prophet* (Cambridge: Cambridge University Press, 1977).
Williams, Deanne, 'Dido, Queen of England', *English Literary History*, 73 (2006), 31–59.
Williams, William P., 'The Castle Ashby Manuscripts: A Description of the Volumes in Bishop Percy's List', *Library*, 6 (1980), 391–412.
Wilson-Okamura, David Scott, *Virgil in the Renaissance* (Cambridge: Cambridge University Press, 2010).
Wilson-Okamura, David Scott, 'Virgilian Models of Colonization in Shakespeare's *Tempest*', *English Literary History*, 70 (2003), 709–37.
Wiltshire, Susan Ford, 'Aeneas in America', *Vergilius*, 25 (1979), 2–9.
Wood, Henry, 'The Beginnings of the "Classical" Heroic Couplet in England', *American Journal of Philology*, 11 (1890), 55–79.

Worden, Blair, *The Rump Parliament, 1648–1653* (Cambridge: Cambridge University Press, 1974).
Worth, Valerie, *Practising Translation in Renaissance France: The Example of Étienne Dolet* (Oxford: Clarendon Press, 1988).
Woudhuysen, Henry, *Sir Philip Sidney and the Circulation of Manuscripts, 1558–1640* (Oxford: Clarendon Press, 1996).
Ziolkowski, Theodore, *Virgil and the Moderns* (Princeton: Princeton University Press, 1993).

Index

Albertus Alasco, Prince, 73
allegory, 3, 136, 166–70
Allen, Don Cameron, 69, 72
amatory poetry, 79, 81, 85, 87–8, 101–3, 105, 107–10
anachronisms, 23, 26, 43, 45, 72
Anguillara, Giovanni dell', 92
Anne, Queen, 119
anti-Catholicism, 154–65
Appian, 137
Ariosto, Ludovico, 79, 86, 92–4, 95, 189
Aristotelian logical system, 39
Aristotelian physics, 37
Aristotle, 9, 14
Arundel, Earl of, 88
Augustan *Aeneids*, 7–8, 12, 149–50, 158, 160, 164, 165, 170, 177, 181, 187–8
Augustine, Saint, 89, 97
  City of God (De civitate Dei), 95–6, 113n, 161
Ausonius, 137, 141
Avicenna, 21

Bacon, Francis, 139
Badius Ascensius, Jodocus, 22, 29, 30, 67, 68, 146n
ballad metre, 23–4, 26, 33, 189
balladeers, 153
Baswell, Christopher, 58
Beal, Peter, 80
blank verse, 24, 189
Bloom, Harold, 47
Boccaccio, 138
Bono, Barbara, 74
Bothwell, Earl of, 1, 2
Bowers, Rick, 21–2
Braden, Gordon, 6, 8, 9, 10
Brahe, Tycho, 37
bravery, 29, 30, 163, 178–80
Brinsley, John, 83
Brooks, R. A., 7
Bruni, Leonardo, 11
Buckley, Emma, 57, 60
Budé, Guillaume, 89
Burrow, Colin, 5, 6, 36, 69, 80, 84, 86, 94, 151, 158
Butler, Captain Nathaniel, 120, 125
Butler, Samuel, 150–1, 152, 153, 187

Cambrensis, Giraldus, 38
Campion, Edmund, 39, 40, 45
Carew, Thomas, 169
Carleton, Dudley, 125
Caro, Annibale, 19, 92
Carthage, 36, 64, 66–7, 73, 117, 137, 160, 163, 166–7, 169–70
Castle Ashby translation *see* manuscript translations
Catholicism, 5, 22, 28, 36–7, 40, 43–4, 45
Cauchi, Simon, 79, 80–1, 85, 92–3
Caxton, William, 23, 24
Cerda, Johannes Ludovicus de la, 105
Cerretani, Aldobrandi, 92
Chaloner, Thomas, 88
Chamberlain, John, 125, 129
Chapman, George, 119
Charles I (Prince Charles), 132, 157–60
  dedications to, 102
  parliament and, 176
  peace treaties and, 168–9
  Spanish marriage plan and, 133
Chasseneux, Barthélemy de, 90
Chaucer, Geoffrey, 58–9, 60
Chaucerian English, 41–2, 48, 189
Cheney, Patrick, 57, 62
choruses, 57, 72–3, 74
Christianity, 97, 135, 138, 161, 162; *see also* Catholicism; Protestantism
Cicero, 11, 14, 167, 168
Civil War, 150, 151, 152, 154, 172, 177, 179, 180, 191
Clausen, Wendell, 7
Coffee, Neil, 169
colonialism, 40–1, 116, 119–20, 125, 130, 141–2, 191; *see also* Virginia Company
commentaries, 3, 22, 29, 39, 57–9, 61, 67, 79, 95–7, 105, 118, 123–4, 166, 168, 184n
  Harington, 89–93, 94, 95, 98–9, 100, 161
  Sandys, 134, 136, 137, 140–3
common good, 13, 83, 164
commonwealths, 142–5, 166–7
Compton, James, 79
Compton, William Lord, 79

Conington, John, 151
Conley, C. H., 4, 5
Constantinople, 137
Conte, Gian Biagio, 71–2
Cope, Jackson I., 62
Coryat, Tom, 152
court culture, 7, 86–8, 170, 174
Cowley, Abraham, 38, 44
Craig, D. H., 80, 94
Crosland, George N., 172
Cummings, Robert, 152

dactylic hexameters, 8, 23, 24–6, 32, 34, 42, 43, 140, 189
Daniel, Samuel, 92
Dante Alighieri, 59, 177
Davis, Paul, 7, 12, 44
Denham, Sir John, 38, 44, 78, 149, 187
Digges, Sir Dudley, 83, 116, 117, 144–5, 150, 168, 192
  Aeneid translation by, 131–3, 160, 170
  Didos Death, 125, 126, 131, 159, 160, 166, 170
  Foure Paradoxes, 126–9
  Heaths and, 171
  parliamentary speech against Spain, 130–1
Digges, Thomas (father), *Foure Paradoxes*, 126–8
Dolce, Lodovico, 71, 72, 92
Dolet, Étienne, 24
domestications, 65, 121, 132, 145, 160, 174, 176
Donatus, Tiberius Claudius, 61, 64, 67, 166
Douglas, Gavin, 5, 19, 20, 23, 24, 25, 58, 59–61, 78, 83, 102, 189
Dowland, Robert, 119
Drayton, Michael, 92
Dryden, John, 5, 6, 8, 15, 44, 131, 178
Du Bartas, Guillaume, 173
Du Bellay, Joachim, 56, 87
Dugres, Gabriel, 173
Dyer, Sir Edward, 87

East India Company, 126, 130
Eclogues, 3, 22, 83
education, 83, 158, 164
Egypt, 135
Elizabeth I, Queen, 1–3, 9, 37, 71, 126, 127, 132, 156–7, 191, 192
Elizabeth of Bohemia (Elizabeth Stuart), 130, 132, 156
Ellison, James, 139
empatheia, 71
emulation, 13–15, 18n, 23, 36, 47, 94–5, 100, 133, 160, 181
English language, 31, 38, 41–2, 47–8
English Pale *see* Ireland
epideictic readings/rhetoric, 13, 59, 60, 62, 74, 91–2, 142, 144, 189
epigrams, 119–20, 154
Erasmus, 89
eroticism, 63, 84–6, 86, 119
Erskine-Hill, Howard, 149
Essex, Earl of, 87, 95, 126
ethics of translation, 14, 78, 96, 103–4
ethics of Virgil's poetry, 63, 87, 104, 109, 133, 155, 161–2

exemplars, 14, 27–8, 180
exile, 9, 12, 38, 40, 42, 44–5, 48, 169

Fairfax, Edward, 92
Falkland, Lord, 133, 134–5, 144
Fanshawe, Sir Richard, 81, 189
Fawkes, Guy, 155
Feeney, Denis, 61, 98, 161
Ferdinand II, Emperor, 130
Fitzmaurice, Andrew, 125, 142–3
Fleming, Abraham, 83
fourteeners, 24, 25, 34, 42, 93, 94, 121, 189
France, 71, 117, 168
Fraunce, Abraham, 119
Frederick I, King of Bohemia, 130, 156
free translation/invention, 14, 55, 56, 63, 65, 74, 81–3, 101, 103–4, 156
Frost, William, 5, 172

Gager, William, 71, 72, 73
Galen of Pergamon, 21
Galinksy, Karl, 98
Gardiner, Stephen, 9
Gellius, Aulus, 104
Geoffrey of Monmouth, 27
Georgics, 3, 22, 83, 104, 157
German Romantics, 72
Gill, Roma, 56, 57–8, 68
Gillespie, Stuart, 6, 15, 17n, 78, 110, 185n, 188
Giraldi-Cinthio, Giambattista, 71, 72, 93
glosses, 26, 28, 30, 33–4, 35, 36, 85–6, 123, 168
Godolphin, Sidney, 160
Goeurot, Jean, 21
Goodwin, George, 154
Googe, Barnabe, 20, 21
Gorges, Sir Arthur, 87
Gournay, Marie de, 117
Grafton, Antony, 136
Great Comet (1577), 37
Greenblatt, Stephen, 62
Greene, Thomas, 20, 23
Gregg, Pauline, 168–9
Greville, Fulke, 87
Grimald, Nicholas, 20
Guicciardini, Francesco, 167–8
Gun Powder Plot (1605), 154–5, 156

Hall, Arthur, 20
Hall, Joseph, 46, 47, 48
Halliwell, Edward, 71
Hamilton, Donna B., 6
Hardie, Philip, 98
Harington, Sir John, 10, 19, 161, 187, 192
  Aeneid translation by, 81, 83, 88–100
  attribution of BL Add MS 60283 to, 79–81
  glosses by, 85–6
  Orlando Furioso, 93–4
  A Tract on the Succession to the Crown, 90
  tumultuous year of, 95
Harrington, James, 151, 159, 174, 187
Haynes, Jonathan, 138
Heath, John, 173
Heath, Robert, 15, 160, 190
  Aeneid translation by, 174–81
  attribution to, 172–3
  Clarastella, 172, 173, 177, 178, 185n

Heath, Robert (*cont.*)
  humour in, 175–6
  and Vicars compared, 175–6
Heath, Sir Robert (father), 171, 172, 176, 177
Heinze, Richard, 71, 124
Heneage, Sir Thomas, 88
Henry, Prince, 78, 88–9, 90, 94, 95
hermeneutics, 58–9, 60, 62
Herring, Francis, 154, 155
Hill, Christopher, 4
Holinshed's *Chronicles*, 39, 40, 41, 47
Homer, 20, 29–30, 137
  contrast between Virgil and, 71
  Iliad, 20, 30, 71, 92–3
  Odyssey, 30, 109–10
How, William, 32–3
Huet, Pierre-Daniel, 10
Hulubei, Alice, 145
humanism, 11, 22, 23, 29–31, 35, 89–91, 128, 142–5
humanist *Aeneids*, 145
  Gavin Douglas, 59–61, 75
  Phaer-Twyne, 22–37, 49
humour, 99–100, 175–6, 177
Humphrey, Lawrence, 39, 47, 49, 78, 94, 175
  on free translation, 56, 103–4
  Interpretatio linguarum, 8–15, 17n, 56, 190
  metaphors for translation, 12, 49, 192
  The Nobles; or, Of Nobility, 35

iambic pentameter, 140, 175, 189
Iliad, 20, 30, 71, 92–3
imitation, 10, 23–5, 46, 71, 121, 174
  Dido Queene of Carthage, 55–6
  emulation and, 13–14
interpolations, 58, 84, 101, 104–8, 122, 140
Ireland, 38–9, 40–2, 47–8

James, Heather, 6
James I and VI, 119, 127, 139, 157, 191
  Basilikon Doron, 89–90, 98, 149
  European crisis (1621) and, 130, 131, 132, 133
  foreign policy of, 126
  Harington's presentation to, 78, 88–9
  letters between Queen Elizabeth and, 1–3, 192
  warfare and, 128–9
Jamestown massacre (1622), 139
Javitch, Daniel, 92
Jodelle, Étienne, 71, 72
Jones, Howard Mumford, 116–17
Jones, Robert, 119
Jonson, Ben, 73–4, 149, 152, 153

Kallendorf, Craig, 6, 7, 29, 72
Kelliher, W. H., 185n
Kelly, L. G., 166
Kelsall, Malcolm, 57
Kerrigan, John, 42
Kilroy, Gerard, 89, 111n
Kinney, Clare R., 57
Kläger, Florian, 40

Lally, Steven, 21–2, 32
Landino, Cristoforo, 67–8, 124
language, 12, 21, 22, 31, 40–2, 45, 47, 48, 62, 140, 142, 158
Lee, Sir Henry, 88
Lennon, Colm, 38, 40, 45
Lenox, Katherine Stewart, Duchess of, 158
Levin, Harry, 62, 68–9
Lewis, C. S., 37, 189
Lindsay, Maurice, 102
Llwyd, Humphrey, 27
'loftiness', 21, 22, 23, 25–6, 31, 37–8, 46, 48, 49
Longiano, Fausto da, 11
loyalty, 177–8
Lyne, Raphael, 5, 83, 99, 136–7, 140, 191, 193n

Machiavelli, Niccolò, 128, 167
Magdalen College, Oxford University, 9, 10
Manetti, Giannozzi, 11
Manuche, Cosmo, 79, 80
manuscript translations, 78–9, 110, 174–5, 189
  BL Add. MS 60283 (Castle Ashby), 79–88, 110
  Robert Heath, 171–81
  Sir John Harington, 81, 83, 88–100
  Sir William Mure, 100–10
Marcellus, 98
Markham, Thomas, 95
Marlowe, Christopher, 76n, 188
  Dido Queene of Carthage, 4, 55–7, 101: additions to, 105, 106–7; dramatic and epic voices in, 70–5; and the Renaissance *Aeneid*, 57–62; translations of the *Aeneid* in, 63–70
  Ovid's *Amores*, 65
  Tamburlaine, 62, 68
Martial, 120, 173
Martindale, Charles, 188
martyrdom, 45, 48, 49, 102
Mary, Queen, 9, 36, 121
Matthiessen, F. O., 4–5
May, Steven, 87
Menni, Vincentio, 92
mercenaries, 167–8
metre, 8, 189
  ballad, 23–4, 26, 33, 189
  experimentation, 42, 80
  fourteeners, 24, 25, 34, 42, 93, 94, 121, 189
  George Sandys and, 140
  hexameters, 8, 23, 24–6, 32, 34, 42, 43, 140, 189
  ottava rima, 80, 81, 87, 92–3, 94, 112n, 189
  Richard Stanyhurst and, 42–3
  Robert Heath and, 175
  Thomas Phaer and, 23–6
  Thomas Wroth and, 121
  see also stanzas
military *Aeneids*, 7, 149–81
  Dudley Digges, 125–33, 150, 159–60
  John Vicars, 154–65
  Robert Heath, 160, 171–81
  Robert Stapylton, 165–71
Milton, John, 178
monarchy, 98, 112n, 149–50, 163–4, 176–7, 183n, 192
Montgomerie, Alexander, 101, 102
More, Sir Thomas, 23

Mornay, Philippe de, 161
Moseley, Humphrey, 172
Mure, Sir William, 78, 100–10
Musaeus Grammaticus, 168

Nashe, Thomas, 20, 21, 46, 48, 69
neologisms, 42, 47, 158–9
Netherlands, 40, 44, 45
Norbrook, David, 127, 159
Northwest Passage, 129
Norton, Glyn P., 17n, 56

Ogilby, John, 3
oratory, 60–2, 142
Otis, Brooks, 71
ottava rima, 80, 81, 87, 92–3, 94, 112n, 189
Ovid, 5, 62, 65, 88, 134, 135, 137, 139, 191
Owen, John, 154
Oxford, Earl of, 87
Oxford University (Magdalen College), 9, 10

pagan gods/saints, 28, 36, 43–4
Parker, Martin, 152, 153
parliament, 125, 130–1, 154, 157, 176, 177
'parliament' in translations, 26, 163–5, 176, 183n
parliamentarians, 125, 130–1, 132, 133, 150–3, 159–60
Parry, Adam, 7
Parry, William, 16n
patriotism, 4–5, 13
patronage, 89, 118–19
Pazzi, Alessandro, 71, 72
Pearcy, Lee, 139, 140
Peele, George, 15–16n, 69
Peletier, Jacques, 10, 56
Pembroke, Countess of, 92
Percy, Bishop, 89
Périon, Joachim, 9, 11, 14
perspicuity, 11, 15
pessimistic readings of the *Aeneid*, 7, 13, 75, 106, 189, 191; *see also* Marlowe, Christopher
Petrarch, 102, 108, 138
Phaer, Thomas, 15, 19–37, 88, 93, 180, 188, 190, 191, 192
  Catholicism, 36–7
  fourteeners, 94
  Stanyhurst and, 38, 41, 42, 43, 44, 46, 47
  word 'parliament' and, 163
  young readers and, 83
'pietas', 30, 162, 183n
piety, 90, 91, 108, 128, 143–4, 155, 160
Pigman III, G. W., 13
Pigna, G. B., 93
pilgrims, 36, 44–5, 49, 162, 182n
pity, 70, 107–8, 162
'pius', as epithet for Aeneas, 30, 34, 37, 143, 162–3
Pliny, 21, 168
Pocock, J. G. A., 128
politics *see* monarchy; parliament; royalism
Polybius, 167–8
Pope, Alexander, 44
Potter, Lucy, 74
Powell, Thomas, 119
print culture, 87
prophecy, 27, 63, 65, 124, 136, 138, 141, 162, 170, 176
Protestantism, 4, 36, 37, 119, 131, 132, 133
Proudfoot, Leslie, 6, 8, 18n, 131–2, 158, 159, 170
providentialism, 37, 64, 155–6, 160, 161, 162
Prynne, William, 151, 153
puritanism, 151–2, 154, 160, 162
Putnam, Michael, 35
Puttenham, George, 20, 48
Pythagorean transmigration of souls, 94, 97, 100

quantitative verse movement, 42, 50n
Quint, David, 69, 70, 166–7

republicanism, 98, 151, 187
Reynolds, Matthew, 11
rhetoric, 30, 61–2, 67, 69–70, 87, 93, 106–7, 135, 137, 143, 157
  epideictic, 29, 35, 59, 74, 136, 142
Rich, Sir Nathaniel, 120
Roman Empire, 26, 127, 143, 161–2, 167, 187
  decline of, 94, 96, 97–8
Roman nobility, 22, 26–8, 31, 34
Rosier, James L., 47–8
Ross, Alexander, 157–8
royalism, 3, 5, 8, 13, 170, 172, 175–7, 181, 191
Rubin, Deborah, 140

saints/pagan gods, 28, 36, 43–4
Sallust, 96, 97
Sandys, George, 27, 99, 100, 116, 117, 133–45, 148n, 149, 150, 157, 192
  Aeneid translation by, 140–5, 162, 170
  Ovids Metamorphosis, 139–44
  A Relation of a Journey, 134–9, 140–1, 147n
  style of translation, 158
satire, 42, 45–6, 47, 151, 154, 170, 178
Scaliger, Julius Caesar, 47
Scots language, 19, 24
Scott-Warren, Jason, 86, 111n, 112n
Sebillet, Thomas, 24, 56
seditious material, 78, 86
Servius, 61, 96, 123–4, 184n
Sessions, W. A., 24
sestets, 79, 87, 101, 189
Shakespeare, William, 87, 191
Sharpe, Kevin, 170
Sidney, Henry, 39
Sidney, Sir Philip, 30, 127, 128, 129, 142
Sidney, Sir Robert, 118–19, 120
similes, 34, 36, 49, 82–3, 104, 108, 111n
Skinner, Quentin, 89
Skinner, Sir John, 95
Smith, John, 116–17
Smith, Mary E., 57, 76n
Smith, Sir Thomas, 119, 129
Smythe, Thomas, 119
Southey, Robert, 42
Sowerby, Robin, 8, 149, 165
Spain, 40, 130–1, 132, 133, 168
Spanish Armada, 156
Spenser, Edmund, 30, 62, 81, 87, 92, 153, 191
Spiller, Michael, 102

Stanyhurst, Richard, 10, 15, 19, 21, 23, 36, 37–48, 189
stanzas, 155
  ababcc six-line, 79, 87, 101
  Harington, 79–82, 84, 91, 92, 94–5, 112n
  Mure, 101, 103, 107–8, 110
Stapylton, Robert, 123, 159, 165–71, 192
Steane, J. B., 66, 68
Steiner, George, 9, 25, 65
Stewart, George, John and Bernhard, 158, 164
Strachey, William, 116
Strange, Lord, 88
Sturm, Johann, 89
Surrey, Henry Howard, Earl of, 19, 20, 23, 24, 25, 32, 78

Tasso, Torquato, 104
Thomas, Richard F., 7
Tough, William, 100, 102
trade, 129–30, 169–70
translation(s)
  didactic, 83, 88–9, 92, 158, 164
  emulation and, 13–15, 18n, 23, 36, 47, 94–5, 100, 133, 160, 181
  ethics of, 14, 78, 96, 103–4
  flexibility, 189–90
  free, 14, 55, 63, 65, 74, 81–3, 101, 103–4, 156
  'gentleman's language' in, 22
  imperfection of, 12–13, 15
  incomplete, 134–45, 173–4
  innovation, 24, 42, 47, 74, 80, 158–9
  interpolations, 34, 43, 58, 84, 86, 99, 101, 104–8, 122, 140
  manuscript, 78–110, 171–81
  metaphors for, 12, 44, 49, 102–4, 192
  mirroring the Latin, 24–5, 31, 34, 42–3, 140, 165, 175
  modernisation, 43–4, 99–100, 101
  multiple renditions of single line, 173–4
  paraphrase, 56, 87, 104, 134
  partial, 92, 133, 145, 190
  as rhetorical interventions, 69
  simile 'trespass', 82–3
  single book, 116–45, 188–9, 190
  utilitas of, 11–12, 13, 28, 49, 192
translators, 99
  active role of, 103
  anonymous, 79–88, 125–6
  attribution, 79–80, 87, 172–3
  competitive, 15, 18n
  duties of, 8–15, 56
  Humphrey on, 8–15, 17n, 18n, 94, 192
  predecessors, 47, 121, 160, 170, 174
  self-examination of, 44
  storyteller, 100
  'transfiguration' by, 65
  virtues of, 10, 12, 175
Trevet, Nicholas, 95
Trojan horse, 155, 156
Troy, 25, 27, 44, 66, 67, 71, 137, 141, 155, 163
Trundle, John, 152, 153
Tudeau-Clayton, Margaret, 5, 6, 22, 28, 36, 41
Tudor culture, 26, 27, 48
Twisleton, Lady Catherine, 165, 170
Twyne, Thomas, 15, 19, 20, 22–3, 31–49, 180, 190, 191, 192
  comet of 1577, 36–7
  fourteeners, 94
  Phaer and, 36
  Stanyhurst and, 38, 39, 42
  word 'parliament', 163

Valvassori, Clemente, 93
Vaughan, Henry, 38, 44
Vegio, Maffeo, 20, 32, 35, 36, 37, 190
Verstegan, Richard, 42
Vicars, John, 15, 19, 37, 83, 169, 189, 190, 191, 192
  Aeneid translation by, 157–65
  anti-Catholic publications by, 153–7
  Butler's criticism of, 150–2, 187
  Dudley Digges translation and, 160, 174
  Heaths and, 171, 174, 175–6
  'ramshackle' style of, 158, 174, 182n
  'Virgiliae Vindiciae' and, 152–4, 165
Vickers, Brian, 69
Vida, Marco Girolamo, 98, 104, 114n
'Virgiliae Vindiciae' (E. C.), 152–4, 165
Virginia Company, 116–45, 191
virtue, 35–6, 37, 128, 177
  in the *Aeneid*, 13, 14, 28, 29–31, 35–6, 37
  of good translators, 10–12
  kingly, 29–30, 90–2, 133
  nobility and, 35, 86
  religious, 108
  state and, 98, 143–4, 166
  warfare and, 128, 177–80

Wales, 27
Waleys, Thomas, 95, 97
Waller, Edmund, 149, 187
Walsham, Alexandra, 155
warfare, 127–9, 131, 177–8; *see also* military *Aeneids*
Warwick, Earl of, 120
Watkins, John, 6, 138
Webbe, William, 20, 21, 25, 26
Weber, Clifford, 57
Weil, Judith, 63
White, Peter, 39
Wightman, William, 20, 31, 35
Williams, Deanne, 57
Williams, William P., 79, 80, 87
Wilson-Okamura, David Scott, 6, 104, 117, 166, 190
Wiltshire, Susan Ford, 116
Wimpfeling, Jacob, 89
Wither, George, 119, 151, 153
Wood, Henry, 147n
Wordsworth, William, 15, 18n
Worth, Valerie, 56
Woudhuysen, Henry, 78
Wroth, Sir Thomas, 10, 19, 83, 116, 117, 118–25, 144, 145, 192
Wyatt, Thomas, 23

EU Authorised Representative:
Easy Access System Europe Mustamäe tee 50, 10621 Tallinn, Estonia
gpsr.requests@easproject.com

Printed and bound by CPI Group (UK) Ltd, Croydon, CR0 4YY
16/01/2026
02036314-0002